WHERE
NO
ROADS
GO

WHERE NO ROADS GO

A Devotional Biography

TRUSTING GOD
THROUGH CHALLENGES
AND CHANGE

Carin LeRoy

ANEKO
PRESS

We love hearing from our readers. Please contact us
at www.anekopress.com/questions-comments with
any questions, comments, or suggestions.

Cover Design: Jonathan Lewis
Editors: Sheila Wilkinson and Ruth Clark

Aneko Press

www.anekopress.com

Aneko Press, Life Sentence Publishing, and our logos are trademarks of

Life Sentence Publishing, Inc.
203 E. Birch Street
P.O. Box 652
Abbotsford, WI 54405

BIOGRAPHY & AUTOBIOGRAPHY / Religious

Paperback ISBN: 978-1-62245-744-1
eBook ISBN: 978-1-62245-745-8

10 9 8 7 6 5 4 3 2

Available where books are sold

Contents

Introduction

I screamed and jumped from the chair to run for cover under our bed's mosquito netting. Not another night of dive-bomb roaches. I'd had enough! One of the epic-sized, ugly bugs had launched from the wall and glided toward me. Under the safety of the net's cover, I would read for the rest of the evening. I never thought I'd have to share a house with many critters, but here I was. The nocturnal activity of these creatures made for many sleepless nights, and I soon realized this jungle setting was no place for a wimp. I needed to toughen up fast if we were going to live here and raise a family.

I didn't know that trekking through the jungle meant hours of muscle-shredding exhaustion, or that our firstborn son would overdose on malaria medicine. Who knew that my family would become the focal point for an entire village, or that running water would become a luxury? I didn't anticipate that malaria chills, flights on small aircraft, and watchful eyes would be a part of everyday life. There was a lot I didn't know, and that was a good thing.

I also didn't yet realize the calm of listening to a tropical rainstorm on a metal roof, or the joy of a life changed by the power of the gospel. I didn't know that extreme isolation would mean the adoption of a jungle tribe who became our family-away-from-family. And, who knew that the people we had gone to help would come to our aid many times through those years!

My husband and I were young and zealous, excited for an adventure with God but without knowledge of what that would require. Choosing to leave the comfort of my Southern roots, I found myself tossed into a primitive culture where suffering was common and fear of the spirit world reigned. In our interactions we could go from heartfelt tears to peals of laughter as we lived with our tribal friends. The complexities there blindsided me as a young twenty-three-year-old missionary wife. Life would never be the same, but that would be a good thing.

This jungle would be where our roots of faith would grow deep as we learned to call on and depend on God. I would learn to cling to an ever-loving Savior while seeing him provide and protect many times. A myriad of unique experiences taught us countless spiritual lessons. Following God to this remote place seemed like a risk, but it was the "risk that wasn't" because of God's faithfulness.

The bougainvillea – a tropical, vining shrub – displays its magnificent color better in times of drought and intense sun than when grown in the shade or when heavily watered. But it needs both. As the cactus thrives in the desert, so can our difficulties create something beautiful in our lives. As our faith is forged in God, our transformation mirrors a reflection of him. By stepping out in faith, we will experience his blessings in a new way and learn dependence on God, who will love and lead us without fail.

In our journey with God, the question is not *"Can I trust God?"* The question is, *"Will I trust God?"* God is active, always working out his purposes, and forever faithful in big and small ways. Come, join me in a place where no roads go, where challenges and change reveal God's amazing grace.

Section One

Jungle Beginnings

Living in a foreign land excited me. As a young girl, I was fascinated with stories of missionaries. I'd hoped to go to a faraway place someday and live among a people who had never heard how Jesus loved them – even if that meant rough living. God put that passion in my heart at a young age, but I soon realized that passion and reality can collide.

New beginnings challenge our faith and stretch our emotions. Packing up our belongings for a new location, arriving in a vastly different environment, eating unfamiliar foods, and making new friends were all causes for extra stress. It's uncomfortable to adjust, and yet, adjust we must. Change can bring out the worst in us, or we can allow it to make us stronger.

With every fresh start also comes a sense of adventure. The country of Papua New Guinea (PNG) is the eastern half of the large island off the northern coast of Australia; it is appropriately called "the land of the unexpected." My husband and I jumped headlong into this strange land together, leaving our family behind to embark on this journey with God. This far-flung area of the world would change me forever.

New beginnings are a part of God's plan; I believe they give us a greater sense of who he is. Walking by faith into life's changes is a journey, but we don't walk alone. The God of all beginnings goes with us.

Necessities Only

So be careful how you live. Don't live like fools, but like those who are wise. Make the most of every opportunity in these evil days. Don't act thoughtlessly, but understand what the Lord wants you to do. (Ephesians 5:15-17 NLT)

"Why are you taking that big thing? That's going to take up too much space in the crate. We don't need it," I said.

"Yes, we will need this," my husband, Dale, said.

All of our material possessions for our journey across the ocean were contained in one small two-by-two-by-four-foot crate, one footlocker, and four suitcases – all the things we needed for the next several years. The crate and footlocker would be shipped, and the luggage would go with us on our flight. Leaving one life behind to begin another required preparation. We purged, discarded, or gave away what we could live without. We packed and stored wedding presents in my parents' attic, and we set aside important things to pack.

My husband and I agreed upon most things. But this one item became a point of hot, energetic discussion: the five-gallon yellow water cooler with a tap. Not only was it huge, but it was also round and would be hard to pack around.

"We will need this for the storage of clean water. This has to be packed," Dale said. Grudgingly, I shoved it into the crate and packed clothes and little things inside it and around it. This dumb thing prevented me from taking a few other items, and I was sure we would never need it.

Only essentials would go: three years of clothes, kitchen items, books to read, bedding, two pillows, a few personal items, office supplies, tools, and a chain saw. Some of the most essential items were our books and tools. In the days before Internet and computers, books would nourish and entertain us; tools would help my husband fix, build, and repair.

In the extreme tropical heat, 100-percent-cotton clothes were essential. We packed them after checking all the labels. We included only a few warm items for the times we would travel to cooler mountainous areas. Flip-flops. Tennis shoes. Hats. Umbrellas for tropical storms. I packed five pots for cooking: two skillets and three lidded pots in various sizes. I took an eight-piece place setting of dishes and silverware, a supply of plasticware given by friends, and two sets of sheets and towels. We also put essential baking tins, first-aid items, and a few decorations and pictures in the crate. Packing for a life overseas required careful thought and planning. We didn't have a second chance to repack once things were shipped, so this was our only chance to get it right.

Life is the same; it requires careful planning and wise decisions. We don't get a second chance on this earth. We must make it count. Leaving behind one part of our life to follow God into a new stage may require purging. Some questions to ask are, What ungodly clutter do I need to discard? Do I have unresolved emotional pain, an anger problem, an addiction, or ongoing unforgiveness toward someone? What part of my life is not pleasing to God? What friends or habits don't lead me toward holiness? What lifestyle choice is harmful to me or my family? Or, what good thing should I leave behind in order to grasp something better that God may be nudging me toward?

Life is all about choices.

And choices affect everything. Ungodly clutter affects our closeness to God and reduces our ability to serve him faithfully. And when we leave behind something good for something better, it may be just what God desires to help us reach the potential he planned for us.

Purge. Plan. Prepare. Follow God.

Then, who knows what God might have in store for us. And I'm glad I listened to my husband and packed that yellow cooler! It came in very handy later.

Prayer

Father, thank you for guiding me into wise decisions when I walk with you. Give me a heart that will trust and lean on you for understanding and insight into areas I need to purge so that I can serve you faithfully. Help me to seek your direction in all that I do, and help me to follow the plan and purpose that you have for my life.

Personal Reflection

1. What have you discovered as you sought God's purpose for your life?

2. How does Ephesians 5:15-17 speak to you? Are you making wise choices? What changes might you need to make?

3. Read Proverbs 3:5-6. What three things do these verses say we need to do for God's guidance?

Waves of Change

The LORD had said to Abram, "Leave your native country, your relatives, and your father's family, and go to the land that I will show you. I will make you into a great nation. I will bless you and make you famous, and you will be a blessing to others." So Abram departed as the LORD had instructed. (Genesis 12:1-2, 4 NLT)

The heat slammed us in the face the moment my husband and I disembarked from the air-conditioned plane at Jacksons International Airport in Port Moresby. It felt as if I had walked straight into an oven as the scorching air hit my skin. The asphalt radiated heat from its ebony surface as we walked toward the terminal. While we stood in line for the customs inspection with a pile of luggage, the humidity and temperature change smothered us.

I had expected the tropics to be hot, but this jolted my senses. It reminded me of sitting too close to a burning-wood fire and needing to move to a more comfortable place. Sweat gathered on my face as we waited in line.

We'd just arrived in the island country of Papua New Guinea. Finally, we were here on this God-appointed adventure. I had no clue what would lay ahead, but it would be a mixture of the struggles of a different life and the joys of following God's call.

With my passport in hand, I stepped up to the customs counter to enter a country to which I'd never been, to live a life I didn't know, and to meet a people I had yet to love. It would be years before I'd return to my home country.

Beads of sweat soon dripped down the side of my face. Excitement mixed with a little fear of the unknown clung to me as I surveyed the scene around me. Eccentric-looking westerners were scattered throughout the customs line. Some looked as apprehensive as I did. Others looked comfortable, brandishing the country's traditional string bags and the common footwear – flip-flops. Babies fussed as parents tried to calm them.

I've heard it said that misfits, mercenaries, and missionaries are the westerners you find living and working in Papua New Guinea. Whether or not that was true, I didn't know. I knew I was out of my element. Gone were my pampered days of comfort – no more air-conditioning, electricity, hot showers, or store-bought bread. These would now be uncommon luxuries. My high heels had now been replaced with flip-flops.

We planned to live among a remote primitive tribe who had never heard of the love of Christ. I imagined I could make sacrifices, live rough, deal with extreme isolation, and learn a new language. Was I up to the task?

No.

But we trusted in an almighty God who was more than able to sustain us, teach us, and enable us to do the work he had called us to do.

"Next," the customs officer said as he waved us forward. Now our adventure had begun.

When God called Abram out of Ur, he said, "*Go* to a land I will show you." The specifics weren't given because God wanted Abram (later renamed Abraham) to follow him in faith. We don't need to know the outcome before we obey, because God goes before us. We are all called to be like Abram – to listen to God's voice, to walk by faith, and to follow his leading. That journey will look different for each of us, but the calling is the same: go, and you will be a blessing to others.

Answering God's call is our choice. God doesn't force his will on us. Yet he guides us with a gentle hand, leading us forward into a deeper walk with him if we are willing to step out into the unknown that he has purposed for us. Will we trust him? At times, the journey may be difficult, but the blessings will be many.

Prayer

Father, thank you that your promises are true. Just as you were faithful to Abram when he obeyed, you will be faithful to me as I listen to your leading. Help me to learn to walk daily in faith with you. Give me an obedient heart to do your will and be a blessing to others.

Personal Reflection

1. Do you have a willingness to step out as Abram did? Why, or why not?

2. Do you feel God's tug calling you in a new direction?

3. The Christian life is a walk of faith. Read Hebrews 11:6. According to that Scripture, what is it that we must have to please God?

4. Faith in God is not a one-time thing at salvation; it's also a daily commitment of trust in his Word and his promises to us. With what do you need to trust him today?

Stranded on the Curb

Aren't five sparrows sold for two pennies? Yet not one of them is forgotten before God. In fact, even the hairs on your head are all numbered. Do not be afraid; you are more valuable than many sparrows. (Luke 12:6-7 NET)

We looked like two lost souls waiting at the curb with our four suitcases as we searched for our ride. Minutes passed, but we didn't see anyone matching the description of our mission's Port Moresby representative.

"Did you bring the contact information of the person picking us up?" my husband asked as we waited on the outside curb.

"No, I thought you had it."

"All I remember is the guy's name."

It wasn't a great moment. There was no point in starting the blame game of which one was guilty of this oversight. Here we were in a brand-new country, but we didn't know where to go. We had no address or phone number, nor access to a phone, so we couldn't hire one of the local taxi drivers.

"Did you tell him we were arriving today?"

"Of course. I sent a message a few days ago."

Heading through the customs inspection earlier was easy: a few questions, a stamp in our passports, and we were done. I stood near our pile of luggage while Dale tried to search for our ride. Our pickup person would take us to the missionary guesthouse where we would stay while in the capital city of Port Moresby.

We searched the long sidewalk and waited in the heat for what seemed like an eternity. I wiped some of the sweat off that had collected on my upper lip. How could someone forget that new missionaries were arriving?

Apparently they did.

Our excitement at arrival turned to dismay as we stood on the sidewalk. How could we have made such a mistake? I observed my new surroundings with interest. Taxis and cars were busy picking up passengers and loading a mixture of bags, boxes, and suitcases. I heard languages that I didn't know as people bustled to get their rides. In the land of more than seven hundred languages, who could even know which dialect they were speaking? Dale pointed out the colorful string bags that most people carried and the woven beanie hats that were common. I stood absorbing the ambience. The heat, the smells, and the high humidity were new things to which I would need to adjust.

After most of the crowd left with their rides, we still waited. I'm sure we looked like lost, newcomer foreigners when an Australian woman noticed us.

"You look like you're lost or in need of a ride. Where are you headed?" she asked.

"Well," my husband stammered, "we are not sure. We forgot to bring the phone number of our contact here."

I'm sure she wondered how we could forget something so important. "Look, I'll take you to my house, and we'll figure out where you need to go."

After loading our possessions into her car, she drove us to her home and gave us a welcome cold drink. It was refreshing to cool down in her air-conditioned home. With Papua New Guinea's close relationship to Australia, many of its citizens lived and worked in the country. She helped us locate our contact, and we called them on her phone. Within several hours we were installed in a missionary guesthouse for the week. We learned later that they'd been confused, thinking our arrival was the following week, yet the Lord used a stranger to make sure we got to our destination.

Although something went awry that day, something good happened as well. In our first hours on this new adventure, it was as if God said,

"I want you to see how I can intervene when you see no way forward. I won't forsake you in the future either."

Mistakes happen. Communication gets crossed, and people forget. During those times we can still depend on God. There is no need for anxiety or panic. *The LORD watches over all who love him*[1] is a reminder to all his children. God can still care for us even when our plans go wrong. If we are forgotten, we are not really forgotten because our loving Father sees us. Seeing God's provision by using a kind stranger to help us as we arrived in this new country was a foretaste of much more provision to come. His watchful eyes and caring hand would be with us for years into the future.

Prayer

Father, thank you for knowing everything about me – my thoughts and my ways, my coming and my going. You never forget me. May my heart rejoice today because of your watchful care for me.

Personal Reflection

1. We are never forgotten by God. Read Luke 12:6-7 again. If God never forgets the sparrows and he has numbered the hairs on our head, what does that say about his care for all his creation?

2. Have you ever felt forgotten by someone? How did the Lord take care of you in that moment?

3. Read Psalm 139:1-6. What does that passage say about God's care for you?

---

1   Psalm 145:20 NIV

Boo-Eye

But thank God! He has made us his captives and continues to lead us along in Christ's triumphal procession. Now he uses us to spread the knowledge of Christ everywhere, like a sweet perfume. Our lives are a Christ-like fragrance rising up to God. But this fragrance is perceived differently by those who are being saved and by those who are perishing. (2 Corinthians 2:14-15 NLT)

"Guess you are wondering what the red stains are all over the area," the local missionary said as we walked through Boroko, a small shopping district near Port Moresby. Crowds of people moved about the streets on foot. I surveyed the scene, and splatters of red caught my attention – on the sidewalk, along the street, in the dirt, and in strange places, such as on the wall of a building. Was it blood? It looked similar to ketchup, and its random sprays were everywhere. What was it? Trash had been swept into piles for pickup, and the red color had even landed there. I avoided stepping in it.

On this day we would open our bank account with the help of a local missionary. He picked us up to drive us around the area and take us to the bank.

"That is the spit from the betel nut. It's a mild stimulant that many people here chew. The local word is *buai* [pronounced "boo-eye"]. They spit the juice from the nut, and it creates a mess on the streets."

I learned that the user chews away until there is a need to spit, much like chewing tobacco. Its mildly euphoric and addictive quality makes it popular with many in the area. Street vendors sell it on the sidewalks.

However, it seemed acceptable to spit it randomly anywhere. Sadly, I also learned it ruins teeth and gums and can cause oral cancer.

People walked around with red-stained mouths as they chewed, overwhelming my senses with culture shock as we continued our tour of the area.

In contrast to the dirty streets, the market displayed beautifully woven traditional bags in all sizes, shapes, and colors. Made and sold by the women, these string bags were sewn by hand from colorful yarns and woven together in intricate designs. They introduced us to a wonderful work of art that is the trademark of all Papua New Guineans. Baskets and wood-carved items were on sale in the market as well. Other traditional items such as *kundu* drums, bows and arrows, and fighting shields are made by the men. Much of their intricate and beautiful artwork was displayed in the market that day.

By the end of our day, we had set up a bank account, gone to the embassy, and done some shopping.

Living in a new country means adjusting to culture, food, dress, language, and traditions. We would learn what was acceptable and what was not. If we weren't careful, we could unknowingly offend if we ignored cultural standards. Our time of learning had begun, and I was already feeling plenty of culture shock on this day. However, it didn't mar the joy of the arrival at our new home. We would learn and grow as time allowed.

Every culture will have both good and unlovely things. We can love the one while looking beyond the other. Because God deeply loves and creates all people, he sees the potential in everyone. Yet we often get distracted by the unlovely things that make us uncomfortable. God's heart's desire is that we look beyond what we see as unlovely to see the person – the one who needs a Savior, the one for whom Jesus died.

Prayer

Dear Father, help me to be a person who is willing to adapt. Rather than looking at the negatives around me, help me to see the good things in a new situation. Give me a heart to think on those things that are lovely and good, and help me to learn flexibility and to adjust to new challenges that come.

Personal Reflection

1. Have you experienced a difficult change recently? Describe the negative things you looked past and the good things you saw.

2. In every situation, we will find the good with the bad. Read Philippians 4:8. How can this verse help you adapt to changes in your life?

3. How can you look past a person's differences and see them as someone whom God loves?

4. What habits or thinking can you change to respond more like Christ to others?

A Bird's-Eye View

*Therefore go and make disciples of all nations, baptizing them
in the name of the Father and the Son and the Holy Spirit,
teaching them to obey everything I have commanded you.
And remember, I am with you always, to the end of the age.*
(Matthew 28:19-20 NET)

We climbed into the medium-sized twin-engine plane and fastened our seatbelts. The pilot buckled in, checked his instruments, and started the engine. As the whirl of the propellers grew in intensity, it created a deafening sound outside the passenger window. No longer could I hear my own voice, much less Dale's. We looked with anticipation at each other and waited for the next part of our journey. Soon, we taxied and took flight to the mountainous interior of the country.

Many thoughts and questions ran through my mind as we settled in for the next stage of our new journey.

Will I cope in this isolated place away from all I've ever known?
Will the people like us? And will I like them?
Do I have the ability to learn their language?
How will I raise children here?
Can I endure the hardships this life will bring?
Do I trust God enough? And what if we fail?

The future ahead seemed daunting, and the rumble of the engine added to the heaviness in my spirit. As we climbed in altitude, I gazed out the window at the scene below. I no longer saw sprawling cityscapes or the paved superhighways I'd left behind in my home country. A far different scene came into view. This coastal city, Port Moresby, had one airport, a main city center, and a shopping district. The largest building rose only a few stories. Beyond the city and coastal hills, small communities dotted the outlying areas. It wasn't long before tropical jungle occupied the expanse of land below.

This bird's-eye view of the jungle portrayed the harshness of this impenetrably dense rain forest that I would soon come to know well. Muddied brown after heavy rains, rivers weaved and carved their paths through the jungle, creating relief in an otherwise unbroken view of the treetops below. Scattered signs of life appeared when the thatched houses of a small village emerged in the bush. Smoke spiraled upward from a fire below. There were gardens sprinkled on the outskirts of a village, and mounds of dirt nurtured vegetable plants. Someone in a dugout canoe paddled on a river. As we rose above the clouds to clear the mountain ranges ahead, the jungle was lost from view.

In this vast and remote place, small pockets of people lived far into the interior and never had the chance to hear that God exists and loves them. Many lived as they had for centuries – in fear of ancestral spirits and sorcerers and bound by their animistic belief system.[2] Devoid of knowledge of the true God, some still needed to hear of the God who loves them and who could release them from their fear and bring them peace and hope.

From beginning to end, God has a bird's-eye view of human history. Nothing is hidden from his sight. He sees and loves all people everywhere. Yet many still do not know of him. I needed to trust in his enabling power to live in this remote, untamed land. When I think of our experience, I'm reminded of the verse in Isaiah: *Then I heard the Lord asking, "Whom should I send as a messenger to this people? Who will go for us?" I said, "Here I am. Send me."*[3] We had followed God's leading and went where he sent us.

The challenge is to ask myself, How can I best utilize my time on earth? What impact will my life leave? What legacy will I leave for the next generation? Life shouldn't be a random set of choices, because

---

2   Animism is the belief that all things – plants, animals, trees – have a spirit. Those spirits and dead ancestral spirits can help or harm humans.

3   Isaiah 6:8 NLT

each person is created with a purpose. Stepping out in any unknown direction will challenge us. Questions, inadequacies, and fear of the future will invade our thoughts. But we can push those aside as we walk by faith, hand in hand, with a mighty God. He sees all. He knows all. And he goes before me. That truth, when realized, quells my fear and calms my heart.

Prayer

Lord, thank you for creating me with a purpose. Give me a heart that desires to follow and obey your plans for me, even the difficult ones. Give me more understanding about my part in the Great Commission of Christ. Help me to honor you with my life and leave a godly legacy for my children and others. Calm my fears and inadequacies, for I know you are always with me.

Personal Reflection

1. What has God called you to do that is radical or different from others?

2. In Matthew 28:19-20, Jesus' last command on earth was to *go and make disciples of all nations*. What part can you play in the Great Commission of Christ?

3. What impact do you want to leave on this earth? What legacy do you want to leave for your family and others?

4. Read Acts 26:12-18. What had God appointed Paul to do? God appoints all believers to be a witness for him. Who can you share your faith with today?

Praise the Lord Anyhow

And he who searches our hearts knows the mind of the Spirit, because the Spirit intercedes on behalf of the saints according to God's will. And we know that all things work together for good for those who love God, who are called according to his purpose. (Romans 8:27-28 NET)

Disappointment came less than a week after our arrival. My expectations and reality would soon collide in a meeting with the mission leader. We had arrived in the cooler mountainous area of Tari at the mission headquarters in the Southern Highlands Province where the Huli tribe lived.

We bumped our way up a graveled dirt road to our next destination. Large potholes slowed us down as the driver navigated around the worst ones. I looked out the window to see a few men from the Huli tribe wearing elaborate headgear. Until then, I had never seen such a thing, and it looked uncomfortable and itchy. Known for their ornamentation, the men in this tribe put these wigs together with hair, bird feathers, and other local materials.

Some with painted faces held bows and arrows and stopped to watch us pass. Women trudged along the road with heavy string bags slung from their heads, probably returning from their gardens. We passed a small settlement with several thatched-roof huts. From the scenes out the van window, it seemed like we had traveled back a few centuries.

When we landed earlier in the day, I noticed the cooler temperature as soon as we stepped from the plane. Travel in Papua New Guinea takes days when you travel to more remote areas. At each location, you must wait for the next flight out. In most cases, the most remote areas have no roads for vehicles due to huge mountain ranges, difficult terrain, and lack of development, which is why we traveled by air to most locations. Grass or gravel airstrips had become the answer for gaining access to many areas, but this larger mountainous town had both airstrip and road access to several locations and settlements.

We soon arrived at the small mission headquarters where all the administration was handled for those working in remote locations. The main office, a small printing-press operation (for Bible and literacy materials), a mechanics building, and a guesthouse were here, along with houses for missionaries who lived on the base. We would stay in the main guesthouse called Toad Hall for the next few days.

The next morning was sweater weather, a nice change from the heat of Port Moresby. We met with one of the mission leaders in his office. After chatting a while, he said, "We will be sending you to Kiunga to do a nine-month orientation with two of our experienced senior missionaries. They have offered to host you in their house on the mission's base at Kiunga."

Seriously? I wasn't prepared to be told that we would need to share living quarters with an older (nearly retired) missionary couple for *nine* months. We had lived with others for months before our departure, and I had been looking forward to having a place of our own.

We both walked away from that meeting heavy with frustration. I was fine with a time of orientation, but I was not prepared to live in the home of strangers who were decades older. I expected rough living conditions, new foods, language learning, and even intense heat, but not this.

I remembered from childhood how my mom had placed a little plaque as a reminder on our kitchen's windowsill that read, "Praise the Lord anyhow." While doing dishes day after day, the words on that little plaque took root in my heart. Her favorite verse when she dealt with disappointment was *all things work together for good for those who love the God.*[4] I heard her quote that promise from God many times.

---

4   Romans 8:28 NET

In my disappointment, I got a nudge from the Lord and remembered my mom's verse.

How many times in life do we struggle with the sting of disappointment? Things we hope for never happen, and the plans we make are crushed. Instead, changes that are out of our control sweep us into a whole new direction. Rather than allow Satan to create anger and bitterness, we can learn to lean on the knowledge of God's sovereign control.

Will I trust this as God's plan for me? Resting on God's sovereignty in the midst of my disappointment allows him to bring peace to my heart. We can trust in his plans for us, and many times we will look back and be thankful.

Prayer

Father, thank you for the promise that you will work all things for my good. Help me to understand and believe that truth as you direct my steps according to your purposes. When disappointment comes my way, help me to rest in the knowledge of your sovereign control.

Personal Reflection

1. Describe how you feel about an unexpected change when your hopes are dashed. What emotions do you feel, and how do you react to the situation? Why?

2. What promise do you find in Romans 8:27-28?

3. Read Proverbs 16:9. What does this verse say about God's sovereign control of our lives?

The White Fright

Do not be anxious about anything. Instead, in every situation, through prayer and petition with thanksgiving, tell your requests to God. And the peace of God that surpasses all understanding will guard your hearts and minds in Christ Jesus.
(Philippians 4:6-7 NET)

The roar of the engine buzzed in our ears as we journeyed farther inland. Visibility was nonexistent as we flew through thick clouds in this six-seat Cessna 206 plane. Being cocooned in this metal cubbyhole with wings put my nerves on edge, and all I could see were billows of white. I hoped the pilot knew where he was going in these murky skies. We were on our way to our nine-month assignment with the missionaries in the small town of Kiunga.

After about fifty minutes, the pilot turned to look at us and broke the silence.

"Do you see the ground anywhere?"

When your pilot asks that question while you are flying at five thousand feet, it sends you into a panic. Fear swamped me when I realized he couldn't find his way.

What? Does the pilot know where we're going? We're going to die before we make it to our first assignment.

My husband and I looked out the windows to help him locate ground, except I focused more on the fear while my husband looked for trees or dirt – or anything that looked like a place to land. Eventually, toward the left, we saw a break in the clouds that revealed ground far below.

The pilot banked the plane to pop down through the opening and get below the cloud cover. With good visibility, the entire landscape came into view. He easily navigated to touch down on the gravel airstrip. As I stepped off the plane and my feet stood on solid ground again, I took a deep breath of relief. We had arrived at this little town on the Fly River in the middle of vast rain forests in Papua New Guinea.

I didn't know this was normal for air travel in PNG, one of the most dangerous areas in the world to fly in. The difficult terrain and unpredictable weather patterns created challenging conditions for any pilot. Tropical storms could crop up in minutes without warning, and fog-clad mountains weren't for inexperienced pilots. Missionary Aviation Fellowship (MAF) pilots were some of the best-trained in the country. In the 1980s, these pilots didn't have the GPS navigational devices in small planes that most have now. They flew by sight, maps, and their knowledge of the area by using rivers, villages, and other landmarks to find remote locations. Pilots flew at a high altitude, sometimes in dense clouds, until they were clear of the highlands. They descended after they reached the lowland areas.

We were safe all along. Yet my lack of knowledge made me jump to a fast conclusion and react in fear. How many times in life do I react with worry when the situation doesn't warrant it? Instead of enjoying life, I develop an anxious heart by thinking of things that may go wrong.

Many times we sacrifice peace and joy because we don't trust God. Proverbs reminds us that *anxiety in a man's heart weighs him down*.[5] God doesn't want us to carry unnecessary burdens, nor does he want us to pray, only to pick up those worries again. We pray, commit our concerns into his care, and leave them with him.

To this day, I wonder if the pilot was trying to add a little "excitement" to our maiden flight into a remote area. I learned one thing though: it's easy to react in fear from ignorance or lack of understanding. The pilot knew how to navigate the plane; I didn't. With understanding of the intricacies of flying in PNG, I soon learned what to expect on a flight.

God knows how to navigate our lives too. Let's practice giving our concerns, fears, and problems to him in prayer. His understanding is

---

5   Proverbs 12:25 ESV

limitless, and he is more than capable of taking care of us. We can trust him. Let's sit back, relax, and enjoy the journey.

Prayer

Dear Lord, guard my mind from worry and don't let anxiety or fear weigh me down. Help me come to you with my concerns and pray. Thank you for offering peace that goes beyond all understanding and is supernatural in how it works in my life. Thank you that I can trust you to navigate for me.

Personal Reflection

1. When have you experienced an anxious heart in a new or unknown situation?

2. What does God tell us to do about anxiety in Philippians 4:6-7?

3. Read Proverbs 12:25. What does God say anxiety does to a man (or woman)? What cheers up a person? Think of someone you can encourage today.

4. Read Isaiah 41:10 and 1 Peter 5:7. They also speak of God's provision during times of fear and anxiety.

Learning the Ropes

You who are younger must accept the authority of the elders. And all of you, dress yourselves in humility as you relate to one another, for "God opposes the proud but gives grace to the humble." So humble yourselves under the mighty power of God, and at the right time he will lift you up in honor. (1 Peter 5:5-6 NLT)

I didn't know it, but we had moved in with "Martha Stewart" of the jungle. Everything in our hosts' home was done with proficiency and order, no matter who did it. The bed was made the moment someone awoke. The house was swept, the louvered windows cleaned, the floors mopped, and the laundry washed and folded all on a strict timetable. Hibiscus flowers were picked fresh for the coffee table each morning, and the dinner meal was set with a clean tablecloth. Her house helper completed some of these tasks each day, but our hostess made sure things were in order and on a schedule.

With over seventy years of combined missionary service, our Kiunga hosts, Bill and Ruth Merriweather, shared their home with us. Bill was a naturalized British Australian, and Ruth was Australian. "Mrs. Merri," as I liked to call her, was an amazing missionary wife, and I knew zilch about how to live in the jungle.

Taking morning and afternoon tea was our first adjustment.

"Come have a cuppa," Mrs. Merriweather would call out down the hallway toward our bedroom. At first, the interruption was an annoyance. The American way is to grab a drink to carry it back to the desk and work, but our Australian friends loved their hot tea mid-morning and mid-afternoon. To please our hosts, we would arrive in the living room for a cup of hot tea and two cookies – *biscuits* in Australian lingo.

Teatime became a chance to take a break from the endless pile of census material I was typing up for the mission hospital. I soon enjoyed this short time of fellowship and refreshment.

One morning at the breakfast table, Mrs. Merri announced, "I've decided that we should each have a day to do our laundry. Tuesday morning will be your day to wash clothes." A few days before, I had chosen to do laundry on the same day as she did. We kept bumping into each other in the teeny laundry room as we both tried to get laundry finished. Then we ran out of clothespins and clothesline that day.

"That also would give both of us sufficient line and clothespins for hanging our laundry outside," she said.

Gone were the days of throwing things in an automatic washer and dryer. Instead, I learned to use a twin tub. One side washed the clothes while the other side spun out the water. Then we hand-rinsed items in a big sink and spun them again. When we finished washing, we hung everything on the line to dry. I planned my week around laundry day because of the attention and time it took.

"I usually hang my clothes inside out, so the sun doesn't fade them," she said one day when I had left my clothes on the line all day. "I try to bring things in as soon as they are dry because the sun rots the clothes faster if you leave them on the line all day. The sun also destroys the elastic in your underwear."

I still needed to learn so much. Who knew that sun rotted elastic? The stress of this new life overseas wore me down as I dealt with so much change. At times I felt like ignoring all the instructions that came my way, but my rule-following spirit helped me to make most of the adjustments.

"Don't use that tea towel for drying pots; the residue from the gas flame will stain the linen. Use this one. This is for drying pots and pans, and this one is for drying the plates, silverware, and cups." She showed me the difference between the towels.

I grabbed the proper towel.

"Oh, and make sure that you wipe down the cupboards after you wash the dishes because the soapy water that splashes down will make the doors mold."

Mold was a definite problem with the high humidity and heat of the tropics. It flourished in that environment and was a constant battle for homemakers. I learned another new thing one night as I prepared my bucket shower.

"When you finish your shower, pull the curtain closed so it dries out properly and doesn't mold."

Those first few months were a huge adjustment as I lived with many changes. Some days I longed for something familiar. I'm sure that having two not-so-neat Americans living with them unsettled Mrs. Merri's household order. However, she kindly taught me what was expected, and I strived to comply, since we were the guests who had invaded their home. If she wanted a tablecloth for the evening meal, then I set the table with one. If she asked me to do laundry on Tuesday, then I did my washing that day.

Sometimes God puts us in intense learning seasons where he wants to teach us to comply under someone else's authority. It may grate on our nerves and frustrate us, but God desires that we not only obey him, but that we also obey those who are in leadership over us. When we honor that person's position over us, then we honor God. He says to *give respect and honor to those who are in authority.*[6] Although we were simple missionary wives, I believe that concept remained true for me to honor Mrs. Merri by submitting to how she ran her home. Submitting to others creates a humble, obedient heart, and we all need more of that.

Prayer

Father, I ask you to help me submit to those in authority. Give me a humble heart to obey and serve others in leadership over me. Expose any pride in my life and replace it with grace and humility. Remove selfishness and help me to willingly look after the interests of others because it pleases you.

---

6   Romans 13:7 NLT

Personal Reflection

1. How do you typically respond to the authority of others?

2. Do you think submitting to the authority of others helps us to accept and obey the authority of God? Why is accepting the authority of God so important?

3. According to Philippians 2:3-4, how should we think of others? How does humility help create harmony in our relationships?

Still Learning the Ropes

Taste and see that the LORD is good. Oh, the joys of those who take refuge in him! Fear the LORD, you his godly people, for those who fear him will have all they need. (Psalm 34:8-9 NLT)

"I never throw that in the paper rubbish; it doesn't burn properly," Mrs. Merri remarked one day when my confusion landed an item in the wrong container. Who knew that throwing out trash could prove to be so complicated? We had three trash containers, and I never knew what went where.

"It's best if we open the ends of each tin and smoosh it, so we can conserve space in the rubbish hole outside," she said. Mrs. Merri was showing me the best way to throw out the trash.

There was a bucket for food scraps (for composting), a drum for paper trash (for burning), and a container for metal items – things that neither composted nor burned. I soon learned the drill. We opened tin cans at both ends and flattened them before putting them in the container. We threw metal, glass, and non-burnable items down a hole dug on the side of the yard and then covered it with a lid. Every few days, we burned the paper trash and threw the metal trash down the hole. We carried the composting trash out each day so it didn't attract flies.

"After you wash a plastic bag, hang it up *this* way. It dries better," she said. We also washed and reused plastic bags and aluminum foil. Aluminum foil was hard to obtain, and plastic bags weren't common. We reused both for as long as possible.

This jungle life threw me on a large learning curve. I had days when I dreamed of sweater weather, American hamburgers, and a long shower. Yet there was no point in going there; I needed to enjoy other fun things where God had placed me.

After nine months of orientation, we had developed a good rapport with the Merriweathers. Through the earlier days of disappointment and frustration over not living on our own, I realized that God had placed us there for a reason.

Under Ruth's (Mrs. Merriweather's) tutelage, I learned far more than I imagined. From her example, I learned to run a home with efficiency in a tropical climate. I watched her ability to get things done without frustration. She served others – guests, family, and friends – with ease and an attitude of joy and love.

She had become my missionary "mom." After the mission assigned us to another location, I contacted her often for advice or recipes. A few years after they retired to Australia, she passed away. I felt a deep sense of loss but was so grateful that I had shared part of my time in PNG with Mrs. Merri. My time with her was my training ground for many challenges that lay ahead.

God knew I needed her.

When I got my own little jungle home, I found myself doing what she did. I smashed each tin can before throwing it down the rubbish hole – just like she did. I cut out the rotten and bad spots in vegetables and used the rest – just like she did. I gave clothes a morning to dry and ran out to get them before the sun would fade and rot them – just like she did. I only used a can of food when it was a special treat or when there was nothing else to eat – just like she did. I washed plastic bags and aluminum foil – yes, just like she taught me.

My husband also learned from Bill. His wonderful and gentle way with the local people was a great example for Dale. Everywhere Bill went, he had a following of people who desired to talk with him. He was well-loved by everyone, and his influence was obvious. My husband learned the same style of his come-alongside demeanor that was so needed in the local church at that time.

Although the initial disappointment had stung, God knew that living with this couple would be good training ground for our years in PNG. God was not concerned about making us happy in the short term as much as he was about equipping us for the long term. That time of preparation led to more contentment and confidence as we moved forward in the work. He knew what we needed.

Disappointments often turn into blessings. We left after those nine months, excited to be on our own again, but better equipped for the challenges of life in the jungle. We realized how much we had learned from this amazing couple. Our disappointment and frustration had turned into thankfulness. God had a better plan all along.

Prayer

Lord, I praise you for your goodness to me. You know what I need to help me grow in maturity. Help me learn to cling to your promises when I am disappointed, because I know your plans for me are perfect. Thank you for the promise that when we submit to your will, you give us everything we need.

Personal Reflection

1. When disappointments happen, do you still believe that God's plan will turn out to be the best? Describe a time when you had a disappointment that turned to joy.

2. What promise is given in Psalm 34:8-9 that you can cling to during difficulty?

3. Goodness is an attribute of God. What does Psalm 145:9-10 say about the goodness of God? What will all his followers do?

Life-Giving Water

Jesus replied, "Anyone who drinks this water will soon become thirsty again. But those who drink the water I give will never be thirsty again. It becomes a fresh, bubbling spring within them, giving them eternal life." (John 4:13-14 NLT)

A severe drought hit most of the country only months after our arrival. That meant serious water conservation. With no wells or any town water system available, we caught all household water in a water-tank system set up on the house. When it rained on the galvanized tin roof, gutters caught the water and directed it into the two-thousand-gallon water tank. This water was used for all our needs. We used it for our laundry, flushing the toilet, doing the dishes, and for drinking. So, when a drought came, we had to change our habits once more.

As the water level in the tank got lower and lower, we worried we might run out. When washing clothes, we recycled all the water; we used rinse water for several loads of wash, and we used soapy water to water flowers, mop the floor, and flush the toilet. When the water level became dangerously low, we preserved the rest for our drinking and hired help to carry water up from the river in buckets for all household use.

We filled a basin with river water to use for handwashing, rather than using the tap water. We turned the taps on and off while brushing our teeth to save every drop. It didn't take long to realize how important water was in our life.

A galvanized bucket with a showerhead and tap attached to the bottom became our shower. The bucket was fastened to a pulley on the ceiling and could be lowered to fill with water and hoisted up to shower. Each night, we usually filled the bucket with water and added a kettle of hot water, but the drought meant using even less water for our showers. By turning the tap on and off, we learned to use less water: on, to wet my hair; off, to scrub my hair; on, to rinse. When I finished showering, my husband took his shower and used whatever water I had left in the bucket. He emerged a bit soapy on nights when I washed my hair.

After adjusting to this lifestyle for months, the drought finally broke. The rain thundered on the metal roof with that familiar deafening sound, providing us with happy relief. We watched as cool, refreshing, life-giving water filled the tank. What a blessing to see the tank fill up again. Something so simple, yet so important, gave me a new appreciation for this necessity of life. In all our years there, I took joy in watching a rainstorm fill our water tank. A full and overflowing tank made me happy to be blessed with plenty of water.

Just as water is life-giving to our body, Jesus is life-giving to our spirit. When Jesus talked with the Samaritan woman at the well and revealed himself to her, he offered her *living water*.[7] She wasn't even looking for God that day, yet he offered to give her a new life and freedom from the penalty of sin. Jesus knew he had what her soul longed for – peace and love.

When Jesus likens himself to living water, he offers us a lasting spiritual change. Just as water is a necessity for our physical existence, Jesus is a necessity for our spiritual well-being. Without either one, we will die. Jesus offers everyone new life that helps us overflow with joy, peace, purpose, and fulfillment. Is your soul thirsty? Then run to Jesus. He has the living water that brings us new life.

Prayer

Heavenly Father, thank you for sending your Son, Jesus, to us. Thank you for his life, death, and resurrection. I praise you that because of him we will spiritually thirst no more, and through him we are guaranteed an inheritance and eternal life with you. What a great God you are to us!

---

7   See John 4:4-26.

Personal Reflection

1. List some of the small and ordinary things you appreciate in life. What simple things are you thankful for today?

2. In the verses above from John, what does that *fresh, bubbling spring within* us give?

3. Water is essential for life and cleansing, and the Spirit of God is essential to our cleansing and purifying as believers. Read John 7:37-39. Who did Jesus say the *living water* was? Why would that be important for every believer?

4. Read Ephesians 1:13-14. What does the Spirit of God guarantee for the believer?

Section Two

Jungle Cuisine

*W*e all love to eat. No matter what area of the world we live in, everyone gathers around food. It is the passion of societies. Every culture has unique specialties and methods of cooking. Papua New Guinea is known for its *mumu* – a banana-leaf-wrapped, in-the-ground-baked meal. Sago, one of the main country staples, is made from the sago palm; it requires great effort to extract the starch from the pulp of the tree. Many in the village work together to provide this for the community. Bananas are another staple with dozens of varieties available.

Efforts to gather firewood and prepare food is a daily activity that involves the family. Someone gathers wood, another makes the fire, some fish, and the boys and men hunt big game. Husbands and wives work together to plant the garden. If they don't put forth effort, they do not eat. Working hard to provide nutrition for the family is a way of life.

I expected new and unfamiliar cuisine. What I didn't expect is that sometimes it would be more than I could handle. Our taste buds needed adjustment as we tried new things. During our time with the Merriweathers, we learned that meals provide a way to connect with others and build relationships.

Food brings everyone together.

We're Eating What?

No discipline is enjoyable while it is happening—it's painful!
But afterward there will be a peaceful harvest of right living
for those who are trained in this way. (Hebrews 12:11 NLT)

"What's this?" my husband whispered in my ear. I had called him in for lunch, and he stood looking at the table where our host had placed a salad at each setting. It was Sunday afternoon, and a fresh salad plate with lettuce was a special treat. Various items adorned each plate, but one thing in particular looked strange to my husband. Off to the side, he spotted something unfamiliar, even weird looking.

I had hoped he wouldn't ask, but since I had helped wash the vegetables and shred the carrots, I knew the item in question.

"Minced lamb's tongue," I responded.

He grimaced and looked at me but said nothing. I had watched in the kitchen as the small tin of minced lamb's tongue was divvied up onto each plate. It was only a spoonful, so we both managed to eat it buried on our fork with other salad items.

We soon realized that organ food was a cheaper protein for missionaries who wanted to take advantage of that option. That same week I walked into the kitchen as our host prepared dinner. On the counter was a hunk of strange protein that she was filling with bread stuffing. I didn't recognize it.

"What are you stuffing?" I asked casually, trying not to panic at the unknown meat she was preparing for the dinner table.

"Tonight we are having stuffed beef heart."

I gulped, grabbed the silverware, and went to set the table. My worst nightmare as a child was when my mother decided to serve liver one night each week. My brother and I hated it. Smothering a tiny piece in a spoonful of grits or sautéed onions, we forced it down. We were required to eat it for the good nourishment it contained. Thankfully, it went off the menu when Dad later admitted he despised it too.

But now I was an adult on the mission field. I could do this. I went to warn Dale of the upcoming dinner entrée.

When dinner was ready, the stuffed heart was sliced and all the food was portioned out onto each plate. Everyone got two slices of stuffed heart along with the usual steamed vegetables and root potato. Saying a prayer, we started eating. Surprisingly, it wasn't bad, and the addition of the stuffing made it easier on my palate.

Yet the kidney stew served several days later was a different story. I knew that steak and kidney stew was a common dish in some countries, but this had only kidney, no steak. I could hardly get my bites down as the strangeness of its flavor made me want to leave the table hungry. However, I managed to do as my mother taught me and I cleaned my plate.

In the span of one week, we had three different organ foods that our host served to us. We began to dread what next gross thing we might be served. Our American taste buds were screaming for something familiar.

Later that week I visited with an older friend whose husband ran a small store in town. I helped her several days a week teach ladies to sew simple skirts and tops. I loved her and her husband's fun personalities, so during a conversation I said, "Doreen, do Australians eat a lot of organ meat?"

"No, honey," she said, "we never eat that stuff. Why? Are you having that for meals?"

"Yes, we've had it a few times." I wondered if we could expect to see this for more meals in the future.

When I was a child, my mom taught us children to eat what was put in front of us. "Don't complain," she said, "and eat what you are served." Nor would my father let us grumble about a meal my mom cooked. (She was a great cook.) We had to taste a spoonful of everything she made. I remember many a night when my brother or I had to sit at the table long after dinner to finish eating that spoonful of an undesirable something. After a while, I decided to eat that first to get it over with.

"Eat a spoonful of everything," she would say if we went to someone's house for dinner. If we didn't, we were in trouble. I can eat almost anything now because of those lessons growing up. I may not like it, but I can eat it. I might not choose to eat organ meats, but we get through it.

Who knew this childhood discipline would help me overseas?

What are we building into the lives of our children? Do we cater to their desires, or are we building structure and discipline into their lives? It is easier to give in to childish demands, but it takes hard work to teach obedience and self-restraint. Do they respect your authority? If so, that helps insure they will respect others in authority as they become adults. Proverbs says, *A wise child accepts a parent's discipline; a mocker refuses to listen to correction.*[8] Too often we see out-of-control adults who were probably out-of-control children in the home. Our job as parents is to leave a legacy of love, discipline, and faith with our children that will carry them into responsible adulthood.

Happily, we were never served *offal* (viscera) again. We couldn't figure out why it never appeared on the table again after we'd had such a deluge of the stuff in one week. Unbeknownst to us, my friend told us months later that she told our host, "You can't serve those poor kids *offal*. Americans don't eat that stuff."

Prayer

Father, thank you for the gift of children. As a parent, give me patience and diligence. Help me not to be lazy, but to work hard at training my children in obedience, discipline, and self-restraint. Help my obedience and love for you be an example to my children. Help my faith lead them to faith in you.

---

8   Proverbs 13:1 NLT

Personal Reflection

1. What legacy do you hope to leave for your children? Describe how you teach them discipline and self-restraint.

2. Read Deuteronomy 6:4-9 where repetition seems to be a theme. What do these verses say about how parents should train their children? Who needs to obey God's commands first?

3. Do you think parents have contributed to children becoming out-of-control adults? Why is it important for parents to be in charge of the home and for the family to learn discipline and responsibility? Note these verses on parenting: Proverbs 22:6; Ephesians 6:4; Proverbs 29:15, 17; Proverbs 5:23.

The Little Guys

In times of prosperity be joyful, but in times of adversity consider this: God has made one as well as the other, so that no one can discover what the future holds. (Ecclesiastes 7:14 NET)

I opened a forty-four-pound metal drum of flour and gathered the remaining items to bake bread. As I scooped out the flour, something seemed strange, so I took a closer look.

Is the flour moving?

I gasped. Little grubs were squiggling in the flour. I took a step back when the stale odor from the drum hit my nostrils. This was beyond anything I wanted to use for baking. But since I wasn't in charge of the household, I went to check with the lady of the house, Mrs. Merri.

As new missionaries in our twenties, my husband and I were still living with the Merriweathers for a time of orientation in the little river town, Kiunga, which had occasional generator power, a few stores, and even a small hospital. Mission leadership had placed us under their guidance. It became my responsibility to keep the table supplied with freshly baked bread. Store-bought bread was expensive and not easily available, so I enjoyed the new challenge.

I walked to her office where she was working.

"Mrs. Merri," I said, "I just opened the drum of flour. It's stale and has worms. Do we have better flour to make bread?"

She stopped her work and walked into the kitchen with me. Her brow furrowed as she peeked into the drum. I lifted a spoonful to show her the wiggles in the flour.

"Well," she said, "it's all the flour we have. You'll have to sift out the worms."

Really? Sift out worms?

I signed up for missionary service, but I didn't know this would be in the job description. Not only was I dealing with unrelenting heat, strange foods, a new language, and unfamiliar customs, but I also had to sift worms out of flour before making bread.

It was a necessity to be endured.

Although the drum of flour had never been opened, this flour was old and had been in storage for a while. The supplies we found in town were often past their expiration date. We ate chewy cheese puffs, white-spotted chocolate, and other items past their prime. Sometimes older supplies were sent upriver to remote areas once newer supplies had arrived in port cities.

Determined to be a brave new missionary, I reached for the wire strainer. Then I pitched in a cup of flour, grabbed a spoon, and started sifting – slowly. Flour fell into the bowl below. As the sifter emptied, I saw wiggly, little white grubs coated with flour. I dumped them onto a plate on the counter where they squirmed in a heap. Then I gathered another scoopful and started the process again. It took forever to sift the eight cups needed because I didn't want one single worm to escape. If one made it past the sifter, I snatched him out with a spoon and chucked him into the pile with the rest of the little guys. I shuddered to think about one worm in my bread and refused to think about the other additions that came from worms living in flour.

After a few months of bread making, extracting worms from flour became tedious work. Sifting quicker seemed a better option. I knew a few were making it through the sieve when my chuck-out pile was smaller than my earlier efforts. The kneading process was sure to send them on to worm heaven though.

Although she didn't like it, I knew Mrs. Merri had learned over her long missionary career to tolerate many circumstances. She knew that whining and complaining were futile in a situation you couldn't change. I still needed to learn that, but her example and patience helped me learn to make the best of this situation.

I learned that missionaries could adapt to things over time because

I noticed that some long-serving ones didn't worry about sifting flour. One weekend we were invited to another missionary station twenty-five miles away for lunch with another couple. After we sat down at the table, the host prayed, and we began to eat. Lunch consisted of boiled eggs sliced into a white sauce and served on toast. I took several bites before noticing a few cooked worms in the sauce.

Obviously, worm sifting wasn't high on her priority list. She had adapted. Picking them out from a cream sauce wasn't a good option either, although I tried to shove them around my plate. I ate carefully, trying not to be obvious, and I managed to get through the meal. My husband, however, never noticed a thing and ate lunch with gusto. That reminded me of the old saying that "ignorance is bliss."

Months later when the drought broke and the rains started, we were able to get fresh, worm-free flour. With the river high enough for the boats to travel, they brought new supplies to our little jungle town. It was a great day when fresh flour arrived. I never took good flour for granted again, and I learned to be thankful for these little things in life.

If I cannot change the circumstance, the best choice is to learn to adapt and accept where God has placed me. We don't have to like it, but we can learn to accept it.

Challenging times not only give me the opportunity to accept a difficult circumstance, but they also give me more awareness of blessings that come my way. A heart trained to find contentment learns to accept tough times, rejoice in the blessings of good times, and realize that both are given to us by God in his loving sovereignty.

I never liked sifting worms, but I did gain a new appreciation for the benefits of fresh flour. Hard things have a way of giving us a new perspective.

Prayer

Lord, you desire that we live in contentment, even if circumstances are difficult. Give me the ability to adapt to changes and a heart that looks to you for my satisfaction. Remove my complaining spirit and give me a spirit that is trained in contentment. Thank you for the promise that you will never abandon or fail me.

Personal Reflection

1. What is your response in an unpleasant situation? Do you complain, or do you have an ability to adapt?

2. Read Hebrews 13:5. What reason does God give that we should be satisfied with what we have?

3. What are some of the good things in your life that you take for granted? Make a list of some you can be thankful for.

Bananas Galore

After everyone was full, Jesus told his disciples, "Now gather the leftovers, so that nothing is wasted." So they picked up the pieces and filled twelve baskets with scraps left by the people who had eaten from the five barley loaves. (John 6:12-13 NLT)

great thing about living in the tropics is the bananas. Their flavor and sweetness surpass any banana from an American grocery store. We loved them. We would buy the ones that were picked soon before ripening, a stalk at a time (about seven to ten clusters of bananas) and hang them on the back veranda.

Each morning, we would collect a handful of ripened bananas and carry them to the table. They are an essential part of the diet in most areas of PNG. Dozens of varieties are available, from soft, sweeter ones to starchy green ones. They range from finger-sized to large plantains. The locals ate bananas every day. They roasted them on the fire or boiled them in a pot. They preferred the cooking plantains that were more filling, rather than the ripe, sweeter ones we chose to eat. Because they were available all year long in the tropics, we never lacked for a banana.

We sliced them in the morning onto our granola or oatmeal, put them on our toast, smeared them with peanut butter for a snack, or just peeled and ate them. We baked banana bread or made banana sandwiches. We mixed them with papaya and pineapple to make a delicious fruit salad. For desserts we made banana pudding, a version of bananas foster, or fried banana fritters sprinkled with icing sugar. If there was a way to use a banana, we had it figured out.

The problem with all this deliciousness is that the novelty wears off. Eating banana-everything became banana-overload. After a while I craved a fresh apple, a juicy orange, or a crispy pear – none of which were available. Rather than wish for something I couldn't have, I needed to be thankful that I had an overabundance of this sweet fruit that could be used in so many ways.

"We never throw out the whole banana. We cut out the spoiled section and use the rest," the senior missionary remarked one day when I had chucked a bad banana away.

Even though thirty bananas hung on the porch, we still needed to use our resources wisely. I learned to cut out any bruises or bad spots before eating them, rather than be wasteful.

Even Jesus set the example for resourcefulness when he fed the five thousand. After the miraculous feeding of thousands of people, he sent the disciples to collect the food left over. They collected twelve baskets full. Rather than abandon the food to rot or mold on the mountainside, it was taken with them. I'm sure it would feed either the disciples and their families or others who needed food in the days ahead.

Jesus said, "Let nothing be wasted."

Shouldn't we follow his example by wisely using our resources as our appreciation for God's provision? Even overabundance isn't a reason to be wasteful, but a chance to become creative or to share with others. May we be thankful and not take God's provision for granted.

Prayer

Father, thank you for providing for us what we need. Forgive me for the times when I have been wasteful. Help me to be creative and resourceful in using what you have given me and give me a generous heart to share with those who have need.

Personal Reflection

1. Describe ways in which you have learned to be resourceful in your home.

2. Jesus told the disciples to let nothing be wasted. God blessed the crowds with abundant provision that day. Examine ways in which God has blessed your life with extra resources, gifting, or opportunities. Are you wasting some of his provision in your life?

3. Do we take God's blessings for granted? Are we using his provision wisely?

Frugality

I am not saying this because I am in need, for I have learned
to be content in any circumstance. I have experienced times of
need and times of abundance. In any and every circumstance
I have learned the secret of contentment, whether I go satisfied
or hungry, have plenty or nothing. I am able to do all things
through the one who strengthens me. (Philippians 4:11-13 NET)

"I never open a tin of food unless there is nothing else to eat. It's far more expensive to use," Mrs. Merri said.

Unfortunately, I hadn't learned that in our earliest weeks there. While she and her husband, Bill, were away for a two-week ministry trip, I raided their pantry and used many cans of food as I struggled to adjust and prepare meals. When she returned, she noticed the missing cans of food from her cupboard. I had used about a dozen cans of baked beans, peaches, tinned meat, and other items. I'm sure she was horrified at what her young American guest had used, but she only gave me a kind correction.

Since every item in the small store in town had to be flown in or brought upriver on a barge, the cost of these items was three to four times what we paid at home. It didn't take long for me to learn how necessary it was to become a frugal homemaker – especially on our minimal missionary budget.

Lunch consisted of homemade bread, cheese, or local fruit – bananas, pineapple, or papaya. If there were leftovers from the night before, those would be divided and added to our plate. A special lunch treat was a salad, a boiled egg, or a small tin of meat to eat with our bread. Dinner consisted of a chunk of meat with steamed local vegetables cooked in the pressure cooker. Potatoes, carrots, green beans, or cabbage were the most common available. The pressure cooker was quick and used less gas on the stove. Gas bottles for the stove were expensive and came into town on a barge up the Fly River. Life became frugal and simple.

Things that had once been ordinary to life now became luxuries. Coke, a common item in our home country, cost four times more in PNG. A head of lettuce was six times the price, so a salad and a Coke became a lavish treat. Once or twice each month, Dale and I would split one can and savor each sip.

During okari nut season, I watched Mrs. Merri go to the market and buy up every nut she could find. This indigenous edible nut takes work to extract it from its thick outer shell, and we bought them shelled from a local market. This long, thick-layered nut had a unique and delicate flavor. She would bring them home, wash and cut them into pieces, and then roast them in the oven to dry. She preserved them for months in jars; she used them in her cookies and desserts.

Frugality not only meant being careful with food, it meant becoming prudent with other things as well. We learned to re-use envelopes for internal mission mail and to save plastic grocery bags. We washed and dried zip-top bags and aluminum foil to use many times more. Lights were never left on. We cut up and sewed old and frayed towels into potholders and cleaning rags. We washed glass jars and used them for storage. If we collected too many, we passed them on for someone else to use. Nothing was wasted.

The locals were experts at recycling. If an umbrella broke and no longer served its purpose, they ripped it apart for a new use. The material was used to swaddle a baby, and the metal spokes were turned into needles for weaving a string bag. Even a cardboard box was considered useful. Large ones were hauled off and opened to become sleeping mats. Empty tin cans cut open neatly became potential cups or a vase to put flowers in for church. We gave empty drink jugs away for others to use for fetching water. Things that we once threw out without thought were now given to someone who could make use of them. A land of need has a way of changing how we look at things and their potential value.

If we couldn't use it, then someone would figure out a way to recycle it for a different purpose.

I had left the toss-out world of plenty to live in a world where everything had value. I needed to learn to deny myself things that had become expensive luxuries and be content with what we had. God hadn't brought me to this place to live as I had before, but to change my heart, my habits, and my outlook. Rather than focus on what I had lost, I needed to learn happiness in my new circumstances.

Some adjustments are never easy, but a willingness to change shows a heart that fully trusts in God. God isn't concerned with my comfort as much as he is about growth in areas of my life that need it. Contentment can make adjustments when necessary and trusts in the sovereignty of God's plan.

Prayer

Father, change my heart. Whether in need or in abundance, may I find my contentment in you as my Savior. Give me satisfaction where you have me and a hope that trusts in your sovereign plan for me. Transform my thinking so that I can walk in joy with you even when my circumstances change.

Personal Reflection

1. Has your financial standing changed to where you need to make drastic changes in your lifestyle? What things are you doing to be frugal?

2. Contentment comes from within as we learn to trust in God's plan. In what area of your life do you struggle the most with contentment? How will you allow God to transform your heart?

3. Read 1 Timothy 6:6-7. What two things does verse 6 say is great gain for a person's life?

Ants and Apple Pie

Therefore, as the elect of God, holy and dearly loved, clothe yourselves with a heart of mercy, kindness, humility, gentleness, and patience, bearing with one another and forgiving one another, if someone happens to have a complaint against anyone else. Just as the Lord has forgiven you, so you also forgive others. And to all these virtues add love, which is the perfect bond. (Colossians 3:12-14 NET)

Covering the leftover dessert with a tea towel had been a bad idea. With no room inside the small fridge, we placed the leftover half of a pie on the top of the fridge. Then I covered it with a tea towel. The next night, we planned to eat the rest.

Big mistake.

After a store owner gave me a few treasured apples, I had gone through painstaking work to make a special dessert. Imported items not native to Papua New Guinea were expensive. With a few bruises and bad spots, these apples weren't good for selling, so my friend who ran the store gave them to me. I decided to make a pie.

The anticipation and smell of the pie in the oven cheered us up as it baked that night. Comfort food from home was on the menu for dinner. We cut into the warm pie and enjoyed every bite of its warm, cinnamon-spiced sweetness. It tasted delicious.

The following night Mrs. Merri and I went to the kitchen to serve the other half of the pie. I reached for it and removed the towel while she gathered dessert plates.

"Oh no, we can't eat the pie. Ants have gotten into it," I said disappointedly. The pie was swimming with ants.

Looking at the pie, she said, "I'll just pop it in the oven to kill the ants. It will still be okay to eat." Then she turned on the gas oven, jacked up the temperature, and placed the pie inside.

What? Really?

Does she mean to eat the pie with the ants?

Well, yes she did. She had every intention of eating more pie.

I wasn't so sure about the whole idea. I'd heard that some people ate fried beetles, chicken-feet soup, roasted bugs, and other "delicacies," but could I eat pie with ants? My wishful thinking hoped the hot oven would make the ants scurry from the pie.

After five minutes on a high temperature, she pulled the pie from the oven and served it on four plates.

Yep. The ants were dead.

I didn't warn Dale of what he was about to eat. I simply placed his pie in front of him and sat in my chair, but his careful eye caught a problem right away. Our hosts dived into their evening dessert with delight, enjoying their second night of American-made apple pie. We ate timidly. I tried to shove a few dead ants buried in the crust to the side, as I ate tiny bites here and there. I really wanted more pie, but I wasn't a well-broken jungle missionary yet (not that I ever would be).

I had eaten about half of my pie when Dale flipped his slice over to see the bottom crust plastered with dead ants.

With a furrowed brow he said, "Hmmm, I don't think I can eat any more of this."

Then I flipped mine over to find a hidden ant army too. Those little buggers just ruined my appetite. We decided together that we no longer wanted more pie. It was too much to handle.

In true hard-core missionary fashion, Mrs. Merri looked up and said, "Oh, just close your eyes and eat it; it's more protein."

In their combined seventy-plus years of serving as missionaries on far-flung isolated outstations, this was easy to handle. They had lived in the years when supplies and mail came upriver only once every six months. They were tough, and their lives had seen far worse than tiny ants in a pie. I'm sure they almost starved in their earliest years. Never looking at the underside of their pie, they finished it with gusto.

Every. Single. Bite.

But not us; we were wimps.

Rather than berate us or joke about it with us, they let us make our decision. Even later, they never brought it up. Nor did they judge us according to their standard. We had many lessons ahead, and they chose to let this one pass. During those months of mentoring, they showed a kindness and patience that I'm sure tested them or made them chuckle. It couldn't have been easy to have young, inexperienced missionaries living in their home for months.

We will always differ in opinion and actions from others. Will we use those differences as a reason for discord or teasing? A different choice doesn't mean that we cannot get along and respect the other person. Learning to accept others for their differences or their lack of experience is a way to model maturity as a Christian. Helping someone on a journey different from ours may be the reason God put them in our life.

Prayer

Father, thank you for the body of Christ and all those who have had an influence in my life. Give me kindness and patience as I engage with others. Help me to respect and accept others for who they are, even if our opinions differ. When a difference arises, give me a gentle spirit to display Christian maturity. Let me show love as you would.

Personal Reflection

1. How do you treat others when you differ in opinion from them? Do you judge others by your standard, or do you allow them to have opposing opinions?

2. Read Titus 2:1-8. What does this passage say about mature Christians teaching younger ones?

3. Was there a time when you mentored another person? If you are older, have you considered walking alongside a younger person to model spiritual maturity and encourage them in their walk with Christ?

Coconut Sago

Then Peter replied, "I see very clearly that God shows no favoritism. In every nation he accepts those who fear him and do what is right. This is the message of Good News for the people of Israel—that there is peace with God through Jesus Christ, who is Lord of all." (Acts 10:34-36 NLT)

The local pastor's wife walked up to the house with a warm bundle in her hand. She spoke a little English and was one of my first friends in the country. Her outgoing personality helped put me at ease as she tried to help me adjust to our new life.

"I made you some coconut sago."

A few days earlier, she promised to make me some of her sago and let me try the traditional staple of the area. In her hand she held something wrapped in banana leaves. She unrolled her steamy bundle to show me its contents. Inside the leaf, she revealed food in a long tubular shape.

"It's really good. You are going to like it," she said.

She tore some off and handed it to me. It was grayish in color with white flecks of the shredded coconut. I took a bite. It was warm and almost tasteless, though the grated coconut gave it flavor. Its texture was tough and rubbery. Sago was a new food for me, and I wasn't sure what to think. I was not impressed, but it wasn't horrible either. I kept eating. Her face smiled with eagerness as she waited for my response.

"Thank you for making this for me. I like the coconut in there," I said. I wasn't sure what to say, but I wanted to show my appreciation for her gift.

The staple food of the lowland areas in most of Papua New Guinea is sago, which is made from the starch of the sago palm tree. The pith of the tree is beaten, soaked with water, and then squeezed. The starch runs down a trough and through a woven bag to catch the fibers; it is collected in a bark tray. Once the water is drained off, a damp, powdery starch is left, similar to wet flour. The native New Guineans make it into a plain, moist flatbread, or they mix in coconut, greens, fish, and other food. It can also be wrapped in leaves and steamed or cooked in a fry pan. The nutrition content is low, but it fills bellies – which is important when garden food is scarce.

Sago is sold in the market in a large, leaf-wrapped lump and tied with jungle twine. Rather than being dry like flour, it is a starchy, damp hunk. To cook, a chunk is removed and used in a variety of ways for a meal. It can last a couple of weeks out of the fridge but gets tangy as it starts to sour.

Mrs. Merri served this to us at breakfast, but she cooked it a different way. She would grab a handful and break it up into a hot and oiled skillet by rubbing it between her hands. Then she sprinkled it with a smattering of water and let it cook. After a couple minutes, she flipped it to the other side. When done, it was slid onto a plate and sliced into pie-shaped pieces. Then we put on butter, jam, Vegemite, or peanut butter.

At first this new food was strange, but we soon learned to like it. Over our years there, it became a lunch staple. I added either grated cheese or coconut. Mashed banana made it a sweeter option. Sometimes I cooked it plain, and we smeared it with peanut butter. The locals also added greens or seasonal *pitpit,*[9] which we also liked. If I had sago on hand, it was a quick item to cook.

We wanted to adapt to this culture, so we learned to eat this food. The sago in this country was the equivalent to bread in my home. It was served almost every day and was an important part of the meal. The more I learned to cook and eat it, the more I could identify with this cultural food. Sago filled the people's bellies, but it had also saved their lives during times of drought.

Embracing this food was embracing the people and the culture.

While there were some aspects of the culture that we could not

---

9   Pitpit is an edible stalk of wild cane.

accept, we would learn to enjoy sago. The locals loved to see us eat their food. It was a delight to them to hear us say, "I'm hungry for sago," or "When is the pitpit season ready?" While much of our diet was flown in to nourish our family, there were still local seasonal foods that we looked forward to eating: breadfruit, pitpit, hala fruit from the Pandanus tree, bamboo shoots, seasonal nuts, and a type of jungle grape. We also loved papaya, which grew in abundance all year.

When we live in another culture, it's wise to share in the important aspects of the local life. Loving the good things about another's food and culture endeared us to them. As we lived among them to show them God's love and to bring the message of the gospel, we learned just as much as they did. They taught us, and we taught them. It was a mutual relationship of friendship and respect. Love and acceptance make all the difference.

Prayer

Father, thank you for the abundance of food on this earth and the unique opportunity to learn and eat new foods as we travel. Give me a love and respect for those whose culture and food are different, and help me to learn to build friendships. Give me a heart that finds common ground with everyone I meet, so that I can have the opportunity to share the Good News of Jesus with them.

Personal Reflection

1. Have you traveled to another country? What was different about the culture and the food?

2. Often someone needs to feel accepted before we can share the gospel with them. Are you able to build friendships with someone different from yourself?

3. Read 1 Corinthians 9:19-23. How did Paul adapt to different cultures? In verses 22-23, what did he say his purpose was?

The Fat Fellows

So why do you condemn another believer? Why do you look down on another believer? Remember, we will all stand before the judgment seat of God. For the Scriptures say, "As surely as I live," says the LORD, "every knee will bend to me, and every tongue will declare allegiance to God." Yes, each of us will give a personal account to God. So let's stop condemning each other.
(Romans 14:10-13 NLT)

Kritope, the hired house helper, walked over to the table during our lunch one day and said, "Do you want to try a sago grub?" In his outstretched hand he held several fat, little, squirming worms for us to see.

Try one? They are still moving.

These chubby grubs with brown heads were considered a delicacy. I knew this, but I hadn't been face to face with the little creatures yet. They looked disgusting. Their bloated white bodies had ridges and looked as if they might burst at any moment. They are found in the rotting trunks of the sago palm tree; the grubs are hatched from the eggs of a beetle. I'm told they taste like bacon when roasted, but they are also steamed with sago inside banana leaves over the fire, and they are also eaten raw.

"There is a very good juice inside," he said. He then squeezed one grub to show us the "juice."

An awkward moment took over as we hoped the senior missionaries would handle the situation and make it go away.

They didn't.

Perhaps they wanted to let the young missionaries try their hand at eating one. I'm sure in their earlier years they had to eat more than their fair share.

Dale broke the silence. "Kritope, how do you eat them?"

He reached for one between his fingers and put it up to his mouth to show us. Squeezing it between his lips he forced the insides out and shoved the rest into his mouth.

"They are very good," he said with a twinkle in his eye.

By this time, I had lost my appetite. No more lunch for me.

When we arrived in this country and were informed about different aspects of the culture, we were told that if you offer the people's food back to them, then they are not offended. Dale decided to try that tactic.

"Kritope, thank you, but we know this is a favorite food for you. You eat them, and we will eat our lunch."

With that, he was satisfied and went to complete his other chores. We breathed a sigh of relief that eating a live grub had been averted.

Several years later, we went to a traditional feast that the local church held. Their custom is for everyone to place a plate in the center of the room, and everyone shares their food by placing a little on each plate. Then the plates are given back to you, piled high with more than you can eat. On the top of my plate, I saw a warm piece of coconut sago. I loved their warm feast sago when it was dotted with coconut. However, on a closer look, I noticed that this piece had a plethora of steamed sago grubs scattered throughout. I stared at those fat fellows lying there buried in that rubbery warmth, and I could not bring myself to take a bite. Yet I knew they had given me their finest piece. I tore off a couple corners without grubs and ate that. Later, when I was done eating, my plate was passed to someone who wanted the remainder of my food. They ate it with pleasure, I'm sure.

Most missionaries had stories of their grub-eating adventures, yet in all our years there, I managed to avoid eating even one grub. My family ate them, but I never did. I decided I did not need those bragging rights. That was one cultural adjustment I was not making. No grubs for me. Ever. Whether or not I ate those fat fellows didn't define me as a good or a bad missionary. In this instance, I was the "weaker sister" who couldn't eat a grub.

There may be times when missionaries judge their fellow workers in culture adjustment, language ability, willingness to "rough it," ministry methods, and other areas. Yet we each need to find the areas where we can adapt or where we will politely decline.

Some things in life, too, are not right or wrong, nor do they define us as a good or bad person. God gives us freedom to choose. Yet sometimes we can make a big issue over someone's choices – reading a certain version of the Bible, attending a specific denominational church, arguing about vague theological points or style of worship music. The danger is falling into the trap of debating or unnecessarily criticizing others.

Paul says, *Accept other believers who are weak in faith, and don't argue with them about what they think is right or wrong.*[10] Some things do not go against standards of biblical truth and are not forbidden in Scripture, but are only a preference or a choice. In these things we show an attitude of acceptance. We are all on a different journey of maturity, and love and grace toward one another honors God.

Prayer

Father, thank you for your standards of biblical truth that remain true for all generations. Help us to live by those truths. I also thank you for the freedom we have in Christ to make choices in areas that are not crucial to your biblical standards. Help me to not have a critical or argumentative spirit with other believers, but give me a loving and graceful heart toward others.

Personal Reflection

1. In Romans 14:10, who gives an account to God? What do Christians need to stop doing?

2. Do you have a critical or argumentative spirit with other believers you don't agree with?

3. In Paul's day, he called for Christians to show restraint from judging others. Matters that don't relate to salvation

---

10   Romans 14:1 NLT

or biblical truth and are not forbidden in Scripture should be handled with love and grace. How are you at showing grace toward those who have a differing opinion?

4. Has there been a time in your life when you felt wrongly judged? How did that affect you?

Life Is Sweet

Bless the LORD, O my soul, and all that is within me, bless his holy name! Bless the LORD, O my soul, and forget not all his benefits, who forgives all your iniquity, who heals all your diseases, who redeems your life from the pit, who crowns you with steadfast love and mercy, who satisfies you with good so that your youth is renewed like the eagle's. (Psalm 103:1-5 ESV)

One of the great things about the tropics was the abundance of tropical fruits. With the exception of bananas and pineapple, we had new fruits I had never seen nor eaten. I loved to try them all.

One of the first strange fruits we tried was the tamarillo. This egg-shaped fruit came with a red or orange skin which resembled a tomato when sliced. We were shown how to cut it in half and spoon out the insides to eat. Adding a sprinkle of sugar took the edge off its tangy taste. Over the years, my favorite ways to use this fruit was to make it into jam or to mash it up and use it like berries inside a Southern-style cobbler.

Another great fruit we learned to eat was the papaya, or *pawpaw*, as it's called in Papua New Guinea. Several sizes and varieties were available. Several trees full of this fresh fruit grew outside the mission house. These reminded me of cantaloupe but with a much sweeter taste and a softer interior when ripe. Most days we ate sliced papaya for lunch with a squeeze of lemon. When we had an abundance of ripe ones, they also made a delicious jam.

One of my favorites was the soursop fruit, which had a bumpy, green-skin exterior and soft and creamy-flesh interior. Large black seeds dotted the stringy fiber of its interior. Pulling the flesh apart, we used to pop it into our mouths and enjoy its unique juicy flavor. Its sweet taste reminded me of a mix between a strawberry and a pineapple. Our family looked forward to soursop season, but some of our house guests were disgusted by its squishy, fibrous texture. We loved to make a drink with it by pushing its juice through a strainer. We used that to flavor water for a drink (much like how you would make lemonade). This tree and its fruit is now becoming known for its medicinal benefits.

Two fruits that were not indigenous to the area where we were but could be found in other parts of the country were the lemon and the guava. By growing a couple trees from the seeds, we soon had a couple lemon trees at the station and a guava tree growing near our house. Lemons would produce most of the year, but guava was seasonal. When we had a large supply of fresh guava, I usually made a batch of jam – a great way to preserve many varieties of fruit. Mangoes, avocadoes, star fruit, passion fruit, and watermelon were other fruits we ate on occasion as we traveled in the country.

Throughout our years in PNG, we enjoyed all these wonderful, fresh tropical fruits. What an adventure to taste these exotic treasures of another country and learn how to eat and preserve them.

God says that he will satisfy our desires with good things, and these sweet tropical fruits were some of the delicious things he provided for us. Life will have good things as well as difficult things, and it takes a wise person to see that we can learn to live with both. Because God is our creator and Redeemer, we can take joy in these little things. Rather than allow our focus to be on the difficult, let's seek out the blessings that God has brought our way. Life is sweet because we have a great and faithful God. He is active in our lives and gives us everything we need. Let's enjoy all the blessings, even the sweet fruits that God brings our way, and rejoice in his goodness.

Prayer

Thank you, Father, that life is sweet and blessed because you are our creator God. You provide wonderful things for us to enjoy, and you provide us with every spiritual blessing that we need. You have forgiven and healed us; you have redeemed us; you have crowned us with love and mercy; and you have satisfied us with good things. Today I praise you for all you have done for me.

Personal Reflection

1. What are some of the sweet things in your life right now? Or, what are some ways in which has God blessed you in this stage of life?

2. What are the five benefits (five verbs) that God gives his children in Psalm 103:1-5?

3. What are the spiritual blessings that God has given all believers according to Ephesians 1:3-14?

Out-of-Date

*But godliness with contentment is great gain. For we brought
nothing into the world, and we can take nothing out of it. But
if we have food and clothing, we will be content with that.*
(1 Timothy 6:6-8 NIV)

In this small, riverfront town of Kiunga, some things didn't matter
in our new but temporary location. We learned early on that dates
were insignificant, that is, expiration dates. Many things we bought at
the local trade store in Kiunga were past their prime. We used them
anyway – cereal, food, jam, and even some medicine. If the tin wasn't
dented, rusty, or distended, we bought it; but even if it was, we might
consider it! The bottom line was that we could not be picky. If we needed
it, we picked out the best from what was available. As newcomers to the
country, we didn't especially like it, but we had to choose from what
was available.

Milk powder took on a yellowish hue when it was old; chocolate had
a grayish haze; orange apricot jam turned into an undefined color; and
stale cereal became the norm. If it was free of mold and smelled okay,
we ate it. Most of the food was still fine to eat.

Things went stale quickly in this tropical and humid environment.
Sometimes we would heat our stale cereal in the oven to crisp it up
again. We learned to store food in airtight containers for long storage.
In later years when we had children, they grew up eating stale, chewy
cheese puffs, which we ordered a carton at a time from the store. The
great thing is the children didn't know the difference. I'd reach into the

storage pantry and grab them each a mini bag, and they were delighted with their "special" snack.

We also learned that most out-of-date medicine was still good, maybe just not as effective. So if our stored medicine went past its expiration, we used it anyway. And usually it still took care of our problem. We were guided along by our experienced missionary friends in what to do and not do.

This was a challenge for me in the beginning, but I learned that I needed to make these changes in lifestyle if I were to follow God in contentment. Why fuss and focus on what I didn't have? I didn't have beautiful orange apricot jam; I had one brownish in color, but it was still perfectly fine to eat. If I focused on what I couldn't have, then I would lose sight of the goal for which God had sent us. Would I let all these little things create a complaining spirit within me? We had to guard our attitudes to avoid discontentment as we learned this new life.

Change is something in life that we will all experience. A move, a loss in finances, or a new job may be hard on us or our family. Or we may experience a challenge like an empty nest or retirement which brings about a change in daily purpose. It can be difficult to become accustomed to life's changes and look toward a new normal. Satisfaction shouldn't arise from our circumstances, for it comes from a heart that is willing to change and find contentment where God has placed us. Insisting on things the way they once were can bring pain and discontentment. God desires us to do our best to focus on the new opportunities, new friendships, and new adventures before us. Living life where we are and learning to adapt shows a heart that is learning contentment. And this pleases God.

Prayer

God, you have said that godliness with contentment is great gain. Help me to embrace this truth. Help me to learn what it means to experience contentment when difficult changes are happening in my life. Rather than focusing on my circumstances, help me to remember all the blessings you have made available to me as your child. Give me a thankful heart that praises you even amid the changes and challenges where I find myself. Give me joy in your presence and a heart that rests in your love for me.

Personal Reflection

1. Does change come easily to you, or are you resistant to change?

2. What two things does God say is *great gain* for us in 1 Timothy 6:6-8? What two things does he say we should be content with?

3. The world bombards us with what we "need" – to obtain more, to look a certain way, to have a degree, to be married, and much more. In what area of your life do you need to pray for contentment?

4. What promise do you read in 2 Corinthians 9:8?

My Cup of Tea

*So I recommend the enjoyment of life, for there is nothing bet-
ter on earth for a person to do except to eat, drink, and enjoy
life. So joy will accompany him in his toil during the days of
his life which God gives him on earth.* (Ecclesiastes 8:15 NET)

After placing two bowls of oatmeal on the table, I sat down and
noticed lizard poo on my placemat. I paused.

Great. More lizard gifts.

I decided to deal with that later. I didn't want the quietness of this
morning interrupted as I enjoyed waking up with my hot tea. Dale said
the blessing, and we started eating.

The calm of a quiet morning would end soon as others began to
descend upon the mission station where the mission house, the medical
worker's house, and the aid post were located. Some would come either
to talk on the high-frequency (HF) radio or to wait for medicine. The
space underneath our house, which was built on posts seven feet off the
ground, became the favored spot for sitting and waiting. Shaded from
the intense tropical sun, it created a cool spot for everyone to hang out.
At times we endured screaming babies, laughing mothers, and energetic
children, all with the radio blaring in the office at the end of our home.
Sometimes the loudness of morning chaos put my nerves on edge.

Lizard poo was the least of my worries.

One thing I learned is to not let the little aggravations get the best
of me. Pick and choose what matters most. Rats roaming the house
at night to chew on food, lizards getting into fights at the top of the

wall, and the creepy sound of flying foxes (bats) flapping their wings outside our window made for many a sleepless night. Worst of all was the annoying rat that climbed the coconut tree some nights. We would lie in bed, listening to his constant chewing as he chomped his way through the outer husk and shell to reach the coconut meat. The noise he generated in the silence of the night was unbelievable. How could one little creature have such determination?

Coupled with the tropical heat and the creatures who stirred in the night, sleep could be elusive. Some mornings we awoke tired and bleary-eyed. So, who cares about a little lizard poo? Not me. I just want my cup of tea to clear the fog from my mind and wake up.

Some things in life aren't worth the stress or the worry. With so many things happening in life, do we really need to worry about all the little things that annoy us? Can we just learn to sit and enjoy the moment? I feel blessed to have another day to live, to love, and to serve. The more I learn to drop the things that irritate me, the more I gain inner peace. Those little aggravations will become only a comma that makes me pause, but not a period that makes me stop. Life doesn't revolve around insignificant things, and I can choose to ignore them.

Instead, I plan to enjoy my hot, steaming cup of tea with its little spoonful of sugar.

Prayer

Lord, help me choose to ignore life's irritations. Rather than worry and stress over little aggravations, help me learn to take pleasure in the positive things around me. Give me a heart that is thankful for the blessings of each new day. Teach me enjoyment in all of life's little moments.

Personal Reflection

1. How do you react to life's irritations? Do you choose to ignore them, or do they exasperate you?

2. Pastor Chuck Swindoll says, "Words can never adequately convey the incredible impact of our attitudes toward life.

The longer I live the more convinced I become that life is ten percent what happens to us and ninety percent how we respond to it."[11] Why do you think attitude is important in our outlook?

3. Read Psalm 118:24. What does this verse say about how we should face each new day?

11   Chuck Swindoll, www.azquotes.com/author/14373-Charles_R_Swindoll/tag/attitude

Section Three

Jungle Dilemmas

Culture shock creates a sense of anxiety and confusion as we learn to relate to a foreign environment. As our reference of normal is tossed upside down, it doesn't take long to feel out of balance or lack confidence in the new things we experience. Expectations from cultural or tribal traditions, a new language, and even weather may all be different. What might be appropriate in our own country may now be bad behavior in our new culture. What was considered rude in our former home may now be normal in our new one. These sudden changes and differences can be reasons for added stress and can take years to understand.

What's it like to be the outsider, the missionary foreigner? How are we viewed by these people so different from us, and how do we view them?

The gray areas in a new culture will challenge us most when there is no clear right or wrong. Sometimes we may see no easy solution, and we may not get things right. Much of life's changes are about a journey of faith and dependence upon a holy God. We can rely on his wisdom to help us. Things that began with difficulty soon get easier as we adjust to a new way of understanding people, their culture, and their environment. Yet some things (mostly critters) will always be a challenge.

The following stories are from the time after our stay in Kiunga. We were moved to three different remote outstations by mission leadership. Each place had a different house and varied challenges.

Bush Baby

Yet the LORD longs to be gracious to you; therefore he will rise up to show you compassion. For the LORD is a God of justice. Blessed are all who wait for him! (Isaiah 30:18 NIV)

"Before you go out to the bush you really need to see how a baby is delivered. Some day you may need that knowledge to help a woman in labor," the government doctor told me one day when he stopped by while we were in Kiunga. (The term *bush* was used for rainforest areas with no road access.) The bush areas were the most remote and poorest areas of the country. People lived there much as they had for centuries, and we would move there in a couple of months.

"The next time a lady comes in for labor, I'll come pick you up so you can see the process."

"Okay," I said, although I was not sure I wanted to learn about birthing babies.

Sure enough, a week later, he arrived at the house in the hospital's Suzuki vehicle. "It's time," he said. "A lady is in labor." We got in his vehicle, and he drove us the short distance to the local hospital.

He led me to the room where the woman was in labor. No sooner had I arrived at the hospital than my stomach lurched several times. I felt sick and ran for the restroom to throw up. Not wanting a sick lady in the ward, they drove me back to the house. Embarrassed by my lack of control of the situation, I couldn't figure out why I had gotten sick.

But others had their suspicions. I had had a queasy stomach on other mornings, and Mrs. Merri had noticed.

Hmmm, she thought. After a few more of these same "episodes," she suggested that we go get a pregnancy test.

Sure enough, our own little baby was on the way. Soon, we transferred to that remote station in the bush. I had not brought one single baby item with me when we had packed our crate for overseas. We had nothing for this child – no diapers, no bedding, no crib, no clothes, *nothing* for a little one.

The nesting instinct began to set in, and I wanted to prepare for our new addition. A friend purchased a few pieces of material for me, so I sewed a gingham baby blanket and a few nightshirts. It wasn't much, but I had done something to welcome our baby.

I felt sorry for myself and our little baby. I could make no preparations. There were no stores for shopping, no baby showers to attend, and online shopping was a thing of the future. Months went by at this isolated outstation while my tummy grew. Somehow, I knew God would provide, even if by my last-minute shopping in the capital city. Yet I still longed to prepare and have things ready for our little one's birth.

Five months later, my mother wrote us a letter. One of our supporting churches in North Charleston, South Carolina, had held a baby shower for us. My mother attended and opened all the gifts in my place. In the letter, she listed all the presents from the shower. I was overwhelmed with joy at this news. Short-term summer workers coming to the country would bring the items with them to the capital city, Port Moresby, where I was required to fly to for the baby's birth. I could pick up the shower gifts weeks before the birth of our baby.

On my arrival in Port Moresby, trunks, suitcases, and a duffel bag full of items waited for me in the guest room of my missionary host. I sorted through the items, elated at the generosity of this church. Everything was included – a playpen, a foldable crib, dozens of cloth diapers, bottles, toys, shoes, hats, blankets, pacifiers, nursing items, a foldable stroller, and even a travel high chair. Dozens of summer clothes of every kind and size for a boy and a girl were included.

Nothing was forgotten. I was overwhelmed by the generosity of this church, for God had provided through his people in an amazing and extraordinary way. This baby had everything she needed, and I did not need to buy one thing. The timing was perfect. God had abundantly provided more than I thought possible. And these items would be used for years when our boys were later born.

God knows our need. But the waiting and trusting can be difficult when we look at our circumstances. Does he really care? Will he provide? Yes. The times of true and helpless need in our lives create a deeper trust and dependence on God. As we struggle through a trial, our challenge is to learn to wait and lean on promises in Scripture. A heart willing to wait on God will see the perfect provision in his time. He will not abandon us. I believe our heavenly Father takes great joy in overwhelming us with his provision.

Prayer

Heavenly Father, thank you for being gracious and compassionate to me. In a time of waiting, give me a strong faith to believe that you will help me when your timing is perfect. You see and you know all the needs in my life, and you will never abandon me. You are able to accomplish more than I can even ask or think. I praise you today that you are my God.

Personal Reflection

1. Describe a time in your life when God provided for you in an amazing way.

2. According to Isaiah 30:18, what does God long to do for us? When does God say we are blessed? How can this verse change your thinking about God?

3. What does Ephesians 3:20 say about God's ability to accomplish what we might ask or think? Take this verse as a promise for your day.

Mushroom Lady

But if anyone is deficient in wisdom, he should ask God, who gives to all generously and without reprimand, and it will be given to him. (James 1:5 NET)

After our nine-month time of orientation with the Merriweathers, we moved to an outstation where the only way in or out was by foot or small aircraft. We were then under the leadership of another missionary couple.

In this remote location, we lived in what we called a "glorified bush house." Built from local materials, it had a few amenities. Instead of a thatched roof, it had a galvanized metal roof. Running water, which was fed from rainwater collected in tanks, was installed in the kitchen and the shower. The round-timber siding and flooring were made from the local black palm tree. Round timber framed the windows that were covered with sheet metal. With no screening, these windows were pushed out on their hinges during the day and held open with a large stick to allow the breeze to flow through. When the tropical rains came, they were shut to prevent rain from blowing into the house.

Without screens, the wind blew through with ease in the hot season – a welcome relief in this lowland heat. Flies and lizards also came in at will, as well as large green grasshoppers. I could deal with the flies and lizards, but the grasshoppers startled me if they flew close. They gnawed holes in the curtains or jumped out of hiding places and frightened me. I hated them.

While preparing lunch one day, I looked out the kitchen window to see one of the local women standing outside several feet away.

"Gwarume, gwarume," she said with slow, deliberate speech.

Her name was Swalimi. Although I didn't know much of the Motu trade language, I knew she was saying, "Fish, fish." With one motion, she drew her hand to her mouth as if to put food into it. Staring at me, I realized she wanted a tin of mackerel fish. All she wore was a bright orange cotton skirt around her waist and a string of Job's tears seeds – nothing else. The necklace was made from an ornamental grass which produces a pea-shaped seed. When dried, the seed turns gray and has a natural hole through the middle. Strung on homemade string, these seeds are used for making local jewelry.

"Gwarume, gwarume," she said again.

The senior missionary in charge told me not to give anything to her, or it would encourage her to return. She was nicknamed "the mushroom lady" by the locals, because years before she had eaten poisonous mushrooms and almost died. Though she lived, she was left with a deficient mental capacity. Sometimes the locals chased her away or laughed at her if she became too annoying. The resident missionary couple and others provided clothes and food for her, so she was well cared for. But she was known for begging. Today she hoped the newcomer (me) would hand her a luxury tin of fish.

As she stood there, I felt sorry for her but also a bit afraid. I wasn't used to this new place. Her behavior was strange as she waited. What would she do? How long would she stand and stare? She waited for a response and kept giving her request.

Not knowing what to do, I went to another part of the house where she couldn't see me. Before long, she left.

I felt guilty. She had asked me for something, and I did not help.

Now I faced a different reality. Many challenges lay ahead, and this was only the beginning. Many situations would be a struggle. How do we help without enabling wrong behavior? How do we love without causing dependence? When will we know the right thing to do? We were here to help, but when was helping wrong? All of these questions and more rose up within my heart as we learned to live in this new culture. These questions would arise continually as we lived here.

We can all face this dilemma. Sometimes life does not have an easy solution or a quick fix. Nor is everything a right or wrong. People tell us to do something, but we aren't sure if that's correct either. Or we may feel guilty when we do make a choice. To get through these gray areas of life, we need to rely on the wisdom that God offers. He knows how to lead and guide us, and he waits for us to ask. We need to pray for his perfect understanding of our situation.

Prayer

Father, thank you that your wisdom and understanding are limitless. You have the perfect answer for my situation, and you are there to guide and help me. Thank you for hearing my prayer and giving your wisdom generously. When decisions are difficult, remind me to look to you for guidance.

Personal Reflection

1. What decision are you struggling with today? Have you gone to God in prayer to ask for his guidance?

2. Read Proverbs 2:1-5. In this short passage, what are the eight things that God tells us to do? Make a list of what you find. What results will happen for us in verse 5?

3. Now read Proverbs 2:6-10. What are the results of learning to look to God for help and wisdom?

Woodstove Disasters

Work willingly at whatever you do, as though you were working for the Lord rather than for people. Remember that the Lord will give you an inheritance as your reward, and that the Master you are serving is Christ. (Colossians 3:23-24 NLT)

Wood was cheap and plentiful in the jungle. As we moved further into remote areas, cooking on a woodstove became a necessity. A gas stove was expensive to use and freight costs for flying in a large gas bottle to the bush was also costly. Now, most meals would be cooked on the woodstove, and we wouldn't have to worry about the expense. We also used a two-burner gas Primus stove that served only as a quick form of cooking or reheating. The advantage was we would never run out of wood in the rain forest; it could heat water for our bucket shower, bake our bread, and cook our meals – all for pennies.

I had never seen a woodstove, much less cooked on one. This shouldn't be too hard. All I needed was a little kindling, some paper scraps, firewood, and matches. With my can-do attitude I thought, *I can do this.* After all, I had worked my way up in Girl Scouts, so how hard could this be?

That is, until I tried to make the fire.

I scrunched up paper and put on some kindling. Then I lit it with a match. Once the paper was burning, I put on more kindling and a log. Then I started to prepare dinner.

When I came back, the fire had fizzled to nothingness, so I started it again.

And again.

For two hours, I tried to start the fire inside the six-by-six-inch firebox opening – all without success. All those summer campfires I sat around as a girl did nothing to help me get this fire going. I gave up and waited until my husband returned. Dusk arrived, and I did not have dinner ready when Dale came back from his hard day of work building on the station where we helped out temporarily.

The hubby came in worn-out from his day and started the fire without trouble. He said part of my trouble was putting a log on too soon and smothering the fire. He stood there watching things, adding more kindling, and once the kindling was burning well, he added a small log, not a huge one. With a little care, the fire was soon blazing. Then logs were added.

That night we ate a late dinner.

We solved my fire-starting problem by hiring help. We hired a young man to chop wood and kindling, start the fire each afternoon, and help with a few other chores. The locals were experts at making fires.

But I also had to learn to cook food on it. This basic cast-iron stove had no ventilation adjustments and no temperature gauge. I had to learn to fry, boil, simmer, and bake with this stove if we wanted to eat. If I wanted to boil, I learned to place the pan above the firebox for the hottest heat. To fry, I removed a stove grate and placed the pan directly over the fire. To simmer, a pan was placed away from the firebox. To keep food warm, a pan was placed on the far edge away from most of the heat.

Baking day, however, required learning a finely tuned skill. On baking day, as the bread was rising, a rip-roaring fire was lit to get the oven nice and hot. Then I popped both loaves into the oven. After a few minutes, I checked on them and found that the loaf nearest the firebox was already burnt on top. I scrambled to switch the loaf pans around. Soon, the other bread was burnt on top as well. The bread I placed on the table for lunch that day had a burnt crust and a doughy center. The fire was too hot to cook the loaves evenly, so we ate the burnt edges.

In the ninety-degree-plus heat of this tropical location, the fire added to the already steamy environment. This stove was a constant source of annoyance. If the oven was too hot, things would burn; if it was too cool, things would not cook or brown. Baking day became a day of frustration as I learned the skills of baking in this cast-iron woodstove. The fire must burn steady – not too hot, not too cool – for the best baked items. I learned when to put a log on and when not to add one. I learned to switch and turn the pans around for even browning. If we wanted to eat bread, I had to make it. It became a game of strategy to guess the oven's temperature and get out nicely baked food from the oven. After months and months of errors, I gained the skills needed to start a fire, to cook on it, and to bake in it. I had not anticipated this grueling learning process.

Yet I learned to love the versatility of the woodstove. The homeyness of simmering stew, bubbling papaya jam, freshly baked bread, and from-scratch cookies were the simple things in life that we learned to enjoy. The difficulty soon turned to great rewards that filled our bellies and nourished us. Whenever I pulled out a beautifully browned loaf of bread and enjoyed a warm, soft slice with melting butter and a drizzle of honey, it was a great reward. I had accomplished something that had taken many attempts and a learned skill.

Life will never give us everything we need without our effort. Many things will require that we work hard, learn new things, fail, but keep trying. The reward earned is much sweeter when it is born from difficulty. We can all enjoy the fruit of our labors if we persevere.

Prayer

Thank you, Lord, for giving us a sharp mind to reason, think, and learn new skills. Thank you for the ability to work. Give me a heart that works willingly and help me persevere with difficult tasks to see them to completion. Thank you that through effort and hard work, we can enjoy the fruit of our labor.

Personal Reflection

1. Merriam-Webster defines *perseverance* as the "continued effort to do or achieve something despite difficulties, failure,

or opposition." Evaluate your ability at persevering through a difficult task. Do you give up easily, or do you continue to work despite failures?

2. Read Colossians 3:23-24 again. What truths do you learn? How should we work, and whom are we serving?

3. What does Proverbs 14:23 say about work? What profit can you see from your daily work?

Silent Invasion

Jesus responded, "The Scriptures also say, 'You must not test the LORD your God.'" Next the devil took him to the peak of a very high mountain and showed him all the kingdoms of the world and their glory. "I will give it all to you," he said, "if you will kneel down and worship me." "Get out of here, Satan," Jesus told him. "For the Scriptures say, 'You must worship the LORD your God and serve only him.'" Then the devil went away, and angels came and took care of Jesus. (Matthew 4:7-11 NLT)

The tropics are known for their creepy-crawlies, and we had our fair share of encounters. Rats, lizards, flying ants, roaches, earwigs, mosquitoes, and jumping green grasshoppers were of the smaller variety. The scarier creepy-crawlies were snakes. Death adders were the most common poisonous ones in our area, along with nonpoisonous varieties like pythons.

When our daughter was a baby, we moved to a different outstation (our third location) and lived in an old mission house at Debepari station. The house was built six feet off the ground on large wooden posts. It had become our habit to sleep under mosquito netting to prevent malaria-carrying mosquitoes from biting us. In this house, we used a 240-volt generator for lighting at night. We also had rustic kerosene lanterns and one propane pump lantern, which gave off a bright light. Once lit, we hung that from the ceiling in the sitting room. If Dale was up late, he turned off the generator and used the propane lamp to conserve fuel. Battery-powered flashlights were a constant companion too, especially on our nightstand. One evening I crawled under our mosquito netting and went to bed while Dale stayed up to write letters.

Our baby daughter and I were sound asleep while he worked. After writing at the dining table for a while, Dale stretched back in his chair and looked around. Behind him he noticed a snake on the steps that led down to the office, which was on ground level. He ran to grab an axe that we kept near the woodstove. Running back to the office, he placed a few well-aimed whacks on the snake to kill it. Then he placed the snake in a bucket on the porch. He poured in a little kerosene to make sure it was dead.

He sat back down to continue his work, but stretched and looked around some more. A few minutes later, he discovered another snake coming up those same steps. He then gave that snake the same fate as the first one and threw it into the bucket too. Feeling nervous and losing concentration on his work, Dale kept checking out the office just behind him.

I soon awoke when I heard banging noises. Grabbing a flashlight, I rolled out from under the mosquito netting to see what all the commotion was about. By this time, Dale was chasing down a third snake which had made its way into the same little office.

Dale whacked at the snake as I walked into the dining area. He finished him off and headed out to plop him in the bucket with the other two.

"What is all the racket?"

"I just killed three snakes in the office," he said. "They are all in a bucket outside on the porch."

"You killed three snakes in the house? Are they poisonous?" Horrified at the thought that snakes roamed around while we slept didn't make me want to sleep. What if they went into our daughter's room?

"I'm not sure, but I killed them all. I don't know what's going on, but I'll ask someone in the morning what type of snake they are. I'm going to bed before any others arrive," he said as he closed the office door tightly.

He turned off the propane lantern and then walked down the hall. I went into our daughter's room to be sure her netting was tucked in very tightly. Then I checked to be sure all our netting was tucked tightly under each corner of our four-inch foam mattress. The netting was little comfort, but at least I could make sure they didn't crawl in bed with us. I cringed to think that more snakes might come in to roam the house. The rest of the night we slept restlessly.

Around 6:30 the next morning Dale got up and said, "I'm going to check around once more to be sure no other snakes are in the house." He grabbed a flashlight to look around while I started breakfast. He opened the office door and walked in. Shining the flashlight, he investigated every corner of the office.

So far, so good. No snakes.

Then, curled up on one of the office shelves, Dale spotted another snake sleeping. With the axe in his other hand, he placed a deadly hit on the snake. Picking it up with the edge of the blade, he dumped it into the bucket with the other snakes. Now, four dead snakes were in the bucket.

As we made breakfast that morning, the local pastor, Amo, came up to the house and noticed the bucket of snakes.

"Good morning. Did you kill all those snakes?" he asked while staring into the bucket. He spoke to my husband in Motu, the local trade language.

"Yes, they came into the house last night. Are they poisonous?"

"No, those snakes are not poisonous. What are you going to do with them? Do you want them?"

"No, we don't want them."

"Can I have them?" he asked.

"Yes, you can have them, but I put kerosene in there," Dale answered, wondering why he would want kerosene-soaked snakes.

Off Pastor Amo went with the bucket of four dead snakes. He returned later to the house to return the bucket.

"What did you do with those snakes?"

"We ate them," Pastor Amo said.

"But I soaked them in kerosene."

"I washed them before we cooked them," he said with a smile.

We heard later that even the village was creeped out when they learned four snakes had come into our house. Snakes sneaking into the house unnoticed was startling to me. Slithering into the house in the dead of night while I slept made me wonder how many more were outside. What if others were poisonous?

Since the beginning of time, we have equated the snake with Satan. Just as those snakes crept into the house unnoticed, Satan tries to sneak into our lives without notice. Again and again, he will look for any opening to creep into our lives. He does not give up; he is a thief who comes *to steal and kill and destroy* us.[12] He tempts us with sin, tries to lure us into old behaviors, creates fear, or attacks our faith. His ways are numerous as he works to defeat God's people. Just when we think we've conquered his attempts and squashed his lies, he shows up again. His purpose is always the same – to distract, to discourage, to defeat, and to draw us away from God.

But Satan has no power over us unless it is surrendered to him. Just as Jesus caused Satan to flee by using the Word of God in the wilderness,[13] so can we. Just as the axe killed those snakes, God's Word is the powerful tool needed to render Satan powerless. He cannot stand against the truth of God's Word, and he will flee. The importance of knowing and memorizing God's Word and standing on his truth are essential for every believer. We need to be diligent to thwart Satan's schemes to sneak into our lives.

Prayer

Father, thank you that your Word is powerful, and it will cause Satan to flee. Help me not to neglect Scripture but give me a love and desire to study and memorize it to stand against the devil's attacks and temptations. Give me eyes to see his deceit and lies in my life and empower me to stand on your truth.

Personal Reflection

1. Do you recognize when you are under an attack from Satan and his evil realm? Are there specific areas of your

---

12   John 10:10 NLT
13   Matthew 4:7-11 NLT

life where you feel Satan tries to drag you back into old habits and behaviors?

2. According to Matthew 4:7-11, how did Jesus make Satan flee?

3. Read Hebrews 4:12. The Word of God has power against Satan. How will knowing God's Word help us defeat Satan's attacks?

The Missionary Dilemma

Whoever is kind to the poor lends to the LORD, and he will reward them for what they have done. (Proverbs 19:17 NIV)

One night as we finished dinner and dusk was setting in, one of the local pastors came to the house carrying his kerosene lamp. We heard coughing outside, the cultural way of announcing your presence at the door. Once he got our attention, Dale went to see what he needed.

"I have no kerosene for my lamp. Can you spare some for me?"

In the last two locations where we had lived, we'd had no electricity. The only way to have light was to have a small kerosene lantern. Traditionally, people sat by the fire for lighting. Kerosene was flown in by the fifty-five-gallon drum and sold in a small local trade store that carried basic supplies. Kerosene could also be bought at a government outstation's store. That would be a day or two away by foot, depending on the starting point.

"Yes, I can give you some," Dale said. He took his lamp, filled it with kerosene, and gave it back to him. Then he left to return to his village nearby.

Before long, several other men walked up to the house with their kerosene lamps.

"We have no kerosene. Can you give us some for our lamps too?" they asked.

Our own kerosene supply was precious. We ran a small refrigerator with kerosene to preserve our food in this hot climate. If we ran out of kerosene, our food would spoil. We lit our own lanterns with kerosene, and we paid to fly our personal supply in with what little resources we had on a small missionary allowance. Since we had helped the other guy, they hoped we could help them too.

And thus, you have the missionary dilemma: What is the right thing to do? When can I help, but how do I set a limit? Obviously, we cannot provide kerosene for the whole village of hundreds who would also love some kerosene.

In a culture that is willing to give and help each other, we had to learn how to do that without overburdening ourselves as the "wealthiest" people in the area. So over time, one of the things we learned to do was to give to those closest to us – the pastors, our closest friends, and those who worked for us. These were the closest people who would give us advice, go on treks with us, and willingly help us if we needed them. They were in many ways the family we had adopted. They might share a fish with us, and we might give them some rice. A friend might gather some cane from the jungle for us to fix a chair, and we would give him several tins of fish – a special treat. On payday, I would also give my friend some soap to wash her clothes or some other item I knew she would enjoy. If they wanted to share with others, that was up to them.

There is never an easy or perfect solution to this problem. All have needs. Some have more genuine needs, and we were always willing to share with those in greater need, such as a sick person needing good food for nourishment and recovery, or someone needing a flight to the hospital for treatment. When you live within a culture, you see with better perspective and clarity. Each missionary has to decide the best way to handle things in their place of service and according to the culture they work in. Rather than making the blanket statements of "I'm helping no one," or "I'm helping everyone," we looked at the situation at hand to decide. I'm sure we did not meet everyone's expectations. At times, we would also give people work so they could earn a wage for what they needed.

In the end, Dale helped the men with their kerosene lanterns too, but he didn't fill their lamps full like the first fellow. He gave enough for them to use sparingly. They walked away happy for a little help.

The Lord has compassion on the poor, and we should too. Throughout the Gospels, Jesus helped the poor. Even in the Old Testament, the

Israelites had ways of helping and caring for their poor. During harvest time, God commanded that some of the harvest be left behind for the poor to gather for themselves.[14] That's how Ruth gathered food in Boaz's field for her and Naomi to survive.[15] The Lord made sure the Israelites provided for their poor by letting them glean from the harvest fields. Even though we cannot help everyone, we should be willing to help those God may bring our way.

Prayer

Lord, you have compassion for the poor and the outcast. When we help those less fortunate than us, we show compassion and mercy. Give me a generous heart that desires to share and help others in need because I love and serve you. Help me to be a kind and compassionate person in my community to those you bring in my path.

Personal Reflection

1. How might helping the poor apply in your situation or community? Are there specific ways you can help?

2. Read Leviticus 23:22. How did God tell the Israelites to provide for the poor?

3. Read Proverbs 21:13. What warning do you see regarding ignoring the cries of the poor?

---

14   Leviticus 23:22
15   Ruth 2

Planning Ahead

Command those who are rich in this world's goods not to be haughty or to set their hope on riches, which are uncertain, but on God who richly provides us with all things for our enjoyment. Tell them to do good, to be rich in good deeds, to be generous givers, sharing with others. In this way they will save up a treasure for themselves as a firm foundation for the future and so lay hold of what is truly life. (1 Timothy 6:17-19 NET)

Pure jungle rain forest surrounded us. Living remotely meant we lived away from everything we had known – stores, schools, hospitals, cars, fast food, and 24-7 electricity, although we did have some solar power and a generator. All familiar luxuries were gone.

The only way in or out was to walk or fly. To live away from all sources of supply, we stocked up and kept months of food on hand. We stored dozens of tins of food, peanut butter, jam, pasta, fifty pounds of flour and rice, pounds of salt and sugar, jars of oil, plenty of toilet paper, and other necessities in a small pantry. If we ran out, there was no quick replacement, and it might mean weeks of waiting. We also stored medicines of all types for emergencies. Because we only left the station once or twice each year, we needed to keep everything on hand.

Every two weeks, Missionary Aviation Fellowship flew in to bring us fresh food like meat and vegetables, and our mail. Other supplies came as well, including building materials, fuel, and parcels that family sent from home. Medicines for the small medical aid post or supplies for the small trade store might also come on these flights.

Our pilots were missionaries, and their purpose was to serve those living in these outlying areas. Without their ministry, living so remotely would be extremely difficult. If there was a medical emergency – a poisonous snake-bite victim, a woman with a difficult labor, or someone with a severe illness – they would arrive to fly them to the closest hospital. Anyone coming in or out was flown by these pilots.

There was no instant communication, online shopping, or cell phones. We planned ahead for everything. Communication by the slow mail system meant at least six weeks of waiting to get a reply from our home country. If we ordered something, it could take months before it arrived.

Living in such an off-the-grid place meant we had to plan for the longer term and anticipate what might lie ahead. What if we forgot an important staple like salt or didn't keep aspirin on hand for headaches? Both of us kept running lists of items needed for when we did go to a town, even planning months in advance for birthday and Christmas gifts. Long-term planning insured that we had prepared for everything we needed for the future.

In our easy-to-access Western style of living, we tend to think only about the next thing or the next day. In the age of instant gratification and indulgence in the sinful pleasures of this world, remember where true treasures lie. Our long-term plans might be to raise responsible children, live within our financial means, and try to save a little for retirement. These are good and worthy goals. But do we consider what our spiritual long-term plans might be?

Jesus said, *"Store up for yourselves treasures in heaven."*[16] What decisions have we made to live a life that stores up spiritual treasures? What are these lasting treasures?

What counts for eternity? It's a life that chooses faithfulness, purpose, and obedience to God. It's the love we give our family or the patience we show a co-worker. It's in the prayers for a friend or time learning the Word of God. It's the forgiveness we grant or the meal we take to the sick. It's our commitment to our spouse and the generosity we show. It's whenever we choose to do right. It's a life *rich in good deeds*. These, and many more, are the long-term spiritual treasures that we can store up for eternity.

16   Matthew 6:20 NIV

Prayer

Father, thank you for being my Savior and my hope. Help me to stay mindful of where I should put my treasure. I want to store up eternal treasures in heaven. Help me to become rich in good deeds and to be generous and kind to others. Give me a heart that prays and a mind that loves your Word. Help me to be faithful to you in all I do.

Personal Reflection

1. Think about where your treasures lie. Are you storing up earthly treasures or eternal treasures?

2. What are the four directives in 1 Timothy 6:17-19 that help us store up eternal treasures?

3. Read 1 Timothy 4:7-9. Instead of physical training (which is good), what training does God say is much better? How does that benefit us?

4. How will you train for godliness and build up treasure in heaven?

Curious Eyes

Then Jesus said, "Come to me, all of you who are weary and carry heavy burdens, and I will give you rest. Take my yoke upon you. Let me teach you, because I am humble and gentle at heart, and you will find rest for your souls. For my yoke is easy to bear, and the burden I give you is light." (Matthew 11:28-30 NLT)

Little eyes peered through the screen to investigate our small, jungle living room. I sat in a chair on the other side nursing my baby daughter with the window just behind me. Before long, other eyes showed up. Several children stood outside watching. My baby and I had become the new entertainment. We had just moved to our fourth location in three years, so all the inquisitive looks unnerved me.

Didn't your mother teach you not to stare?

Obviously not. Staring was a common thing to do when a foreigner was around, but I had yet to adjust to being the object of everyone's curiosity at such close range. This had not been an issue at our other locations.

This house was built low to the ground, so it was easy for people to stand at the window screens to view inside three rooms of the house: the sitting room, the kitchen, and the office. Many times when I would cook, work, or sit down, someone wandered up to look through the windows and watch. The antics of our baby daughter were entertainment too. While making bread or cooking dinner, curious eyes would come to watch me knead dough or chop vegetables. As I sewed on the treadle machine or typed a letter in the office, the quiet chatter of others standing on the small porch broke my concentration as they watched me work. Even sitting in the living room I would find someone at the window, staring at me reading or relaxing with my daughter. I also gathered an audience on wash day when I used the old-fashioned agitator and wringer machine behind the house.

Being the center of attention was a part of life here because we were the foreigners – the guests in the community who had strange habits. We dressed differently, ate differently, acted differently, and talked differently. Everywhere we went we had a faithful following of inquisitive observers. Little children especially liked to hang around to giggle and stare. It stressed and annoyed me. Coming from a culture where it's rude to stare, I was distressed with so little privacy. I wanted to yell and tell them to leave, but unkindness would create fear. To build relationships with others, I needed to find a way to adapt.

"What is your name?"

Learning names was one way to ease the tension. That in itself was a challenge, since most were unusual and difficult for my vocabulary. At least it was a start.

On days when I'd had enough of curious eyes, I would withdraw to the room in the house where no one could peer in – our tiny bedroom. In there, my daughter and I could take refuge from all the stares, and hiding for a while gave me relief. Soon, children would become bored and leave.

In 1 Kings 19 we read about Elijah. After a great victory over the prophets of Baal, he escaped to the desert to flee death threats from Queen Jezebel. Exhausted, he despaired even of his own life. I think he thought, *I can't do this anymore.* He was weary. He was stressed. He wanted to give up.

In the desert, he fell asleep under a broom tree. Under the scorching heat, the broom tree provided him with shade and a much-needed rest. Then God sent an angel to cook food and feed him.

"The journey is too much for you," the angel told him.

Sometimes our own journey may seem too stressful, and we may long for peace. We might even say, "I can't do this anymore." When stress takes a toll, it is okay to retreat. Elijah fled to the desert for rest; I fled to the bedroom for relief. I believe God understands our frailties and tiredness, and he knows our weaknesses. When life overwhelms us and takes away our peace, where do we turn? Rather than losing heart during times of stress, we must ask God to show us ways to help us cope. Who knows? Maybe he will send an angel to help us too.

Prayer

Thank you for being a Father who understands our frailties. You see our tired hearts and our stress-filled days. You are the one who empowers us with strength to accomplish the purpose for which you have called us. Give us rest, grant us peace, and show us ways to cope when our burden becomes heavy. We look to you, our gentle and kind Savior, because you give rest for our souls.

Personal Reflection

1. In the above verses in Matthew, what must we do in order for Jesus to give us rest? When Jesus takes our yoke and our burden, what does it become?

2. Read Psalm 142:1-3. When we approach the Lord with our concerns, he tells us we can *pour out [our] complaints* to him. Why should we go to him when we are overwhelmed?

3. To whom do you turn for help when your burdens are heavy?

Where There Is No Doctor

"Listen to me, descendants of Jacob, all you who remain in Israel. I have cared for you since you were born. Yes, I carried you before you were born. I will be your God throughout your lifetime—until your hair is white with age. I made you, and I will care for you. I will carry you along and save you." (Isaiah 46:3-4 NLT)

My fifteen-month-old daughter, Janelle, refused to eat her dinner and shoved it off the table and onto the floor. Her chubby cheeks were flushed, and she was grumpier than normal. When I touched her warm forehead, I knew she had a fever. I grabbed a thermometer to check her temperature.

Concern rattled my mind as I realized she was sick again. Her dad was away trekking in the jungle, and Janelle and I were at Honinabi station alone. No one was available to help or give medical advice. I gave her Tylenol to reduce the fever and tucked her into bed.

For the next year, we would base at this outstation so my husband, Dale, could trek into the Gobasi tribal area to make visits. This was the closest location we could live at and be near the area where we hoped to serve. Dale would trek into the Gobasi area for two weeks at a time to oversee work on the airstrip and then walk back for two weeks to recover and re-group for his next time away. During his treks, I was often alone at the station with our small daughter. Several times I flew out to stay with a missionary friend, but this time we were alone.

I was concerned the next morning when I took Janelle's temperature, and it was over 102 degrees. I decided to contact the missionary doctor. The only form of communication with the outside world at the time was by an HF radio transceiver. At noon each day, we were able to talk with a doctor, so I called for help to ask how to treat her fever, because the acetaminophen wasn't helping. Using the assigned radio names for our station, I called the mission hospital.

"Alpha Hotel, this is Charlie Charlie. Can you read me?"

No response.

While I heard everyone engaging in chatter, I tried to interrupt and call again. "Alpha Hotel, this is Charlie Charlie. I have a medical emergency. Alpha Hotel, can you read me?"

Again, no response.

After several tries, I soon realized that our battery signal was too weak for anyone to hear my radio call for help. I waited out the day, hoping the solar panels would charge the twelve-volt car battery that powered the radio. Maybe someone would hear me at the 6:00 radio schedule time that evening.

The station had a small generator for charging the battery if the solar system didn't have enough sun to charge it. Dale had taught me how to start it before he left, so that afternoon I went to the little shed to try to start the generator. My attempts to turn the handle and get the engine turning were unsuccessful. Since I was pregnant with our second child, bending over to get the momentum needed to start the engine was too difficult with my growing belly. I showed a few village men how to start it, hoping they could start the system. Turning a crank in a circle was completely foreign to them, so they were as unsuccessful as I was.

I walked back to the house with discouragement and fear mounting in my heart.

That night during the mission's 6:00 appointed schedule time, I called again, hoping the solar system had been able to charge the battery enough for me to transmit.

"Alpha Hotel, this is Charlie Charlie. Can you copy me?"

Still the hospital station could not hear me.

"This is Charlie Charlie. Can anyone copy me?" I tried to see if any station could hear my call and relay the message for me. But no one could hear my radio transmission. Soon, I heard my husband call me on the portable radio that he had carried with him, but he could not hear my response either.

There was no way to get to a doctor or a hospital. My baby and I were alone in the jungle. The only way in or out was by flying on a small aircraft or walking through the jungle. Neither was an option.

I was totally alone. No one could hear or help us.

The isolation of my situation gripped me with fear as darkness started to settle in for a second night. Holding my sick baby daughter, tears overcame me as I cried out, "God, please help me. What should I do?"

With her fever spiking, I had to make a decision on my own about how to treat my daughter. If it was malaria, leaving it too long could make things much worse. I knew that a long fever of 105 degrees could be dangerous. Her fever wasn't there yet, but I knew acetaminophen would not be enough if she did have malaria.

Living in such isolation meant you went in prepared for any event that could happen, especially carrying in antibiotics and medicines to treat malaria. We had a stash in the house, and the mission hospital had given me a medicine dosage booklet to carry with me. I could check that to see the amount of medicine she needed to treat an infection for malaria. I had also carried in a few medical books as a reference.

I suspected that my daughter had malaria. We all had suffered with bouts of it, and she struggled with leg sores from scratching her mosquito bites. I knew that the doctor would probably put her on a dose of quinine, with the possibility of an antibiotic as well, depending on the symptoms she displayed. I looked up the dosage for quinine in my medical booklet to treat her for malaria.

I crushed the tablet dose and gave it to her in a spoonful of honey along with more acetaminophen to reduce her fever. Giving her a bath to cool her down, I rocked her to sleep. I tossed and turned that night, waking often to pray. Feeling the extreme isolation of our situation thrust me into total dependence on God alone.

Lying in bed that night, I knew he was all I had. I learned a valuable lesson. In our darkest moments of fear, God is with us. When we feel alone, we aren't. He is there working out his purposes for us.

In a society that trusts in so many things, we have many crutches to turn to in a time of crisis – family, friends, pastor, church, doctor, spouse, or counselor. But David declared, *When I am afraid, I will trust in you.*[17] God desires that we turn to him first, but too often we look for other solutions first – like calling on the radio, trying to start a generator, or pulling out a medical book. Do we run to him first – or only after we've exhausted other options?

When I neglect to turn to God first, I miss out on the direction and peace that he gives during difficult circumstances. I miss the blessings of a deeper relationship with him and an awareness of his faithful intervention. Sometimes God may desire to put us in a place where we are forced to acknowledge our dependence upon him. As difficult as that may be, that might be just where he wants us.

Prayer

Thank you, Lord, for making me and carrying me through birth. You will care for me until my death. You have redeemed me, called me by name, and you will always be with me in times of trouble. Even when I am alone, I can depend on you. Help me turn to you first when I face difficulty. Give me trust and total dependence upon you alone.

Personal Reflection

1. Do you turn to God first, or do you tend to wait until you have exhausted other options?

2. In Isaiah 46:3-4, how long does God say he will care for us? List the promises and truths you see in these verses.

3. God tells Israel not to be afraid in Isaiah 43:1-3. What reasons does he give?

4. What promises for your life can you learn from these verses?

---

17   Psalm 56:3 NLT

Tuned In

*As for me, I look to the LORD for help. I wait confidently for God
to save me, and my God will certainly hear me.* (Micah 7:7 NLT)

We had two important lifelines in the jungle: one was the short-wave radio, and the other was our missionary pilot. The radio was our link of communication to the outside world. For the previous two days, I could not transmit on the radio to get help when my daughter was sick. If a station wasn't heard from for several days, then mission headquarters looked into the reason. However, no one had noticed I was absent from the roll call for outstations.

The next morning Janelle was better since I had given her medicine without the doctor's advice, but she was still lethargic with a fever. Stress weighed heavily on me as I got up that morning. With no battery power to transmit, how would I get the generator started? My husband would not be back from his trek for days.

Turning on the radio, I heard everyone's chatter, but again I could not transmit. Then I heard my husband call for our MAF pilot.

"Roy," he said, "I haven't heard Carin up on the radio for a few days, and she is not answering my calls. I think her battery may be dead. She probably can't get the generator started. Is it possible on your rounds today for you to stop in to help her get it started and charge up the solar system?"

"Sure," he said. "I think I can fit in a quick stop there around noon."

Relief flooded my heart when I heard their conversation. Our MAF pilot at the time was Roy Hoey from Australia. He had been our pilot for several years, and he loved his work. Many times he had gone out of his way to help us. Without his ministry, our life as a family would have been far more difficult. He had moved us with all our gear to three locations in the last several years. He flew in our supplies, mail, and food. He was the pilot who flew me out a month before my due date to await our daughter's birth. His mission was to care for the local people and missionaries in his area, and he did it with excellence.

When he landed around midday, I was waiting at the airstrip. Carrying my daughter on my hip, we walked to the generator shed together as several village people followed along. He checked out the generator, started up the engine, and then made sure things were working well before he flew out. After several hours of charging the batteries, the radio was in working order again.

The day before I had been alone with no help and no connection to the outside world. Yet today, the Lord answered my prayers. With a tuned-in husband and a willing pilot, the Lord sent the help I needed. After several days, our daughter was better as well. The malaria medicine had helped.

Husbands, wives, are we aware of what's happening in our families? Are we tuned in to the difficulties our loved ones may be experiencing? A sensitivity to God's spirit and his leading will help us to understand and be aware of the needs of our family. Are you a friend to someone who is struggling or who needs encouragement? Then be willing to serve them. My husband realized my dilemma, and our pilot went out of his way to serve and help. Sometimes it's the awareness and the willingness that will make all the difference in relieving the burden of another. And, you may be the one who becomes the answer to their prayer.

Prayer

Father, thank you for the gift of the Holy Spirit. Thank you that he leads us into all truth and thank you for his guidance in my life. Help me to be sensitive to his leading and respond to his promptings. Give me understanding and guidance for my family, children, and friends who may be struggling. Help me to be willing to serve and help those in need.

Personal Reflection

1. Are you aware when your spouse or child is struggling? Or are you aware when a friend is in need, maybe even a stranger that God has put in your path?

2. Read John 14:16-17. What does the Holy Spirit do in our life?

3. How are you at listening to the Holy Spirit's promptings? Is there a time when he prompted you to act?

The Dreaded House at Honinabi

Don't be afraid, for I am with you. Don't be discouraged, for I am your God. I will strengthen you and help you. I will hold you up with my victorious right hand. (Isaiah 41:10 NLT)

A roach dive-bombed across the room one evening while I sat reading in the little bush house where we lived. Launching himself from the wall, he seemed to aim right for me and came within inches of my head. I screamed and jumped from the chair. These jungle insects weren't wimpy. They could measure as long as one to almost two inches in length.

It wasn't long before several flew across the room.

I ran for cover, dived under the mosquito netting onto our bed, and tucked it in tightly. Staying there for the rest of the night, I read by the light of a kerosene lantern.

Flying-roach nights didn't happen often, but on their active nights, I disappeared to read under the netting. Cans of insect spray didn't help the huge infestation in this house because they lived between the bamboo-platted walls and under the floor. Plus, we didn't want too much poison sprayed around our young daughter or me, since I was expecting our second child.

This bush house had challenges. Built years earlier by a former missionary, it had rounded, split-palm floors and siding. The inner walls of the house were about seven feet high and made from woven bamboo. Looking up, I could see the whole pitch of the roof, and if I sat on a chair, I could look over one wall into another room. Privacy was nonexistent in a house like this, because even a whisper could be heard in the adjoining room.

Since the rough, rounded, split-palm floors had gaps, any number of critters could wander in from the outside. The previous missionary had tacked heavy paper underneath the floor, but that became a hiding haven for the roaches during the day. At night, they came out to roam, look for food, or dive-bomb us. All food had to be stored in tight containers or tin drums to keep bugs away.

The front half of the roof was made from thatch, while the back half was covered in iron to catch the rainwater needed for drinking and household use. The thatch side of the roof had a layer of heavy, wax-covered paper that covered the ceiling, while the iron side had a layer of thick, clear plastic.

It didn't take me long to learn that roaches weren't the only problem in this house.

Sitting another evening in this little jungle house, I heard a strange sound in the ceiling – not once, but several times.

"What's that sound? It sounds like a snake," I said to my husband sitting in the chair next to me.

"No, I don't think a snake would be up there; it's probably a roach," he said, trying to calm my suspicion.

"Well, how come it's a slithering sound then? Can't you hear that?"

"Maybe it's a rat," he said. Well, that wasn't comforting either.

"It's not the sound of little feet; it's a sliding sort of sound," I said.

Then we heard it again.

"Do you hear that? That's got to be a snake!"

Feeling paranoid, maybe my imagination had shifted into overdrive. Finally, because of my worry, my husband grabbed a long bamboo arrow from the corner of the room. With the blunt end of the arrow, he poked above our heads at the heavy paper ceiling where we heard the sound.

While he jabbed at the ceiling, a snake scrambled over to the clear plastic side where it squirmed in protest. Then it slithered back up into the darkness. It wasn't comforting to know that not only did we have roaches in the floor, but there was also a snake in the ceiling. If there were others, I didn't want to know about them!

Later, we learned it was a harmless snake. Every night before putting our daughter to sleep, I made sure to tuck her net in all around her mattress. Not only did it protect her from mosquitoes but from other critters as well.

Weeks later, I froze as I walked out the front door and discovered a small snake near the steps. I turned back into the house to call my husband. We knew some snakes in the area were harmless – like the one seen in the ceiling – while others were poisonous. Not being sure about this snake, we called over a local man to ask him.

He looked at the snake and shook his head while making a long whistling sound. "That one is death adder. If it bites, you die," he said in broken English.

Grabbing a machete, he sent it to where I think all snakes belong.

"It is a small, slow snake, but his bite will kill you."

The snake was no more than fourteen inches long, and it had been lying in the dirt near the front steps of the house. Adder deaths were common in the Western Province. We knew of several people in the last couple of years who had died from its bite.

After that, we never let our toddler wander outside to play unless we or one of the teen girls in the area were watching her. Many times I wanted to run from this place and go home. While we lived in this house, we killed three death adders in the yard. I hated the house at Honinabi station. Would I let these creepy-crawlies and slithering snakes overwhelm me?

Each of us will have times in our lives when the difficulties we experience cause us to lose sight of the goal that God has set for us. Distractions come. Discouragement mounts, and we may think that the struggle is not worth what God has asked of us. Our initial excitement dims as the realities of life weigh heavy upon us. Obedience may seem more like an option, rather than a directive.

Satan loves to use discouragement to draw us away from God's will. Or he may employ circumstances to create a fear that grips us. If we succumb to fear, then he has snatched away our most precious asset – our faith and trust in God.

Just as a runner speeds away at the starting line full of energy, it's not long before his body becomes weary. Yet he endures and forces his physical body to keep moving. His mind knows the temporary pain of the present will be worth it when he reaches the finish line.

Faith in God can waver when we encounter fearful things, and Satan knows that. Yet we have to will ourselves – just like a weary runner – to keep pushing ahead even when we may want to quit. We cannot let Satan prod us with fear or distract us from God's purpose. A determined faith that focuses on the presence of God walking with us gives us peace through the difficulties. In the end, we will be glad we endured.

Prayer

Dear Father, thank you for being my rock and my salvation. You are my fortress where I will not be shaken. When life's circumstances look bleak, don't let Satan's distractions overwhelm me with fear, but strengthen and uphold me with your victorious right hand.

Personal Reflection

1. How does Satan use fear in your life to distract you from doing the will of God?

2. When we experience fear and discouragement, what promises does God give us in Isaiah 41:10?

3. In what area of your life do you need to push ahead in obedience?

Section Four

Jungle Trekking

Trekking is not for the faint of heart. Neither is it a casual hike on a scenic trail, but rather a grueling day through the thick canopy of dense tropical rain forest. It involves crossing streams, navigating rivers, and trudging along difficult trails. Bugs, mosquitoes, leeches, and other critters can make things worse as you walk through unknown territory. The hot tropical weather, high humidity, and muscle-shredding exhaustion create a day that challenges your every step. If a tropical storm begins, you are pelted with endless rain and have to walk a slippery, muddy trail.

What do you pack? How do you find your way through the jungle? What do you eat, and how do you avoid hazards along the way? Join the jungle journey and the spiritual life lessons we can learn from a day of jungle trekking.

Packing for a Trek

"Oh, that we might know the LORD! Let us press on to know him. He will respond to us as surely as the arrival of dawn or the coming of rains in early spring." (Hosea 6:3 NLT)

Trekking into remote jungle villages means that only necessities are packed. With each item carried on someone's back, the weight of every item takes its toll. With no roads for vehicles, the only way into these small villages is by foot on narrow trails through dense jungle.

Supplies were chosen with care. Bedding consisted of a sleeping mat, a thin blanket, a small pillow, and mosquito netting. Basic medical supplies consisted of malaria treatment, bandages and ointment for wounds, a thermometer, aspirin, a dose of antibiotics, and an elastic bandage (for a possible snakebite). Repellent, matches, a flashlight, and a small kerosene lantern were needed along with a couple changes of clothes, a machete for chopping brush, a knife, and a billy pot for cooking, which hung over a small fire. A small Bible and journal were also included.

Food was packed to satisfy basic hunger. The heaviest items were bags of rice and tinned meat, carried in to feed everyone on the trek team – missionaries and carriers. Canned mackerel was the main meat. This fish was mixed into a pot of cooked rice for protein. The carriers loved it; the missionaries tolerated it. Other items were hard, thick crackers (a common item in PNG), seasoning packets for the rice, salt, and an orange-flavored instant-drink powder.

Once the trekkers arrived in a village, people offered garden items – sago, taro, greens, cooking bananas, or whatever was available and in season. People were always ready to share their food with travelers, even us foreigners. Of course, one never knew when a "special" food item might be offered – such as sago grubs. These short, chubby, white worms were given sacrifically since they were considered a delicacy. Once offered, they watched with anticipation as you ate one. Fortunately for us, these weren't readily available!

Sometimes when Dale planned for a longer stay in the village, he packed a few luxuries – canned peaches or corned beef, peanut butter, cookies, and coffee. A long trek boiled down to packing with intention. What must I take, and what can be left behind? It became a calculated decision. I am often reminded that I can live without many things. Now, in a society of great abundance and an attitude of materialism, I am bombarded with what everyone thinks is necessary.

Life is a like a long trek. We live with intention. An important question to ask myself is, What do I need for life's journey? Am I sidetracked by the cares and attractions of this world? Am I working hard to acquire things, only to leave them all behind some day? Do temporal things mean more to me than a life focused on God? It is easy to succumb to the lie that the treasures of this world will bring joy and contentment. But God says to *fix our gaze on things that cannot be seen. For the things we see now will soon be gone, but the things we cannot see will last forever.*[18]

Fulfillment does not arise from the things I possess or the pleasures of this world, but from the blessings that come from a life that walks with a loving Savior. We can discipline ourselves for great accomplishment but fail to attain what is most important – a life that focuses on and acknowledges God. That is a necessity.

In a world that says, "Here, this will make you happy," it's important for me to make another calculated decision – I don't need stuff, I need God.

Prayer

Lord, help me focus my life on you, not riches or material things. May my life be marked by knowing and loving you. Don't let me get sidetracked

---

18   2 Corinthians 4:18 NLT

by the pleasures of this world, but give me eyes to see from your eternal perspective. Give me a heart that is loyal to you.

Personal Reflection

1. What do you need for life's journey? Where are you placing your focus? Are you living with eternal things in mind?

2. What does 1 Timothy 6:10 tell you about money and what can happen to a believer?

3. What does Psalm 49:6-11 say about wealth, death, redemption, and eternal life?

A Guide for the Trail

My child, listen to me and do as I say, and you will have a long, good life. I will teach you wisdom's ways and lead you in straight paths. When you walk, you won't be held back; when you run, you won't stumble. Take hold of my instructions; don't let them go. Guard them, for they are the key to life. (Proverbs 4:10-13 NLT)

We never walked alone in the rain forest. Getting lost in the jungle would be dangerous, even deadly, for a foreigner. Our area was in the middle of a vast jungle. The Western Province was one of the most remote areas of the country and the least developed. Villages tucked tightly here and there in remote places were built along a river, beside a stream, or on a hill. Only a simple path was used by the locals to walk through their territory. They called it a "road," but the obscurity of such a path could be elusive to our Western eyes. We never walked alone. Guides were essential to help us walk from village to village if we wanted to arrive safely.

The locals that lived there knew the trees, every path, the streams, the hills, and every turn along the way. They knew their jungle like we know buildings, landmarks, and street names that mark our way. They are so knowledgeable of their area that one man can tell another where to find something far in the jungle. We knew a man who shot a pig that was too heavy to carry back alone, so he left his precious source of protein and returned to the village. Then he told others the exact spot where he shot the animal. Two other men went to retrieve the animal and bring it back to divide it among the village and roast it.

We needed guides not only because they knew the way, but because they also knew the dangers. Their keen awareness along the trail could spot a snake long before we were conscious of its presence. They knew which stream was safe to drink from and which wasn't. We didn't. Their knowledge kept us safe from danger. They could easily start a fire for cooking or build a makeshift shelter to sleep in. They knew what plants to stay away from and which to glean for food.

A guide was essential for our safety. Without one, our lack of jungle experience might be disastrous. We could have chosen to walk the jungle alone, but it's likely we would never have arrived. We would have suffered the consequence of that decision.

What about our journey through life? There is a myriad of paths we can take, but which is the best path for each of us? What direction will lead us to accomplish the greatest purpose? Where will our gifting be best utilized? We need God's help. Without his guidance, we can become lost or encounter something dangerous to our life. We could miss an important turn in life because we didn't let God lead.

God sees the dangers, and he knows the best path for us. He knows us best and loves us most. His knowledge is far greater than ours, and we'd be wise to let him guide us. Are we willing to let him lead?

Prayer

Father, thank you for teaching me wisdom's ways and leading me along straight paths. Thank you that my obedience to you will give me a life that will be most complete and fulfilled. Help me to listen to your voice and to let you guide me in life. Give me a desire to seek your instructions and to follow you.

Personal Reflection

1. Was there a time when you felt God guiding you in a specific direction? Or was there a time when you ignored God's prompting and suffered the consequences of that choice?

2. What does God say in Proverbs 4:10-13 is the result of obedience to him?

3. Read Psalm 32:8-10. What can you learn from those verses?

Standing Strong for the Journey

"Have I not commanded you? Be strong and courageous. Do not be frightened, and do not be dismayed, for the LORD your God is with you wherever you go." (Joshua 1:9 ESV)

"Tafoli ran away. He left for the village and is not coming to help," Yudobu said. "I'll go and find others." However, we learned later that Yudobu ran away too.

"You are going to die if you go into those villages," others in the community told the two young men.

"Those Gobasi people will do sorcery on you."

Sorcery was an underlying fear all over the area. Their animistic belief system kept them in fear of the spirit world and sorcery, especially from other tribes they did not know or trust. The Gobasi tribe had little contact with the surrounding areas, and the thought of going into this unknown territory frightened the young men.

Dale and missionary coworker, John Fletcher, had planned their first trek into the Gobasi tribe and several other tribal territories for several months, but now it took a disappointing turn when two of the carriers didn't show up to help on the morning of the trek. Carriers are an essential part of a long trek through the jungle because much of the equipment needed for a trip to a village is carried on their backs.

Before each trek, word spread that carriers were needed, and local men were hired to help. Three carriers had planned to come, but now the only man willing to help was Hubay, the local pastor.

Discouraged, the men wondered if they should postpone the trip or continue with only one helper. Although apprehensive himself in trekking into that territory, Pastor Hubay stood strong and chose to go. Dale and John decided to go ahead. They would walk several hours to the Nomad government outpost and try to hire more carriers there. They felt they needed to trust God and move forward with their plan.

Carrying heavy backpacks, the three men began the walk to Nomad. Their condensed, overloaded packs challenged their physical endurance, so they were forced to stop four times to rest. Once they reached Nomad, they dropped their loads and sank down into the local river to rest. With the heat, humidity, and exhaustion from the walk, the water felt cool and refreshing. Then they left to find the officer in charge of Nomad.

"We need to hire some carriers. Do you know of anyone that could guide us into the Gobasi tribe?" They had a short conversation, and then he showed them an empty government house to use for the night. After cooking a few vegetables and a pot of rice, the three ate and went to bed.

How many times in life are we overcome with fear from something God asks of us? The strong young men were more than able to carry the packs, yet they ran away, afraid of what they might encounter. Their anxiety of the unknown and the voices of others influenced their choice more than their faith in God's ability to watch over them. Fear and insecurity can grip us too. Satan may use our own insecurities, fear of the unknown, or the comments of others to influence us.

Fear arises if faith falters. God says *Fear not* many times in Scripture. Moving from fear to faith releases the burden from our shoulders and places it where it belongs – in the hands of God. He is more than capable of walking with us to help us accomplish his purpose. Let's trust God with our inadequacies and concerns. Don't miss that trek into unknown territory where God wants to use us.

Prayer

Lord, don't let fear and insecurity grip me, but I ask that you give me a childlike trust in your ability. Give me confidence in the truths that you are with me, you will strengthen me, and you will uphold me. Whatever burdens I have, help me to leave them in your capable hands. I ask for a faith that does not falter and one that trusts you daily. Make me strong in faith for life's journey.

Personal Reflection

1. What lies does Satan feed you when he uses fear to discourage you?

2. Describe a time when the voices you heard from others discouraged you from what you felt God wanted in your life.

3. Read Deuteronomy 20:1-4. Many times the Lord promised the Israelites victory over their enemies. Some were stronger and mightier than they were. God told them, *"Do not be afraid."* To win those battles they needed to move forward and trust the words of God. How can you apply that principle to your life today?

Jailbreak

*This is what the LORD says—your Redeemer, the Holy One
of Israel: "I am the LORD your God, who teaches you what is
good for you and leads you along the paths you should follow."*
(Isaiah 48:17 NLT)

Breakfast was simple on the second morning of the trek. Crackers
with a smear of peanut butter, bananas, and a cup of lukewarm,
powdered, orange drink. Dale, fellow missionary John, and Pastor
Hubay were just finishing their meal as five men showed up at the house.
After the previous day's exhausting trek, surprise at the creativeness
of God's provision for carriers became evident as they talked with the
men waiting outside.

"Hello. The Nomad officer in charge sent us here to carry your things
and take you to the Gobasi villages you want to visit," said the young
teen who spoke English.

"That's good," they said. "Yes, we need help to get out to those villages. Do you know how to get to Gesumi and Dadalibi villages?"

"Yes, that is my home place. I am a Gobasi from Gesumi village," he
said. "I have been attending high school in Kiunga. They sent students
back to their home village because of the drought and lack of water.
When the rains come again, I will go back to school."

This young Gobasi teen spoke English, and he would become an
important link in communicating with the villagers they planned to
visit that week. This was an unexpected provision from God.

"What is your name?"

"My name is Abi. The officer let these four men out of jail and sent them to help you too. They are also Gobasi men."

The Nomad officer must have thought some compulsory labor was better than sitting in jail, so he freed them with a directive to return afterward and serve the remainder of their jail time. An ordered jailbreak was another of God's unexpected provisions for the guides and carriers. Dale and John never asked why they were in jail because they weren't sure they wanted to know.

Now there was an English speaker and four convicted criminals to guide Dale, John, and Pastor Hubay. The men were a welcome and needed addition to the trek team. Their knowledge of the Gobasi area and Abi's ability to translate for them was an incredible provision from God. Who would have thought we would have a Gobasi man who could speak English? It was obvious the Lord had prepared the way forward.

With five more men to help carry supplies, they divided and separated the items for each man to carry. Now no one would be overburdened with carrying supplies, and the missionaries could focus more on walking the difficult trail. That morning, they set out on their first trek into the Gobasi area. Their first stop would be Gesumi, about a three-hour walk from Nomad station.

The trek had a discouraging and difficult start the previous day when the carriers didn't show up, but God's faithfulness orchestrated something better. He had provided Gobasi men to lead them into Gobasi territory. Who would have thought that God had four criminals and an English-speaking teen waiting at the next outpost?

Don't underestimate the creativeness of God's provision or whom he may choose to use in our life. He loves to work in unexpected and surprising ways when we seek to follow him.

Prayer

Thank you, Lord, for the creative and unexpected ways you can provide for me. I take joy when I see your wonderful provision. Thank you for leading, directing, and giving me exactly what I need. I praise you today that you are my God and my Redeemer.

Personal Reflection

1. In what ways have you seen God's creative provision in your life?

2. When you feel discouraged by a circumstance gone wrong, are you still able to trust God through that difficulty and trust in his provision?

3. Read Psalm 92:4-5. What can you praise God for today?

Bad Feet, Good Heart

Two people are better off than one, for they can help each other succeed. If one person falls, the other can reach out and help. (Ecclesiastes 4:9-10 NLT)

Westerners are not known for agility on the trail. The rough terrain, steep slopes, exposed roots, fallen trees, and slippery paths make us a clumsy sight to our foreign friends. They walk with ease and grace in their environment while we slip, fall, and use walking sticks like old people. When walking with a trek team, sometimes the strong and faster carriers walk ahead with the heavier packs.

"We are walking ahead, you stay back and help them," they'd say to a few. Our companions were always ready to give a helping hand at a difficult place on the trail.

My husband did most of the trekking during these years. Once our children were born, I only went on a few treks. Trudging through the jungle was never something I enjoyed; it was a day I endured and couldn't wait to have end. The sweat, the mud, and the exhaustion were far from my Southern-girl roots. Besides, I never knew so many leg muscles could hurt.

"You're going to slip. Walk slowly," I often heard from a voice on the trail.

Once my legs became exhausted and rubbery, surefootedness disappeared. Lousy at walking in their jungle environment, those feet became even worse with fatigue. An old saying – "Missionaries have bad feet, but good hearts" – proved true when trekking and must be where the phrase originated.

"It's very muddy," another voice said.

Halfway through one trek, we came to the top of a hill. As I looked down the hill, I groaned. The steep slope below was muddy from a recent rain. It would be slippery. I grabbed a firm hold of my walking stick, jammed it in the dirt, and took a step. I slid on the slick mud, but regained my balance before falling, thanks to my walking stick. Obvious that I was inept on the path, two men came from behind me to grab my arms and help me to the bottom. With a man on each side holding on to an arm, my feet still slipped out from under me, but they pulled me upright again. Otherwise, I might have tumbled to the bottom alone. At this point, I was too exhausted to keep myself steady.

We have times in life when we need to accept help from others. Struggling and exhausted from life's burdens, do we allow others to come alongside to help? Or do we refuse help and insist we can manage alone? The humbling process of a difficult circumstance may peel away our pride and help us acknowledge that we need the help of others.

Even Moses, a great man of God, struggled with exhaustion to hold up his arms when Israel was in a battle with the Amalekites. As he stood with his arms lifted and the staff of God in his hand, Joshua and the Israelites prevailed in the battle. When exhaustion overcame him and he could no longer hold up his arms, the enemy prevailed. Then his brother, Aaron, and his friend Hur came beside him, each one holding up an arm *so his hands were steady until the going down of the sun.* With their help, Moses held up the staff of God, and the Israelites won the battle (Exodus 17). Moses withstood the burden because others came to help.

We are not meant to bear our burdens alone. When we allow others to share our burden and to help us walk through a difficulty, that burden is lightened. When life's path gets slippery and exhaustion overwhelms us, we don't need to tumble to the bottom alone. We can allow a trusted person to walk with us, hold us steady, and be our friend. It can make all the difference in winning the battle.

Prayer

Thank you, Father, for our families and friends. Two are better than one. We are not alone when we face trouble, and you are able to send us someone who will comfort and help us in a time of need. Give me sensitivity to hear your voice prompt me when I have a friend who needs help. Help me become a person who helps and encourages those going through a difficult time.

Personal Reflection

1. We need the help and encouragement of others. Do you allow others to come alongside you when you are struggling? Or do you refuse their efforts to help?

2. Do you try to encourage others during a difficult time in their lives? Think of someone today that might need encouragement.

3. What advice did King Solomon give in Ecclesiastes 4:9-12?

4. What insight does God give in 2 Corinthians 1:3-5 about life's troubles?

Crossing Logs

The prudent carefully consider their steps. The wise are cautious and avoid danger; fools plunge ahead with reckless confidence. (Proverbs 14:15-16 NLT)

Walking through the jungle challenges balance and coordination. After several hours on the trail on my first trek, we arrived at a bridge. It wasn't a bridge in the Western sense of the word, but a tree chopped down so that it fell across a stream. The top landed on the other side and created a log bridge. Instead of climbing down the hill, crossing the stream, and going up the other side, the local people simply walked across this log.

As I stood at the edge looking at that log, I froze in a panic. At twenty-five years old, not only was this my first major log crossing, but I was also almost six-months pregnant with our second child. Old and narrow, the log was worn from years in its jungle environment. The top of the log had a slick surface smoothed out from many crossings. On the sides clung moisture-loving moss. I saw no room for error – either I walk the straight-and-narrow or suffer the consequence! The carriers who led us on the trail would never ask me to cross something that wasn't able to hold my weight, but I questioned the wisdom of crossing on a worn, damp log, and worried whether I could get myself across safely.

"It's okay," one of the men said.

That was easy for him to say when he'd grown up his whole life sprinting across these scary death beams. How do I keep my balance on a round log without slipping? I surveyed my two options: climb down the small ravine, wade through the stream, and climb up the other side, or walk across the log. The ravine – about ten feet down – was slick with thick vegetation. The stream was shallow but quick, with a slippery rock bottom. I knew one slip on the log could mean a fall onto the rough ground below. Yet the log seemed like the best option. Far from civilization, I needed to make sure I made it safely across to the other side.

With a skill and balance retained since their childhood, the locals walk across these logs with ease. One of the male carriers stepped onto the log first to assist me across. Overcome with nervousness, I shifted my right foot onto the log with my left foot close behind. Moving one foot at a time, I moved step by step. Holding on to my arm to be sure I stayed balanced, the local man walked across with me.

"Walk slowly," he said as he coached me. No worries there; I intended to be the queen of slow.

I shuffled along the log, foot by foot. I hoped there weren't more of these to cross that day. Finally, with a sigh of relief, I stepped onto the other side.

Rushing across the log by myself would have had disastrous consequences, but taking it slowly, step by step, with a helping hand made the difference. Isn't life the same? Do we rush into a decision that we later regret, or act overconfident only to fall flat with disappointment or shame? Has our impulsiveness or have our thoughtless words hurt me or someone else? Or, have we turned away from a difficult challenge and failed to move forward because we were paralyzed by fear?

Fear, impulsiveness, and overconfidence can give us an outcome we may not desire. Just as walking across that log took focus and deliberate steps, each choice we make should be made with a purposeful decision. Acting with wisdom and care only comes when we walk with the help of our loving Father. He is there to step out with us, and we can seek his help. Times may come when fear will overwhelm us to a standstill, but we can start with small steps and follow his leading. With prudence, we make those calculated steps to follow his guiding hand. Joy comes from knowing that we are led by a faithful God whom we can trust.

Prayer

Father, give me a life of wisdom and a heart of prudence. Help me to consider plans and take careful steps in accordance with your will. I pray for your help that I do not rush into decisions, act in overconfidence, or let fear overwhelm me. Give me a heart that seeks your will and a mind that commits my steps into your hands. Let your Word guide me and help establish my plans so they honor and glorify you.

Personal Reflection

1. When you plan for the future, what careful steps can you take? Think about a time that a rushed decision caused you regret later. What did you learn from that?

2. Are you willing to seek the Lord in your decisions, or do you rush into things without praying for God's leading? Do you consider advice from godly friends?

3. Read Psalm 119:105. What does God say will lead us along the path of life?

Blindsided on the Path

I pray that God, the source of hope, will fill you completely with joy and peace because you trust in him. Then you will overflow with confident hope through the power of the Holy Spirit. (Romans 15:13 NLT)

Hazards along the trail can often take someone by surprise. Massive trees in the jungle have large tree roots protruding along the path, and unless a person pays close attention to where their foot is placed, it's easy to end up face-first in the dirt. Steep slopes slick from rain can send a person sprawling if inattention, overconfidence, or fatigue become the enemy. Navigating fallen trees and crossing over narrow logs challenge balance and coordination.

Yet sometimes no matter how focused we are, we are still blindsided. Once, with my husband's eyes focused down to miss tree roots that might trip him, he failed to see a tree suspended across the path at head height. Fallen in years past, its giant root system on one end and the large branches on the other kept it lifted off the ground. With the brim of a baseball cap blocking his upper vision, he walked at a fast pace, taking some pride in his acquired trekking skill, when his head suddenly smacked into the large tree.

The impact knocked him off his feet, and he landed on his backside, stunned. Since the village was close, his fellow trekkers had split off to stop at a garden and had hurried off in different directions to leave him to get to the village on his own. With the incident unobserved, he was thankful it would not be the main topic around the cooking fires that evening. After gathering his wits, he stood to continue the last of the walk to the village with a broadened focus.

Dale missed an obvious danger overhead while his attention was focused elsewhere. How many times in life have I been focused, endeavoring to follow God and striving to live a life of honor, when I am blindsided by an event from an unexpected direction? No matter how careful I am, life can still send a sudden and hard blow. Surprised and stunned from the pain and shock, what do I do when life knocks me down?

Take comfort in knowing that ultimately God is the one in control, and this did not take him by surprise. Whatever he allows in my life, he has a purpose in mind and lessons I can learn. He offers comfort and strength to get me through each difficulty. Prayer and quietness before the Lord will allow him to speak to my heart, and reading his Word will remind me of truths that give me hope.

In a difficult time, I love to claim a promise he has given that fits my hardship. I have seen how God has remained faithful and stayed true to his promises. Trials don't come to hurt us; they come to make us stronger and to help us see our great need of God. Lastly, trust in his deep love. These truths of the Christian faith are things I need to remember every day because they give me hope.

Prayer

Thank you, Father, for you know me by name, and you know everything about me. Thank you for your sovereign control in my life. When I go through deep trials, you comfort and help me. Through difficulties, teach me your ways and help me to stand on your promises in Scripture. Help me to overflow with confident hope as I trust you. Give me joy and peace because of your deep love for me.

Personal Reflection

1. When you are blindsided by a difficulty, where do you turn? Do you seek God to get through it?

2. Trials help us see our great need of God. Read Isaiah 43:1-2. What hope does God offer in these verses?

3. When facing difficulty, ask, "What does God want to teach me through this?"

Snakes on the Trail

Stay alert! Watch out for your great enemy, the devil. He prowls around like a roaring lion, looking for someone to devour. Stand firm against him, and be strong in your faith. Remember that your family of believers all over the world is going through the same kind of suffering you are. (1 Peter 5:8-9 NLT)

Dale knew something on the trail didn't seem right, even though the carriers had just walked past the same spot. As he took his next step, he realized a snake was on the trail where his foot was headed, so he jumped over it. Then he stopped, bent over, and looked at it. A death adder waited on the edge of the trail.

Dale's heart rate quickened when he realized how close he'd been to stepping on it.

"Snake!" he yelled to the others.

He whacked it several times with his walking stick and threw it into the bush.

One more step and Dale would have been within striking distance of its poisonous venom. He was on a survey trip deep into a mountainous area of the jungle, far from any possible help if he'd been bitten. Shaken by such a close call, he realized how the Lord had watched over him and the others on the trail.

Watching for poisonous snakes on a trek meant everyone had to stay alert. Death adders were common in this part of PNG. With a short, thick body, these snakes have a triangular-shaped head and a skinny tail. Brownish in color, they often hide in dead leaves or branches on or near the game trails. They blend into the ground as they wait for prey. These game trails were often used by the people as ready-made paths if they headed in the right direction. Many snakes slither away when encountering a human, but these slow-moving snakes tend to wait patiently to strike prey along a trail. Camouflaged well in the jungle environment, everyone had to stay watchful.

Fatalities were not uncommon. One bite from a death adder in the remoteness of the jungle with no access to a hospital or easy evacuation for medical help could mean death. This was especially true on this trek where the nearest airstrip was a couple days' walk away.

Two days later, another death adder was killed on the trail. This time a carrier walking ahead of John, our missionary friend on the trek, spotted it and killed it. An old saying about death adders is, "The first man walking on the trail wakes up a snake; the second man makes it angry, and the third man gets bitten." These adders tend to have a lay-in-wait style, and their strike is quick and often deadly. By the end of Dale and John's three weeks of trekking in the remote northern area through rough and mountainous terrain, three death adders had been killed along the trail. Yet each time God protected everyone.

While the men were away on that trek, I remember feeling burdened to pray for protection from venomous snakes. I wasn't worried so much about them trekking or going into tribal areas, but I worried about encounters with snakes. I knew they might not make it home alive if anyone was bitten. May we always pray for what the Lord burdens us with.

Just as trekking requires vigilance in watching for poisonous snakes, we also should stay alert in our spiritual lives. If we are not diligent, Satan's cunning ways may become a deadly trap for us. Scripture tells us he actively seeks out someone to destroy; he pursues us with lies as an animal stalks its prey.

Satan will attempt to lure us into wrong behaviors, speak lies to us, or cloud our sense of direction from God. If I grow careless in my walk with God, tune out his voice, and fail to heed the warnings he speaks to my spirit, I may fall for Satan's deception. Failing to resist Satan means that I let him twist my thoughts away from truth, or I allow him to persuade me that God's Word does not apply to my situation. He will try to convince me that God is not good or doesn't care, or he will try to entice me into a wrong lifestyle. His lies penetrate my mind like a deadly poison as I succumb to his attacks.

May we recognize Satan's lies and attempts for what they are: an effort to draw us away from God. He wants to destroy us. What steps can we take to protect ourselves?

Stand on the truth of God's Word. When Jesus was tempted in the wilderness, God's Word caused Satan to flee. God's truth abounds in Scripture and protects us from Satan's lies. When our thoughts dwell on truth, then those lies will not penetrate our minds. We need to learn God's Word, dwell on it, study it, and believe his promises to us.[19]

Trust in the goodness of God and his love for you. Satan loves to feed us the lie that God is not good or that he doesn't love us. Yet Scripture is rich with verses of God's goodness and everlasting love for his children. He wants a vibrant relationship with us. He desires to give us a life that is full of faith, hope, and joy as we follow his purpose for us.

Jungle trekking meant walking with alertness and caution; it didn't mean walking in fear. The men were on the lookout for deadly snakes. We do not have to walk in fear of Satan's attacks either, but we do have to stay spiritually alert and aware of his schemes against us. God has blessed us with all the tools we need to stand strong in faith.

Prayer

Thank you, Father, for you have provided us with tools to fight our enemy, Satan. Help me to stand firm against all of the devil's schemes. Keep me alert to his lies and his attempts to deceive and tempt me. Help me to be diligent to study the truths and promises that you have given in your Word. Help me to pray at all times and on every occasion, and give me strength to stand firm in my faith.

---

19   Decades ago, I loved a Bible promise book I had. In it, topics were laid out so I could read about God's promises and truths in Scripture – fear, faith, love, hope, confession, forgiveness, etc. What a great way to find many verses with truths that help us when we struggle.

Personal Reflection

1. In what ways does Satan attack you with his lies? What truth from God's Word can you stand on to counter those lies?

2. What does God say in 1 Peter 5:8-9 that Satan is looking for? What does that Scripture say we need to do?

3. Do you ever doubt God's love for you? These Scriptures may help: Psalm 103:11-14; 1 John 4:9-10; Ephesians 3:17-19.

4. Read Ephesians 6:10-18. Who are you fighting against in this world? How are you to fight against those forces?

Trail Food

For God is not unjust. He will not forget how hard you have worked for him and how you have shown your love to him by caring for other believers, as you still do. Our great desire is that you will keep on loving others as long as life lasts, in order to make certain that what you hope for will come true. Then you will not become spiritually dull and indifferent. Instead, you will follow the example of those who are going to inherit God's promises because of their faith and endurance. (Hebrews 6:10-12 NLT)

Rising early one morning after sleeping on the trail, one of the carriers spotted a large fish hiding under a big rock in the river. An opportunity like this was never passed up. Calling out to the others, everyone ran to see the hoped-for prize – a good, solid meal while trekking on a long, arduous trail. Success depended not only on the skill of the hunter but also on the escape capabilities of the prey.

Several men worked together. They scattered themselves in different areas around the fish which hid in a shallow area of the river. One man tried to spear it, but missed. After about thirty minutes of effort, someone else shot it with a spear, but it escaped. Finally, another man hit it with his bush knife, and they were able to pull their prize to shore. They wrapped the dead fish in large leaves and placed it in a string bag for the evening meal later. The fish was about five feet long and would make a great meal for the fourteen men on the trek. Then they broke camp and left for the next part of their journey.

Survival skills are a vital part of jungle life. If gardens fail from a drought, or wild pigs ravage and eat garden produce, the locals survive by finding other sources of food. They are adept at survival. Our friends and carriers knew how to spot food along the trail. If they saw something they could eat, they stopped to gather it – bamboo shoots, greens, wild fruits, or other edible finds familiar to them. Turtles, snakes, or small animals might also be caught. In one isolated area, a nice catch of prawns was hauled in for a meal.

The staple foods they might carry along with them were bananas, local potatoes, or sago. The staples we took were tinned fish and rice. Anything freshly caught or harvested was a great addition to the meal, and it stretched food supplies.

Some men are more skilled at hunting than others, but everyone had to persevere at it if they wanted to feed their families. In our first year in the country, Dale and fellow missionary, John, went to visit an isolated tribe in a mountainous area. A pastor from the Biami tribe, Feagoni, who was helping John in a new work among the Kubo, went along. He proved to be one of the more skilled hunters. While crossing a stream, Pastor Feagoni spotted a fish and tried to spear it, but it escaped. Searching around in the water, he tenaciously grabbed it with his hand and held up his prize for everyone to see. Another morning he announced, "I am going to go hunt for crocodiles." A few men went with him, and sure enough, they returned with two small crocodiles for dinner.

Everyone could have settled for the boring tin fish and rice, but most of the men were industrious and willing to work for more. It was their life, and diligence in hunting provided them with a reward that filled their bellies.

As we go through life, let's not settle for the mundane and just getting by. Let's not be lazy or indifferent, but let's work hard and strive for more. Trust God to open up the doors he has for us and watch him provide. Let's train ourselves for success. Ask God for the patience and determination to finish our goals. God wants to use our best abilities so that we can serve others and honor him. Let's be diligent and keep working toward our heavenly reward.

Prayer

Thank you, Father, for being a just God and not forgetting your people. Thank you for not forgetting the work I do to love and serve others. Help me to be wise and use my time on earth wisely. Don't let me be lazy, but I ask for a life trained in diligence. Thank you that one day I will receive my heavenly reward.

Personal Reflection

1. What life goals have you been working on?

2. According to Hebrews 6:10-12, what will God not forget? What does God want you to have as long as life lasts? What should you not become?

3. Read Ephesians 5:15-19. What guidelines are in this passage for how we should live life?

Keep Pressing On

But I focus on this one thing: Forgetting the past and looking forward to what lies ahead, I press on to reach the end of the race and receive the heavenly prize for which God, through Christ Jesus, is calling us. (Philippians 3:13-14 NLT)

Trekking challenged every fiber of my physical strength. I only did a few treks because it was easier for everyone if I stayed behind with the children. Those walks became some of my most exhausting days. The locals walk the trails with ease, but by the end of each trek day, every ounce of my strength was depleted. Legs that began strong soon screamed for rest. Weak from fatigue, I feared they might collapse as my body begged for relief. For me, those were the most grueling days of my life. I wanted to meet the little tribe God had called us to, so I walked several times to see them.

The thick canopy of trees in the jungle covers like an umbrella overhead blocking out direct sunlight – a blessing in the intense heat of the tropics. However, humidity is trapped underneath, and it surrounds like an oppressive wet blanket while mosquitoes and insects annoy. If a tropical storm begins, then rain pelts you without mercy in the open areas and creates a slippery, muddy trail to slog through.

The first hour into the walk I wondered, *Will I make it?* We had hours to go. I longed to stop, but if we were to arrive before dark, we had to keep walking. Forcing my body to move, I focused on putting one foot ahead of the other to continue forward. Rest wasn't an option. *Just move. Just keep going.*

Mercifully, there were a few times when the carriers allowed me to rest for a couple minutes. They were anxious to get to the village, and I was already the slowest one at the end of the trail of carriers. Exhaustion overwhelmed me when we finally arrived. I was a sweaty, bedraggled, and muddy mess. The exertion of jungle trekking demanded more than my body wanted to give.

But I made it!

This was the first time I would see the Gobasi tribe in their own village. I had only met a few men previously, never the women or children. For years we had strived to get here, and now I could meet the ladies and their children.

On this trek, we took our fifteen-month-old daughter, and later we took her again as a two-year-old, along with our six-month-old son. Locals carried our children for us. Our daughter rode in a backpack carrier, and our son lay inside a traditional string bag that hung from one of the carrier's heads. Both children did amazingly well – either snoozing along the way, or snacking, or stretching their necks to make sure they could see us.

Sometimes life brings us into exhausting circumstances that seem beyond our ability to bear. It may be weariness of caring for a loved one, exhaustion of working two jobs, a debilitating illness, or the stress of being a single parent. Whatever it may be, we feel stretched beyond what we feel we can endure. The emotional or mental exhaustion from these trials overwhelm us, and we long for rest. Instead, we determine to plod forward as best as we can, day after day. What do we do under the strain?

Pray for strength. Isaiah 40:29 says, *He gives strength to those who are tired; to the ones who lack power, he gives renewed energy* (NET). God will help us to endure. Just as my legs were faithful to move me forward, how much more is our God able to sustain us! In fact, I'm sure God kept my legs walking. Life can be messy. We may be exhausted, but God is able to carry us through to the end.

Early in our years in Papua New Guinea, a dear friend and the founder of Pioneers, Ted Fletcher, wrote us letters of encouragement as we experienced many struggles. He always closed with the words "Keep pressing on." I pondered those words. Life requires work and effort. When life isn't easy, we will ourselves to push forward. Endurance comes as we learn to accept the place where God has us, and we use that time to learn from God and draw on his strength.

Remember, it's not only how well we accomplish something, but also the perseverance it takes to get there. Keep pressing on.

Prayer

Lord, when I am tired and weary, give me strength. When I am over-burdened, give me endurance. When I see no end to my circumstances, give me hope that only comes from you.

When I want to quit, help me to move forward step by step. Help me to press on through difficult times, knowing that your love and presence are with me.

Personal Reflection

1. Have you ever felt like your circumstances were too heavy to bear? How did you get through those times?

2. According to Philippians 3:13-14, what should we focus on?

3. Read Habakkuk 3:17-19. What does the prophet Habakkuk say when the Israelites experience difficult circumstances? Where are they to find joy?

Section Five

Jungle Tribe

After we found a suitable airstrip site located central to the Gobasi tribal villages, we moved as close as we could to an established mission station. That base was within a day's walk from the tribe, and it was our fourth move in less than three years. We were given permission by mission leadership to pursue a more permanent move into the area, but an airstrip had to be completed first.

If I had thought my earliest years were challenging, these were even more. We had finally reached the place where we felt God had called us, and it was a joy amid hardship to be here. We had no running water, and the only conveniences were kerosene lanterns and a small cooking Primus.

During our trips out to the airstrip site, Dale organized the work on the airstrip and spent many long hours chainsawing felled trees. He also worked to level out the cleared land on a tractor that was flown out by a helicopter. I trekked out several times with him during this time. It was good to meet people, gather words and phrases in the language, and learn names.

The following are stories from the earliest years of meeting and living isolated with the Gobasi tribe.

Stepping Back in Time

"There is no one righteous, not even one, there is no one who understands, there is no one who seeks God. All have turned away, together they have become worthless; there is no one who shows kindness, not even one." (Romans 3:10-12 NET)

Today was the day to meet the Gobasi tribe in some of their villages for the first time. Thatched houses came into view as the trek team drew closer to the Kume River. The eight men – Dale, co-worker John Fletcher, and six carriers – led by the young Gobasi teen who spoke English, arrived in Gesumi village. It was September 1982.

Walking down a forty-foot embankment, they arrived at the deep and fast-flowing Kume River. Because it was about fifty feet wide, they would need a canoe or raft to paddle across to the village on the other side. High banks rose on both sides of the river. Spotting them coming, a tribal man paddled across in a raft to pick them up. In a couple trips, the eight men and the gear were paddled across.

The men climbed up the forty-foot bank and walked into the village to greet everyone. Most wore traditional dress; the men wore loincloths, and the women wore grass skirts. Before long, a woman brought a bark platter of cooked bananas for everyone to eat. Bananas were a staple food in the area. Most were picked while still green and roasted in their skins on the coals of a fire. Tossing a hand of green bananas on the coals, they turn them until the skin is charred. Once roasted, the charred skin is scraped off with a knife. With many varieties in the area, bananas are eaten most every day.

After a quick wash down in the river to remove the day's trekking dirt, the men changed into dry clothes. Abi, the English speaker and guide, showed Dale and John around the village to greet everyone, while he interpreted for them.

When they were invited to sit down in the house with some of the village men, an older man pulled out a traditional bamboo smoking pipe. Several men smoked it and passed it around for others to partake. A fire burned slowly while a few women roasted more bananas and root vegetables over the charcoal. The haze of smoke filled the longhouse. The scene gave the feeling of stepping back centuries; the only reminder that they hadn't was the few modern items in the village – a couple pots, machetes, and a few tattered clothes.

The trek team walked to several Gobasi areas and spent a couple days visiting the people in each village. Each time, they met with the leaders and others to ask if they would like to have a missionary come and live with them. Even with an interpreter, there was still some confusion about what they answered. However, in the end, they said we could come, and they would search for a suitable airstrip site.

This tribe, comprised of several villages in the area, was estimated to have seven to eight hundred people. Another four hundred people with two close dialects of this tribe also lived nearby. They lived isolated and forgotten as they had for centuries, with little help from the outside world. They struggled for survival in a harsh land, and they lived and died without the knowledge of the Savior who loved them.

The Gobasi lived in a bondage that even we didn't understand in our earliest days. They were controlled by their animistic belief system. Every aspect of their life – hunting, gardening, sickness, childbirth, and death – was focused on appeasement of the spirit world. They would remain healthy, have enough food, and be protected from sorcery and death only if they did not anger these many spirits. Their lives were lived in fear as they tried to keep the spirits happy and avoid a spiritual attack from one of these unseen beings.

The spirit mediums in the village were men who entered the spirit world through a trance during a séance. They were feared, respected, and sought after in times of sickness and death. When someone was extremely sick or had died, relatives would ask the medium to do a séance. Then the "spirit people" would reveal to the spirit medium who the sorcerer was that had harmed or caused the death or sickness of this family member. It might take multiple séances, but usually it led to the revelation of a specific person.

Incapacitating sickness and death were always considered a spiritual attack. Someone in the village had either performed magic against that person because of anger over a wrong action, or the sick person had committed a taboo and angered a spirit. If a sorcerer was named during the séance, then that person had little hope. They would be attacked at some point and killed, usually in an ambush. The village believed there was no chance a mistake had been made, because the spirit world did not make mistakes. In their minds, this death was required to stop others from being harmed through that person's sorcery. They viewed it as protection for others in the village, ignoring the fact that it was a brutal and violent murder.

Every death in the village demanded an answer of who did the magic, and it had to be dealt with in the harshest way possible. Their lives were lived in a cycle of fear: Would they break a taboo? Would they anger the spirits? Would someone commit sorcery against them? Fear and violence, fear and violence were their way of life.

Spiritual healing and freedom can only be provided by Jesus. It was this message of Christ and freedom from the lies of Satan that we hoped to bring. If Scripture says *all have sinned and fall short of the glory of God,*[20] then the Gobasi needed this message. A Savior had set them free from their sin, their hopeless fear, and their vicious violence. Jesus is their Redeemer, and he could release them from their bondage to the spirit world. He paid the penalty for their sin, but they lived in ignorance of the God who loved them.

If Jesus' last commission to his disciples was, *"go and make disciples of all nations",*[21] then that included the Gobasi tribe that was living lost and without hope. God loved and died for them too, and they needed this message of life and peace.

---

20   Romans 3:23 NET
21   Matthew 28:19 NET

Prayer

Father, you have said that none are righteous and none seek you. Yet despite our rebellious sin, your great love sent your Son, Jesus, to set us free. Thank you for giving me new life in you. Help me to be a witness of your truth to others. Give me a burden for those around the world and in my own community who are lost without anyone to tell them the good news about you.

Personal Reflection

1. How do you feel knowing there are people in the world who have never heard the good news of Jesus? Should everyone have a chance to hear of God's love?

2. Many say, "I'm a good person." Yet Romans 3:10-11 says that no one is righteous and no one seeks God. What does that say about the idea that we are good?

3. Read Romans 3:23. Who *falls short* in this verse? Does that include a small tribe in the jungle that never heard of God's love?

4. Jesus said, "Go and make disciples of all people in the world." How are you sharing the gospel with others? Are you in any way involved with a mission outreach in another area of the world?

The Longhouse

But God demonstrates his own love for us, in that while we were still sinners, Christ died for us. Much more then, because we have now been declared righteous by his blood, we will be saved through him from God's wrath. For if while we were enemies we were reconciled to God through the death of his Son, how much more, since we have been reconciled, will we be saved by his life? (Romans 5:8-10 NET)

We stepped over several stacked logs at the doorway to enter the longhouse. About seventy-five feet long, this huge, thatched-roof house was the traditional dwelling for the villagers to live together. Larger villages might have two longhouses. The fear of an impending raid meant everyone lived together for safety.

These stacked logs at the main doorway served an important purpose. Once the villagers were inside for the night, they stacked up more logs between upright posts to cover the entire doorway for protection from raids. This opening was the only way in or out. Barricading themselves inside for the night gave them protection from their enemies. Historically, the Gobasi tribe was raided by a larger neighboring tribe to the east, and they were nearly wiped out by these cannibalistic attacks in years past.

Although they could laugh, joke, and live in community, a raid was never far from their minds. This is how they had survived for centuries.

The longhouse was divided into three sections and was used for different purposes. As we entered through the door, we stepped into the first section, the cooking area. On each side of this room were several cooking fires. Against the walls were platforms for sitting, about eighteen inches off the ground. Long sheets of strong bark stripped from a local tree covered the platform. This room was a large gathering place for the men, women, and children to tend the fires and cook their food. A large pathway down the middle led to the next section of the longhouse.

The middle section of the house was raised about four feet off the ground. On the right side a walled-off area was built for the women, small children, and baby pigs to sleep (separated from the men by the wall). Against the left side of this section was another platform where the married men slept. Again, there was a walkway down the middle of this section to the veranda area, the third area of the longhouse.

This last section was a large space walled off from the previous sleeping areas with its only access being through a small doorway. No women were allowed in this area; it was the meeting area for men and the sleeping area for young unmarried men. Inside this third area was a large and open space with no outside end wall. Typically, they built longhouses on the edge of a hill with the veranda end high off the ground. This open wall on this end of the house created a way of escape should they be attacked by a neighboring enemy tribe.

Life gradually changed in these villages when the colonial government established outposts in the remote areas. Patrol officers enforced peace in the area and discouraged the killing raids. As the fear of attacks lessened, the government also encouraged individual family houses, rather than the traditional longhouse.

On this trek in 1982, after visiting all the villages, we estimated that the population of the tribe was around seven to eight hundred, although others estimated a higher population. The last known cannibalism had occurred only two years before this visit.

The traditional longhouse served an important purpose: it provided protection for everyone in the village. The stacked doorway of logs prevented intruders, the vast house provided sleeping room for everyone, and the open-ended wall provided an escape plan. They felt safe together. If an enemy tribe managed to breech their security with a successful raid, some could escape death through the open wall and down the side of the hill. However, many would still die a brutal death. This was something to fear in this violent culture of raids and cannibalism, and protection for everyone was not possible.

We will all face death. Life does not have a guarantee, but we have assurance as believers in Christ that we are protected. Our safety and security rest in the hands of Jesus. It is his death, his shed blood, and his resurrection to life that spares us from sin's brutal consequences of eternal death. We can escape from our enemies – sin and death – through faith in a loving Savior. His sacrifice will never fail us, and the life he offers grants us lasting peace within.

Jesus provides protection and escape from God's wrath. He is our liberator, our Redeemer, and our freedom. Let's rejoice today in the God of our salvation.

Prayer

Thank you, Father, that because of Jesus, I no longer need to fear death. I have been reconciled to you through faith, and I have been declared righteous by the sacrificial blood of your Son. I rejoice that I am safe and secure from sin's eternal consequences. Thank you for the peace and the security you offer me as your child.

Personal Reflection

1. In Romans 5:8-10, how are we declared righteous before God? How do we escape from God's wrath?

2. According to Merriam-Webster, one definition of reconcile is "to restore to friendship or harmony." Our sin has separated us from God. How are we reconciled to God according to the Romans verses?

3. The longhouse served as a way of protection and escape for the tribe; Jesus serves as our protection and escape – protection from eternal death and escape from God's wrath. What does 1 Timothy 2:5-6 say that Jesus is for us?

The Gobasi Tribe

Then God said, "Let us make mankind in our image, in our likeness, so that they may rule over the fish in the sea and the birds in the sky, over the livestock and all the wild animals, and over all the creatures that move along the ground." So God created mankind in his own image, in the image of God he created them; male and female he created them. (Genesis 1:26-27 NIV)

Traditional clothing was the main form of attire when we first met the Gobasi tribe. The men wore loincloths made from their jungle environment, and the women wore string skirts. The men's grass skirt covered their back side and tied around the waist. Then a loincloth, made from beaten bark, was tucked through the string to cover the front. The ladies wore a string skirt that covered them from the waist to above the knees. These string skirts were made by stripping off long fibers from underneath the bark of a tree. Then the fibers were twisted into string to make their skirts. If any of them had Western clothing, it was tattered and worn from years of use. If they obtained any cloth, the men used it for the front loincloth or the women for a skirt. Nose and ear piercings were common, and long bamboo sticks protruded through the nasal septum of many.

Shell or bone necklaces adorned many necks, while others had necklaces made from the dried gray seeds of the Job's Tears bush. Found in many tropical environments, this plant makes a perfect little bead from nature. Once dried, the seeds harden to a shiny gray with a hole through the center. Shaped like a teardrop, they are strung with home-made string to make simple necklaces for wearing.

Woven jungle fibers crisscrossed the men's chests, while armbands woven in intricate designs embellished their upper arms. The women had capes made by beating the bark from a tree until it was soft and pliable. These were used to stay warm on cold mornings or to protect their babies from the elements.

Ceremonial dress was more elaborate. Using clay, charcoal, animal fat, and other natural materials, they painted themselves in distinctive designs as part of their bodily decoration. Elaborate headdresses made from bird feathers, waistbands from bark, and headbands from animal fur were some of their adornments. Cassowary bone daggers were also tucked down arm or leg bands for added decoration. *Kundu* drums – carved, painted, and topped with the skin of a lizard – kept the beat during their dance ceremonies. A few men and ladies were chosen to be the main dancers and the center of the celebrations.

One of the things that amazed me about this isolated tribe was how they used the environment around them for what they needed – which is mostly lost in our Western culture. They gathered many things from the jungle to create what they needed: soft grass to make their skirts, stringy fibers from tree bark that could be stripped and rolled into string, and bark that could be beaten to make a cape for warmth. Clay was used for ceremonial paint, fur from a small animal was used as a decorative headband, and feathers from birds were used for elaborate headdresses. Seeds, shells, and bones were made into jewelry, and a variety of light- or dark-colored reeds were woven into armbands with elaborate designs.

The Gobasi had the God-given ability to be creative and innovative in their environment. Isolated as they were, they knew how to use the resources in their surroundings. In Psalm 139, David reminds us that we are *fearfully and wonderfully made*.[22] God has given all of us minds for creativity, design, and innovation. From an elaborate feather head-dress to the launching of an aircraft to the moon, man is amazing in his efforts. We are not an accidental jumble of molecules, but are designed for a purpose by our heavenly Father. God gave us our minds and our

---

22   Psalm 139:14 NIV

abilities. He is the most creative of all – the One who put the stars in place, set the planets in motion around our blazing sun, carved the mountains, painted the stripes on the zebra, and gave us the wonder of a newborn baby. He crafted our eyes to see, our heart to beat, and our lungs to breathe. His creative ability is in us because we are made in his image.

Prayer

Father, you have made me in your image and likeness, and you designed me with a purpose. You have given me a creative mind and the ability to achieve great things. It's amazing to think that you desire a vibrant relationship with me. Help me to mirror the likeness of who you are to those around me and to walk faithfully with you.

Personal Reflection

1. Being made in the image of God means you can have a relationship with him. In what ways did you change and begin to bear his likeness when you became a believer?

2. According to the verses in Genesis above, how was man set apart from other living things when God made him?

3. We are not created like other living things, but we are made in God's image. Yet sin has distorted that image. Read Colossians 3:9-10. What is the contrast in these verses as it relates to the image of God?

Peanut Trouble

Then our mouth was filled with laughter, and our tongue with shouts of joy; then they said among the nations, "The LORD has done great things for them." The LORD has done great things for us; we are glad. (Psalm 126:2-3 ESV)

Life deep in the jungle meant that medical help was not readily available for us. With no airstrip and only jungle paths out, we could not get immediate treatment if we had an emergency. A snakebite, a chain-saw accident, or a major sickness could be life-threatening. A helicopter evacuation was an expensive possibility, but was no guarantee of timely assistance. Before the airstrip was built, we took every precaution to stay healthy and safe.

On my first trek out to visit the Gobasi tribe, we took our fifteen-month-old daughter, Janelle. I was also almost six-months pregnant with our second child. We planned to stay about one month to continue work on the airstrip. Our daughter was carried by our friend in a child-carrier backpack while I walked behind. As we walked through the jungle, Janelle would turn around to make sure I was following. With the difficult terrain, I did not have the agility or the strength to carry her the eight hours it would take. It was much safer for a sure-footed tribal friend to carry her.

Taking snacks and a water bottle along, I would hand her snacks to munch on while we walked. She also napped along the way. She was a great little trekker. If she could see one of us, she was happy. After a full day of walking, we arrived at the location of the Gobasi airstrip site.

Our daughter was quite the attraction with her blond hair. While her daddy worked all day on the clearing work for the airstrip, my daughter and I tried to greet everyone. She and I would sit outside, walk around to meet the ladies, and hang out to learn some of the language. We had planned to be there about one month, and then we would walk back to our temporary base.

The locals had built a traditional thatched hut where we lived while at the airstrip site. We lived in two rooms, and two other rooms were used by a pastor's family from another tribe who walked out with us. A fifth room was where we all gathered. Dale built a simple round-timber bed frame on which we placed our four-inch foam mattress. For our daughter, he built a little rustic bed next to ours. The only place in the house to sit was on the grass-platted floor mats or on the bed. During the middle of the day, I usually took Janelle inside for a nap while I rested from the tropical heat.

One thing we hauled out by carrier was a can of roasted, salted peanuts. After her nap one day, Janelle and I sat on the bed together to eat peanuts for our afternoon snack. I gave her one peanut at a time to chew. While we munched together, she suddenly jammed a peanut up her nose before I could stop her. The more she picked at it the further up it went. I tried to see if I could get it out, but I couldn't even locate it. How would I get that thing out? Now aware of her uncomfortable situation, she started to fuss.

I'd brought every other necessity out here, but not a pair of tweezers. Sitting on the bed with her, I panicked. That peanut wasn't coming out.

How could I forget tweezers? . . . What am I going to do? . . . Are we going to have to hire a helicopter for a medical evacuation because she jammed a peanut up her nose? . . . Really, how ridiculous is that? . . . The mission is not going to be happy with us for that expense . . . I'm such a stupid mother; I should have known better than to give her peanuts. What was I thinking? . . .

As we sat on the bed, I sent up a panicked prayer for help. Janelle whined even more about her uncomfortable nose while I contemplated what to do next. Suddenly, she let out a big sneeze, and the peanut popped out and rolled onto the bed.

Amazingly, in a time span of less than ten minutes, her body got rid of it the easiest way possible. All my helicopter-rescue plans were averted by a simple sneeze. I laughed in relief at our good fortune and God's simple answer to our dilemma. I put that can of peanuts back on the shelf with no further plans for her to eat more.

There are situations we face in life where God has the simplest of solutions. While we panic and come up with elaborate plans, God already knows how to fix them. Forget the stress and panic; watch God answer our prayers with an unexpected answer. He loves to bless us and show us his kindness and mercy. He sees our concerns, and he may solve them with something as simple as a sneeze. We don't need to worry; God's got it under control.

Prayer

Thank you, Lord, for surprising me with the simplest solution. Even when I panic, you are in control of my situation. You see all my concerns, and you love to bless me with answers to my prayers. You take joy in looking after your children, and sometimes we laugh at your provision. You alone are worthy of our trust and praise.

Personal Reflection

1. Describe a time when God surprised you with his provision or help.

2. We see God's provision to pay the temple tax in Matthew 17:24-27. How did the Lord supply Peter with the money to pay their taxes?

3. What creative way did the Lord provide for Elijah in 1 Kings 17:2-6?

Language Learning

I rejoice in following your statutes as one rejoices in great riches. I meditate on your precepts and consider your ways. I delight in your decrees; I will not neglect your word. Be good to your servant while I live, that I may obey your word. Open my eyes that I may see wonderful things in your law. (Psalm 119:14-18 NIV)

"*Kemane, Kemane,*" a young mother said. Sitting on our doorstep one morning, Mina repeated the word, hoping I'd understand. I had no clue what the word meant.

"I don't know," I said in the tribal language.

"*Ke-ma-ne,*" she repeated slowly, emphasizing each syllable.

"I don't know that word," I said.

"Give me my string bag," she told her daughter. This traditional bag was made from tree bark. Fibers stripped from a specific jungle tree were twisted and rolled by hand into string. Then weeks are spent weaving a bag, which carries their babies, chopped firewood, garden produce, or other things. Large ones to small ones are made to suit the need.

Inside this woven bag, she pulled out a scrap of old cloth. All her little treasures were carefully stored inside. Unrolling the cloth, she searched until she pulled out a fishhook. Then she held it up for me to see and said again, "*Kemane.*"

Then I knew she wanted fishhooks.

A new word thus learned. I wrote it down in my language notes. Such were the struggles of learning an unwritten language. We could not run to a dictionary and look up a word's meaning, nor could we go to language school. We were on our own in learning this language.

In our first year during our orientation time, we learned basic phrases from one of the few Gobasi teens who had attended the government high school where they taught English. He helped us learn basic and important phrases.

What is your name?

What is this? What is that?

Where are you going?

What are you doing?

I don't know.

Yes. No. Come. Go. Walk. Cut. Chop. Cook. Wash. Laugh. Cry, and many more.

These and other basic words and phrases helped us to learn other new words and to start communicating. Even when we could not form a proper sentence, we could use a word. It took time to gather vocabulary and understand sentence structure, but we still did not know much of the language. With some training from the Summer Institute of Linguistics (SIL), we wrote down sounds by their phonetic symbol to remember how to pronounce the word. Our pastor helper, Dafo, from a nearby tribe with a similar dialect, also helped translate meanings for us. We learned to listen carefully to dialogue exchanges as people went about daily tasks to extract meaning from what was being said.

We were confused daily on what words and phrases meant. We forgot words, pronounced them incorrectly, used the wrong word, or stumbled our way through a sentence to make ourselves understood. You know you've gotten it wrong when you see a puzzled look on someone's face that says, What is she trying to say? No doubt, the Gobasi tribe had many laughs at our attempts to learn their language.

One of the challenges of the language was their use of diphthongs, combinations of vowel glides that have different meanings. In gathering our vocabulary list, we wrote down the word *pig.* It sounded much like our English word *boy.* Later, we learned the word for *snake,* which also sounded like the word *boy.*

"The word for *snake* is like your word for *pig,*" we said. "Is it the same?"

"No. It's a different word."

Was it a tone that made it different? We asked the language helpers to say it several times while we listened. The word sounded the same to us. We simply could not tell the difference between *pig* and *snake* – not a good thing in PNG! What was the distinction? The tone did not seem to change, nor did we think the language had tonal contrasts. After much confusion, we finally figured out that the contrast between the two words was the use of a different diphthong: *Boi* versus *Boe*. Our ears barely discerned it. We had to listen carefully to each diphthong to get the sounds correct.

Language learning was a tedious process. It took time, commitment, and years of hard work. We would hear a word but not be sure what it meant. Or why did they use certain endings on a verb? Was it past, present, or future tense? We needed to look at the context to understand its meaning. This was our greatest challenge – to learn this language and be able to communicate God's truth. There was so much we didn't know and so much more to learn. It was an on-going task until God called us away.

As Christians, we should never stop learning the language of God – his Holy Scriptures. God's Word has so much depth and meaning that we will never attain or fully grasp all of its knowledge. Many rich treasures are buried in God's Word, and we can search for a lifetime and still discover new things. The great preacher Charles Spurgeon once said, "Nobody ever outgrows Scripture; the book widens and deepens with our years."

How am I at learning God's language? Do I study his words to gain better understanding? Do I ponder the meaning of a passage for what it means to me? Do I memorize verses that remind me of truth? Psalm 119:11 says, *I have hidden your word in my heart that I might not sin against you* (NIV).

As we continue in our walk with the Lord, he reveals to us new truths and understanding, because his Word is living, powerful, and relevant. Press on, friends; God has a wealth of treasures for us to learn and discover in his Word that will keep us centered in his will.

Prayer

Thank you, Father, that you have given us your Word. We can read, study, and understand rich truths that you desire to teach us. I want to be faithful in studying your written Word. Help me to meditate on it, obey it, and take joy in it. As the psalmist prayed, I ask that you open my eyes that I can see the wonderful things in your law.

Personal Reflection

1. How does the study of God's Word affect your life? Describe the practices you use to study Scripture.

2. In Psalm 119:14-18, what does the psalmist say you should do with God's Word?

3. According to 2 Timothy 3:16-17, what is God's Word useful for? What does God's Word do for the man or woman of God?

4. What does Colossians 3:16 say about how God's Word is to be an integral part of your life?

Suwaliba's Thankfulness

Therefore, just as you received Christ Jesus as Lord, continue to live your lives in him, rooted and built up in him and firm in your faith just as you were taught, and overflowing with thankfulness. (Colossians 2:6-7 NET)

In the early hours of the morning, I heard the soft chatter of those waiting for me. I had only dressed and had time for quiet reading when people gathered outside our bush house. My two young children had not yet awakened, nor had I fed them breakfast. With no medical worker here, the villagers came to me – not because I was a trained nurse, but because they had no one else. I was their best hope. I could dress sores and dispense aspirin. I also gave out medicine according to a missionary doctor's directions.

It had become an exhausting and overwhelming task to know that several villages depended on me – especially when I felt so inadequate for the task. Yet they needed the help. They suffered needlessly because of a lack of medical care. A simple cut could turn into a horrible oozing ulcer if it was not cleaned or bandaged. Malaria could kill a small baby within days, and a woman with an after-birth infection could go septic and die when simple doses of medicine could have saved her life.

How could I not help them? I would not ignore their suffering.

Knowing little of the tribal language at the time, I did my best to communicate by sticking with simple phrases. Although I sensed that the people were happy that I helped them, no one conveyed this to me.

Day after day, every morning and every evening for months on end, I worked to help them with their pain and sicknesses.

I experienced times, though, when I wished for a place where I could disappear from the watchful eyes of those who needed me. I suffered from days when I was drained of compassion and wanted to escape and run to some faraway place where I might find some comfort of my own.

One day a lady named Suwaliba came and said that both of her ears hurt.

"I have big pain," she said in the local language.

I looked in her ears and saw pus oozing from both. She was in obvious pain from a severe infection. Giving her antibiotic pills and some pain medication, I told her what time of day to take them.

"Eat two in the morning and then eat two more before sleeping," I said.

Then she left for the village with her little packet of pills.

Days later she returned. It was obvious she felt much better. In her hand she held a bundle wrapped in leaves and tied with jungle twine. She smiled and held it out to me.

I opened the bundle at her request and saw a small pile of galip nuts, edible seeds taken from a large tree in the jungle. My husband and I loved them. They were a large, elongated nut about two inches long that was seasonal in this tropical environment. Under its brown peel, it revealed delicate milky-white layers with a smooth, subtle taste.

"Do you want money?" I asked. We paid them when they brought us food. Then they could purchase rice, salt, or some other item they needed.

"No," she replied.

I asked again to be sure, "Don't you want money?"

"No. My ears had big pain, and you gave me medicine. Now they are better, and I'm giving you these nuts. You take them."

She pushed the bundle toward me to insist that I take them and said, "Eat."

There was no word for *thank-you* in their language, but clearly, that is what she was saying. I was touched. Out of the many people I helped every day, she alone had returned to thank me.

Suwaliba's simple act of kindness touched my heart and encouraged me to persevere. She had worked hard to collect those nuts from the jungle and crack open their hard shell. They were a delicious and treasured nut only in season once each year. She gave me something special. I had made a difference for her, and she was grateful. My worn and weary spirit needed rest, and God knew I needed her encouragement.

I wonder how often Jesus went thankless for the many healings he had done. Out of the ten lepers completely healed from their dreaded disease, only one man was touched enough to return and thank him. How are we at showing gratefulness to others? When we receive a gift, do we respond to the giver's generosity? If someone shows us a kindness, do we let them know our appreciation? A thankful heart shows your respect and love for others.

Thankfulness expressed is powerful, both to the one who offers it and to the one who receives it. We often neglect or forget this simplest of ways to encourage and acknowledge what someone has done. It can make all the difference in someone's day.

Just as the one leper thanked God for the blessing of his healing, do we thank God for the ways he blesses us? It is easy to take his salvation and provision for granted. Let's not be like the nine lepers who didn't return to thank Jesus; be the one in the ten that did! Look for opportunities and follow Christ's command to be thankful, not only to Christ, but also to all those who show us kindness and make a difference in our lives.

Prayer

Father, we look to you with grateful hearts for all you have done for us. We thank you for the great love and faithfulness you have shown us. Thank you for the ways you have blessed my life. Give me a heart that overflows with thankfulness and give me opportunities every day where I can show encouragement and appreciation to others.

Personal Reflection

1. When has someone's encouragement made a difference in your day? Have you gone to God in great thankfulness?

2. According to Colossians 2:6-7, what measure of thankfulness does God desire that we have?

3. What do you learn about giving God thanks in Luke 17:11-19? List the ways he has helped you and then thank him.

Bread: Steamed or Fried?

In all hard work there is profit, but merely talking about it only brings poverty. (Proverbs 14:23 NET)

If we wanted bread, I needed to learn a different way to cook it. With no oven for baking, I could cook food two ways: on the small Primus or over an open fire. In the previous years, I had finally mastered the struggle of cooking on a woodstove and baking bread, but at the airstrip site, we only had the basics for cooking. We had no stove. I had to learn a whole new way of putting bread on the table.

For lunch, I learned to fry bread. After mixing up a batch of biscuit dough, I placed little rounds of dough in a fry pan with a small amount of oil. I fried them over low heat to be sure the center would fully cook. Once one side turned toasty brown, I flipped them over for the other side to cook. With a bit of practice, nicely crusted biscuits soon became a lunch staple, which we topped with jam, peanut butter, or canned margarine. A sprinkle of cinnamon sugar was also a favorite. We used leftovers from lunch as an afternoon snack for our children.

After longing for softer, less crusty bread, I also learned to steam bread. An older missionary told me how the earliest church workers would steam their bread over a fire.

"You can make bread by steaming it over the fire. Put the raw dough in empty tin cans inside a larger pot containing an inch of water," she said. After explaining the process over the shortwave radio to me, I thought it would be worth a try. We had one large pot with a bucket-like handle and a lid that would hang on a stick over the fire.

After saving cans from our tinned food, I made a batch of bread and filled the cans halfway with dough. Then I let them rise. The dough rose and crested in a little dome above the top. I filled the large pot with one inch of water and placed the four fifteen-ounce cans inside. I placed its lid on and carried it outside to the little house where our pastor's family lived. I asked his wife, Selebadi, if she could help me cook the dough over the fire. She had helped me cook other food over the fire many times.

Blowing on the embers, she prepared the fire. Then she added a few sticks of wood. It needed to be hot enough for the water to boil and steam the bread. She slid the handle of the pot through the stick that hung over the fire. We learned not to put in too much water, or the bread would get soggy from the boiling water splashing up and ruining it. If the water boiled away, the bread would burn. The fire had to burn exactly right. Did I need more water or less water? Should there be a hot fire or embers? It was a big learning curve. Each time I would try something different to see if the result made better bread. I failed many times in this cooking process as I turned out soggy, burnt, or doughy bread. Yet I wanted fresh bread!

Soon, I learned the method. With Selebadi's help, we turned out nice tins of steamed bread in about thirty minutes over the fire. After cooling in the tin, I ran a knife around the inside to release the bread. Then I sliced it into small rounds. Once I had success, I also made banana bread and other sweet breads this way. Soft and delicious, we gobbled them down. What a joy to have more bread the family could enjoy.

Sometimes life forces us to learn something new, and out of necessity we take on a new challenge. Success comes as we put forth effort. I failed many times while learning from my previous mistakes. Each adjustment helped me learn to turn out perfectly cooked bread. When we fail but keep trying, we learn the joy of accomplishment. Whatever challenge we face, the sweet joy of success is worth all our effort.

Prayer

Father, thank you that in all work there will be profit. In the challenges that I face today, I ask for your favor. Give me the ability to work hard and see the joy of accomplishment. If I fail, give me the diligence to keep trying. Help me to seek you for help and success in whatever task I am given.

Personal Reflection

1. What new challenge are you facing today? In what area do you need more perseverance?

2. How does Proverbs 14:23 speak to you?

3. Moses prayed for the nation of Israel in Psalm 90. What does he ask God to do in verse 17? How can you implement prayer in your life, even in daily tasks and challenges?

Singing Dogs

My dear brothers and sisters, take note of this: Everyone should be quick to listen, slow to speak and slow to become angry, because human anger does not produce the righteousness that God desires. (James 1:19-20 NIV)

With the stealth of an expert thief, a village dog nosed our bush-house door open, walked through the house, and jumped on our rickety table to steal food. The creak from the table gave him away. I rushed out to see him just as he bounded out the door with two biscuits in his mouth. We often chased dogs away that were trying to enter our house to search for food.

On this day, I had made fried biscuits for lunch. With two as leftovers, I placed them on a plate and covered them with a tea towel for later. I planned to put jam on them as a snack for our two children when they awoke. During their afternoon nap, I enjoyed a few minutes of peace when I heard the commotion in the kitchen.

Most village dogs starved because their owners let them fend for themselves.

Papua New Guinea is known for its "singing dogs." These medium-sized dogs are unique and native to the country. Also called "stone-age dogs," they may be a close relative of the Australian dingo. They make vocalizations that sound similar to a wolf's howl. When one dog starts "singing," others often join in until there is a united chorus of dog howls. They can start their dog music at the most awkward and random moments – during the morning church service, in the quietness of the early morning, or anytime that several dogs are together. Once they get started, there seems to be no way to quiet them. It's a part of life in the village. They never bark, only vocalize.

I saw them as annoying, half-starved village dogs. Everyone had one, so wherever they went, the dogs followed. When the men went hunting with bow and arrow, their dogs went along to help locate and catch the prey they shot. They were valued for their hunting skills.

They are not treated as we treat our dogs though; we fuss, baby, and overfeed our animals. We put clothes, Halloween costumes, and sunglasses on our animals. Most of these animals are skin and bones – always scrounging looking for some opportunity to eat. In an area where people struggle to feed themselves, their dogs are the last to eat. They scrounge for potato or banana peelings around the fire and anything else edible they find or steal.

One morning before airstrip work started, we held our usual early morning service with all the workers. As they gathered and sat down, their dogs followed to hang around. Partway through the morning Bible lesson, one of the men walked over late from the village with his bow and arrow in hand, unusual since he was arriving for airstrip work and not going out to hunt. Instead of sitting down to listen, he looked around the scene. Before anyone could react, he pulled his bow taut, readied his arrow, aimed, and shot a dog. The arrow went straight through the dog and out the other side.

In the ensuing chaos, everyone broke out in shocked chatter, wondering what had just happened. The service came to an abrupt halt while loud and angry discussion followed. The dog stumbled around bleeding for a few minutes until it succumbed to its fatal wound. While still new at learning the language, we were unclear as to why he shot the dog. Later, we were told the dog had rushed into this man's cookhouse and stolen his morning sago. It was not his dog but belonged to someone else in the village. Anger abounded that day in the village between this man and the dog's owner. No doubt, every dog in the village had stolen food at some point without receiving this outburst of fury.

This man, who seemed a bit peculiar to us, would later be in the middle of several difficult events. We found that most people in the tribe had a fun side to them; they laughed, joked, and were fun to be around.

But they also displayed quick anger that could result in violence, not only toward animals but also toward each other. This incident was a reminder to Dale of how quick things could take an ugly turn.

Most of us have probably suffered from someone's angry outburst. Rash anger and actions are something the Bible often speaks of. King Solomon said, *Do not let yourself be quickly provoked, for anger resides in the lap of fools.*[23] Anger breaks relationships, destroys a Christian's testimony, and can deeply hurt the best of friends and family. The great English preacher Charles Spurgeon said, "Do not say, 'I cannot help having a bad temper.' Friend, you must help it. Pray to God to help you overcome it at once, for either you must kill it, or it will kill you. You cannot carry a bad temper into heaven."

Instead, God desires that we embrace and allow the nine fruits of the Spirit to be displayed in our lives – love, joy, peace, patience, kindness, goodness, faithfulness, gentleness, and self-control. These enable us to live in community and harmony with one another and to express the love of Christ.

Prayer

Dear Father, forgive me for days when my outbursts of anger produced hurt and sorrow for others. Help me to overcome anger because your Word says that it does not produce the righteous life that you desire. Give me the strength to overcome. I want to walk in righteousness and obedience. I ask that your Holy Spirit help me so that the fruits of the Spirit are displayed in my life.

Personal Reflection

1. Describe a time when you became the brunt of someone's anger. How did that affect you?

2. What are the three things in James 1:19-20 that God desires believers to have? How would those three things help in

---

23   Ecclesiastes 7:9 NET

our relationships with others? Evaluate yourself in these three areas. What can you do to change?

3. What warning do you find in Proverbs 22:24-25?

4. The Holy Spirit within a believer's life can produce fruit. Read Galatians 5:22-26. What are the nine fruits of the Spirit that should be displayed in your life?

Airstrip Work

*Cast your burden on the LORD, and he will sustain you; he will
never permit the righteous to be moved.* (Psalm 55:22 ESV)

"Whoop–Whoop–Whoop–Whoop–Whoop!"
Excitement rang out as men shouted this familiar war-like
cry in a united chorus. A tree was ready to fall. Everyone within hearing distance knew what was happening and waited for its loud thump
to the earth. Once felled, the men continued whooping as they took
pride in their accomplishment of downing another tree.

Airstrip work had begun.

A few years earlier, everyone discussed where to put the airstrip. An
older village leader said, "We should find a good place for this airstrip. We
need to look for a place on a river." His opinion was important. Sawgay's
foresight influenced the search. Water was an important resource, and
life would be better for everyone if they had quick access to a river.
Because they were semi-nomadic, this airstrip site would become the
permanent location for one of the larger villages in the tribe. For us,
building an airstrip meant organizing, raising money, and building it
in the heart of a thick jungle.

Looking for a place with level ground, the village men located a spot
on the beautiful Siu River. The river snaked its way around the area; it
would provide travel, fishing, and an abundance of water. Dale walked
out with another missionary to inspect the location before work started.
Was it suitable for the length needed to land an airplane? A minimum
of nineteen hundred feet was needed to land a small aircraft. They

measured the length to be sure. It seemed to be a good, mostly level spot, so the men determined it to be a suitable site.

The Gobasi knew an airstrip would provide them with a permanent way to help their community. It would provide air travel for emergency medical situations and eventually bring schoolteachers and a medical orderly. This work would benefit them for years into their future. Yet it was a monumental task for this small tribe of people to do all the clearing work by hand.

We lived temporarily at the closest mission outstation, Honinabi, while Dale trekked in and out to the airstrip site. Two weeks each month he would leave to check on the progress. He worked alongside everyone digging out trees and chainsawing. I usually stayed behind at Honinabi station with our two young children.

First, the work started by clearing out the underbrush and small trees. The women cleared the underbrush while the men worked on bringing down the trees. The only tools used were bush knives for the clearing work, pickaxes, six-foot pry bars, and shovels for digging around the tree roots. Axes chopped off the smaller limbs of the felled trees. We had one heavy-duty chain saw that only Dale operated to limb the trees and to cut tree trunks into small sections for rolling off the airstrip. Dale marked off three hundred feet at a time for the workers to complete. When a mark was finished, everyone received their pay and then left for a break to work in their gardens.

A gigantic undertaking was the removal of several massive buttress-root trees. These huge roots proved to be a challenge to dig out by hand. Digging down with shovels and pickaxes, the men worked until each root was exposed and cut off, and the tree fell over. It was important to remove the root system so that future rotting would not collapse the level of the airstrip and leave dangerous holes on the airstrip surface.

Small crews worked on several trees at a time to clear one section of a three-hundred-foot marker. It was slow, backbreaking work. The men were smart in the process of using the power of one falling tree to knock down three or four others in its path, which they had partially dug out. Using the weight of one large tree, they instinctively knew which direction the tree would fall so it would knock the other trees down and yank all their roots out with it. Their garden-clearing skills in the jungle had served them well for learning that technique.

Months after the initial work had begun, a helicopter flew a tractor in that was disassembled into several pieces. Dale had the monumental task of putting its pieces back together again. This would be used to level out the surface once it was cleared. A cultivator, a scoop, and a blade were also flown in to use for leveling the ground. When a section of the airstrip was down to bare dirt, then the tractor would smooth its surface by bringing down high spots and filling in low spots.

After half of the airstrip was cleared, a huge dip, not so obvious when covered with thick jungle, became more apparent on one side of the airstrip. That low spot required a massive amount of fill. We fought discouragement when we realized it would take months to fill in the low area. The tractor scoop gathered dirt from one area to carry and dump in the other place. The airstrip surface had to be as smooth as possible for a plane to land safely. During one summer, the tractor went night and day when a team of short-term helpers came to assist in the work. They were a huge help as each took shifts during the night to help us complete the work.

Later, we hired two national workers to drive the tractor and continue lengthening the airstrip. We found a man skilled in tractor work from the Gogodala tribe in the south of the country who was willing to help. He lived at the site for months and worked with us.

The airstrip took almost three years to build. Everything about the task screamed impossible to us. We had never built an airstrip; never driven a tractor, much less put one together; never used a chain saw; and never managed a group of stone-age tribesmen.

Yet God gave the victory. At times we felt as though a plane might never land there. What seemed impossible wasn't, because of the faithfulness of God. He helped and sustained us. He provided everything we needed – workers, finances, and a tractor. He kept everyone safe while doing the work. Everyone worked little by little as a team to get the job done, and God was with us all the way.

Sometimes the Lord places a task before us that seems beyond our experience and capabilities. We know if we do it, it will bless our family and others in the future. Whatever that task may be, it will stretch us beyond what we feel capable of. We may want to walk away in defeat. Yet if we walk in obedience, we have the promise that *it is God who works in you, both to will and to work for his good pleasure.*[24] We do the work, but God goes beside us. When we labor through to the end, we learn that God is our Sustainer. He will carry us, and his grace and strength will uphold us for the task.

Prayer

Thank you, Father, that you alone are my Sustainer, and you give me the strength for the tasks you set before me. Help me to trust you with these "impossible" tasks. Give me hands that work hard and a heart willing to follow. Thank you for enabling me and helping me to complete the task.

Personal Reflection

1. What are you facing today that seems beyond your capabilities? Are you trusting God to be your Sustainer?

2. What two promises from God do you find in Psalm 55:22? What do we need to do?

3. Read Philippians 4:13. What encouragement does that verse give you as you look at the future?

---

24   Philippians 2:13 ESV

Casting the Net

"I have compassion on the crowd, because they have already been here with me three days, and they have nothing to eat. If I send them home hungry, they will faint on the way, and some of them have come from a great distance." Then he directed the crowd to sit down on the ground. After he took the seven loaves and gave thanks, he broke them and began giving them to the disciples to serve. So they served the crowd. They also had a few small fish. After giving thanks for these, he told them to serve these as well. Everyone ate and was satisfied, and they picked up the broken pieces left over, seven baskets full. (Mark 8:2-3, 6-8 NET)

We are all familiar with this beloved story of Jesus' miraculous feeding of thousands. God has great ability to amaze us with his provision. And that was true for us too, while building the airstrip. The work to clear the land was hard, and food was scarce. Displaced from their gardens and living in makeshift homes, the tribe worked with diligence on clearing the land. Most weekends everyone needed to travel to their gardens to gather food for the coming week. The long spells of work exhausted everyone.

One day while standing on the cliff enjoying the view of the river, we looked down to see an area teeming with fish. In one section of the river was a large, shallow shelf of rock a few feet under the water. When the river was not flooded from the rains, we could see fish swimming in the clear water above this rock shelf – large, beautiful fish. Hundreds of them! But they were difficult to catch with a simple hook and line.

On our next trip out of the bush, we purchased a small fishnet at the village's request. At dusk after our return with the net, the national pastor who assisted us in work and another man loaded up the net. Tying one end to the bank, we watched as two men paddled out into the river in a dugout canoe. After they spread the net over the rock ledge, they anchored the other end of the net to a rock. The net reached about halfway across the river. That night we all hoped for fresh fish.

The next morning as they pulled the net into the canoe, fish after fish came with it. Dozens of large mullet fish were hauled in and divided up for everyone. The smell of smoking fish over the fire permeated the air that night.

Several times during the work on the airstrip, the Lord provided an abundance of large fish that fed everyone who was working. It reminded me of the story of Jesus feeding the multitudes. He looked at the hungry crowd, and he had compassion for them. Then we read of the miraculous provision of food for everyone from seven loaves of bread and a few fish. Jesus knew they needed food for their journey home, and his compassion for them satisfied their need for food.

Jesus is our compassionate Savior. He sees our weariness, our hunger, our discouragement, and our longings. Just as he saw that the crowd needed sustenance for their journey home, he also knows what we need. He is not only a God of great power, but he is also a God who is full of compassionate love. He can provide in extraordinary ways for us too.

Those hauls of fish only happened during the time of airstrip work. We never saw such an abundance again. I have no doubt that God saw a displaced little tribe working hard with barely enough food and a young missionary family hungry for fresh food. He provided everyone with the blessing of his provision. Many thankful tummies sat around the cooking fires that night. No doubt, Jesus smiled as he looked on.

Prayer

Thank you, Lord, for your compassion. You see our needs and struggles every day, and you take joy in providing in amazing ways. If you care for the flowers in the field and the birds of the air, you will care for me. Your faithfulness never ends, and your mercies never cease. Thank you for this great hope that we have in you.

Personal Reflection

1. It is important for us to reflect on the Lord's provision. Think about a time when God provided for you in an unexpected way.

2. What do we know about God from Lamentations 3:22-25?

3. Read Matthew 6:25-33. What do we learn from this passage about God's provision for us?

Section Six

Jungle Home

After we returned from our first home assignment in the United States, we trekked out as a family to live at the airstrip site while work was completed. Dale made our traditional jungle house as comfortable for us as he could. He built our daughter a bed from round timber, while our son slept in a foldable playpen carried out by one of our Gobasi friends. He made a table with a small piece of plywood and legs from chain-sawed timber. Dale also installed the shortwave radio for communication and built rustic shelving for pantry supplies and clothing. Months later, he fixed a small bucket shower in one room to make it easier for me and the children to wash. It was rough, but livable.

I learned how to live without running water and cook on a kerosene Primus or over the coals of a cooking fire. We were the wealthiest people there. We had a four-inch foam mattress while everyone in the tribe slept on pieces of pounded bark on their floor. We had pots to cook our rice in a place where one pot was a prized possession and rice was a luxury. Our children wore diapers and t-shirts, while local babies had neither.

Yet it felt like the never-ending camping trip.

One day, one of the ladies came into our rustic sitting room. We had two folding lawn chairs, flour drums for sitting at our rough-hewn table, and a couple leaf mats on the floor. I had hung our umbrellas and a few bags on four-inch nails.

She looked around and said, "Your house is very good."

Throughout our years in PNG, this was one reminder, among many, that we needed to consider other perspectives when ministering the Word of God, not just our own.

Thatched Home

*Bend down, O LORD, and hear my prayer; answer me, for I
need your help. Protect me, for I am devoted to you. Save me,
for I serve you and trust you. You are my God. Be merciful to
me, O Lord, for I am calling on you constantly. Give me happiness, O Lord, for I give myself to you. O Lord, you are so good,
so ready to forgive, so full of unfailing love for all who ask for
your help. (Psalm 86:1-5 NLT)*

A traditional "bush" house in Papua New Guinea lowlands meant several things: a thatched roof, split round-timber floors, no screens, no running water, no bathroom, no electricity, and no appliances. Our traditional house was built on posts about five feet off the ground.

We built an outhouse, and each day we bathed in the river. In the earliest stage, I cooked on a one-burner, pump, kerosene Primus and over an open cooking fire in a small cookhouse next to our home. These were interesting challenges for us, especially with two small children.

But there were good things as well. The floor never had to be swept because everything fell through the cracks of the floorboards, including pens and utensils. We didn't have to wait our turn for the shower because our family all washed in the river at the same time – in our sweaty clothes. Although extra light was convenient, we didn't really need windows because we could peer through the cracks in the siding to look outside. The kitchen window was useful for throwing out the basin of dirty dishwater.

On our return from a furlough in the United States, we noticed the bad condition of the floor. Termites had caused major damage in many parts of the house. We tried to be cautious where we put our weight until we could replace the floorboards. One morning in a distracted hurry, I forgot to step over the bad board in our bedroom. One leg crashed through the floor just as several men walked past to gather black palm wood for its repair. My leg dangling through the floor was another sign that they needed to help the inexperienced foreigner living among them, and it reinforced the necessity of their morning's work. I sported a huge black-and-blue bruise for weeks.

Until the airstrip was completed, carriers brought in everything we needed from the closest neighboring mission station. It was a long day's walk from us. They carried in our four-inch foam mattress, all our food, clothing, tools, and simple household items. They brought two partial sheets of thin plywood to make a small table and a kitchen counter. Dale made rough, round-timber shelving and a round-timber bed frame for our mattress. He created a bookshelf for an office area by using cut logs as supports and chain-sawed timber as shelving.

A hired helper chopped firewood, hauled in water, and completed other tasks too difficult for me to do. We stored drinking water in a large yellow cooler with a tap, and two buckets were filled for other household use: cooking, washing dishes, cleaning up our kids, or medical work.

Months later, we built a tractor shed with a metal roof. Then we caught rainwater that drained from the roof into two carefully cleaned, old fuel drums. Rather than hauling water up the hundred-foot embankment from the river, we only hauled it forty feet across the yard. Once the airstrip was completed, things would get easier little by little. We lived over a year without running water with two young children in cloth diapers. I struggled to make this rustic life work, and I had my gloomy days. It challenged and stretched me every day. I knew we would not be forever in this stage because we would build a more permanent house, and that gave me hope. Things would improve, and I focused on that.

In this hard season, I learned to appreciate the simple joys: watching the antics of our young children as they learned new things, or gaining excitement as I learned new words in the language. It also helped to sweeten things up by making dessert: cobbler with canned peaches baked over the fire, or fudge boiled on my little Primus. I learned to reduce my expectations and adapt. I didn't need hot water for dishes; cold water worked just fine. I added a drop of bleach to the rinse water to disinfect things.

Years ago, someone told me, "Whenever you are in a hard place in life, ask yourself, What is God trying to teach me?" Even though I may want to complain and feel sorry for my circumstances, God has a purpose for every stage of my life. He is full of compassion and has some lesson to teach us. It's a choice to look for the simple blessings each day.

Looking for those little joys will help our heart discover contentment. As we look to God to persevere, we learn to make the best of where he has placed us. Then, when that season changes, we can look back and realize that God was with us all the way, helping us grow to be more like himself. He gave us the courage, he gave us the strength, and he taught us so much about trusting him through the challenge.

Prayer

Thank you, Lord, for being faithful in difficult seasons. Thank you for giving me the strength to persevere as I look to you. Show me what you desire to teach me during this season and give me the courage to get through challenging days. Give me a heart that will choose joy in simple things. Thank you for your abundance of compassion and unfailing love for all who call on you.

Personal Reflection

1. Are you in a difficult season right now? If so, then ask, What might God want to teach me in this season?

2. What does 1 Peter 1:6-7 say hard trials can do for us?

3. Think about this: Am I willing to reduce my expectations and adapt to where God has me? What simple joys can I be thankful for today? What blessings do I see despite my difficulties?

Fast Little Feet

In peace I will lie down and sleep, for you alone, O LORD, will keep me safe. (Psalm 4:8 NLT)

The worst drawback of living in a bush house was the floor with gaps and the walls that let in critters at night – mainly rats. Since this house was close to the jungle, they entered as soon as the lights were out and the home was quiet. Scurrying around the house, they would hunt for food. They chewed through plastic containers, ran on the shelves, and knocked over whatever got in their way. Their noise often woke us from our first slumbers of sleep. Fighting with each other over a scrap, their screeches were an unsettling sound in the dead of night.

These rodents made for sleepless, exhausting nights.

Although we had rat traps, we couldn't entice them. We woke to hear them scrambling through the house. My husband, frustrated, would grab his flashlight and machete and jump from the bed to chase them from the house. I listened to his murderous-inspired whacks while I stayed tucked under the bed's mosquito netting. I dared not venture into the chaos that ensued. His strikes never killed them because of their fast little feet, but it scared them so much that they dashed back into the jungle. At least all that pandemonium was therapeutic for my husband's frustration.

Because of the high incidence of rats in this house, every night before bed I started a nightly ritual to secure the kitchen from these little invaders. I stored every food item that wasn't in a can or jar in two giant metal flour tins and clamped on the lids. Otherwise, they would find it. Rice, jars of peanut butter, pasta, crackers, and bread were all stored in those metal drums at night. If something was left out, they found it.

Some nights rats scurried by on the wall support behind my head or under the bed. Months of sleep-disturbed nights exhausted us. We needed a better solution than Dale jumping out of bed with his machete. Then, the idea of a cat came to mind, but we knew that cats were not common in the area. When several men left to trek out for more supplies, we asked our friend to look for a cat at the government station. We were thrilled when he returned a few days later with a kitten. Delighted to have a pet, our daughter named her kitty Bubbles.

After a few months of growth, he became a great ratter. Naturally attracted to the hunt, he chased or killed any rodent that wandered into the house. Soon, we were left with quiet nights and better sleep because of his constant vigilance.

With the extreme challenges of jungle living and airstrip building, the sleepless nights led to an ineffective solution – chasing rats with a machete. When we lack sleep, exhaustion takes a toll on our mind and body. Our reactions to things may become impulsive, rather than purposeful and thoughtful. One of the crucial needs in life is for peaceful rest, and we desperately needed sleep. When we prayed and searched for a solution, the Lord graciously answered. Our furry, little, feline friend was a definite answer to our prayer for sleep.

Prayer

Thank you, Father, that you have the answers I need for any large or small difficulty I face. Help me pray and look to you for help because you have the perfect solution for my need. Thank you that I can be confident you hear my prayers, and you are faithful to provide for me.

Personal Reflection

1. Are your mind and body exhausted from lack of sleep? Have you prayed and sought God's help for a solution?

2. Where should you turn first?

3. What does God say about our prayers in 1 John 5:13-15?

Jungle Meals

But let the godly rejoice. Let them be glad in God's presence. Let them be filled with joy. Sing praises to God and to his name! Sing loud praises to him who rides the clouds. His name is the LORD—rejoice in his presence! (Psalm 68:3-4 NLT)

Life at the airstrip site meant simple meals. The carriers hauled all our food for us from another location when it was dropped by plane at the other mission station. With no refrigerator to preserve food and no proper stove, we ate food that had long storage capabilities.

Daily we ate rice, dried beans, and canned meat or tin fish. I also made bread. Our treasured stash of instant potatoes was pulled out for variety once or twice a week. Oatmeal was a staple for breakfast with the occasional bowl of cornflakes with reconstituted powdered milk. On weekends I might cook pancakes. We made syrup by boiling sugar and water with a dash of maple flavoring added, which I had brought from America. Other canned items we used were margarine and drippings (fat), powdered milk, and jam. It was a dismal menu, but we got used to it. At the airstrip site, we definitely ate to live; we didn't live to eat.

Occasionally we would get a hunk of wild meat from someone or a fresh-caught fish from the river. Any fresh meat was a treat and a delicious addition to our boring menu. Tied up in a section of split bamboo, newly caught fish was cooked over the fire. Slowly smoking over the coals, it rotated and baked for a couple of hours. When we knew that a fish was slow-roasting over the fire, we anticipated a great meal. Its smoky flavor and soft flesh were a special treat as we picked it from the bone.

Sugar makes everything better, so we hauled that out there too. Peach cobbler became a favorite when we craved a dessert. When our craving for something sweet hit, I'd open up a can of peaches and dump them into my frying pan. Then I would make a cake batter and pour it over the peaches. Putting on the lid, I cooked it either over the coals of a fire or over a low flame on my little kerosene Primus.

I often made chocolate fudge and no-bake oatmeal cookies. Both were boiled on my kerosene Primus until they came to soft-crack stage. Fudge was cooled and hardened in a small pan, and the oatmeal cookies were dropped onto a tray to cool and harden. If the recipe ended up a flop and the treat didn't harden, we ate it by the spoonful. For our daughter's second birthday, I made her a pan of chocolate fudge and placed two candles on it. Although not too fancy, she didn't know the difference, and we all enjoyed her pan of fudge.

Sunday became the day for treats – whether it was dessert, a tin of corned beef (still not all that great), cornflakes, or an extra glass of orange-flavored drink. I learned to keep a little stash of things just for our Sundays. It was our day of rest, and something special on that day seemed appropriate. We kept this custom in our family for many years.

We had left behind an easy-access, food-rich society, and had exchanged that for eating rice most days. Yet it doesn't take much to create happiness for family. To our children, it was all they knew. Life for them was an adventure every day. Whatever they were served, they ate it with joy – a fried biscuit with cinnamon sugar, a smoked fish from the fire, or a sweet tropical banana. They could enjoy and be thankful for these simple things, and so could we.

Some things we cannot change, so we adapt and learn thankfulness. That gives honor to God. As we learn to make the best of things wherever we are, God will help us find ways to be creative with the little we do have.

And it's amazing what a little sugar will do!

Prayer

Lord, thank you for everyday simple pleasures. Give me a thankful heart for even the small things I can enjoy each day. Help me in times of need to be content with where you have placed me. Give me creativity to make the best of my situation so I can honor and glorify you. And Lord, thank you for little blessings such as sugar.

Personal Reflection

1. Have you had times of need? How did that affect you? What positive things did you learn during those times?

2. What is the repeating theme in Psalm 68:3-4? Is that a part of your life?

3. What three things in Romans 5:3-4 does God say will develop from difficult times that we experience?

Predator to Plate

Always rejoice, constantly pray, in everything give thanks. For this is God's will for you in Christ Jesus. (1 Thessalonians 5:16-18 NET)

Our six-month-old kitten, Bubbles, screamed with vigor. The noise woke me after midnight. Sleeping in this thatched-roof house in the jungle had interesting moments.

That's not normal. The cat must have gotten wedged between the gaps of our black palm floor.

Then he screamed a second time.

Nudging my husband, I said, "Go see what's wrong with the cat." Too afraid to budge, I wanted him to go. Bush houses concealed creepy things at night.

"He'll be fine," he said and rolled over.

Ten seconds later, the intensity was gone, but now he yowled a pitiful sound. I shoved my husband in the bed.

"Go see what's wrong!"

At my persistence, he got up and grabbed his flashlight. After walking into the adjoining room, he dashed back seconds later to our bedroom, throwing our young daughter onto the bed with me.

"There's a big python on Janelle's bed," he said as he ran back to get our little son. He grabbed him and put him on the bed with the rest of us. Now we were all startled awake. Dale grabbed a machete and raced back into the kids' bedroom.

Our daughter's bed was under a mosquito net which hung over the bed; I tucked it in each night under the mattress. Our son's bed was a foldable playpen with netting over it. Our new kitten had pushed the net over a little on our daughter's bed, so he could sleep on the soft mattress. The python gripped our cat by the neck between its jaws and wrapped itself around its body to squeeze the life out of it – all while lying on Janelle's bed. I suppose he hoped for a midnight snack. Instead, Dale swung the knife and put a deep cut in the side of the snake. Startled, the python let go of the kitty.

Dale made one more trip to the bedroom, handing over Bubbles by the scruff of his neck – a little worse for wear, but still alive. He was wet, ruffled, and dazed from the snake's grip. One more squeeze, and it's not likely our pet would have survived.

Meanwhile, the python slithered under our daughter's round-timber bed. Roughly made from jungle materials, it had no legs, so the frame of the bed sat on the uneven floor. But with enough space to crawl underneath it, the snake found a place to hide. Unable to lift the bed and kill the large snake at the same time, Dale yelled out to the local pastor who was sleeping in the house next to ours.

"Dafo, come help! There is a big python in the house," he yelled. Our friend grabbed his bow and arrows and ran over to the house. I wondered how they would get it out from under the bed.

"You lift up the bed and hold it, and I will shoot," he told my husband.

That sounded fine to Dafo, but to Dale it sounded like a sure way to get bitten on his hands or feet by an angry snake. He grabbed the nearest corner and lifted. Dafo stepped back, pulled his bow taut, and aimed for the python. On his first shot, he pierced the snake with a five-pronged arrow. They dragged the snake out, and Dale finished him off with the machete.

"This is plenty of meat," Dafo said. "I will cook him tomorrow." Our friend carried the snake out as he left to go back to his house. This would provide his family and a few friends with a good meal of protein for the next couple of days. Nothing was wasted in the village, and we were relieved to get it out of the house.

The next morning, we went to find out the length of the snake. It measured nine feet. Knowing such a huge reptile was slithering around the house while we were sleeping was a super-creepy thought. Would I let this incident overwhelm me with fear? Could this happen again?

If I let my mind wander, my heart would become anxious and fearful. Yet as I pondered the events in the weeks that followed, I realized that I could be thankful for many things.

- Yes, the snake was on our daughter's bed while she was sleeping, but he was outside the mosquito netting, while she was underneath the net.

- I heard Bubbles cry before the snake had squelched his screams.

- We had a kitty that the snake went after, instead of one of our children.

- The kitten lived, so our daughter still had her beloved pet.

- The children were unaware that a snake visited their bedroom and they didn't become fearful.

- My husband was the one who got out of the bed. If I had gotten up, major screaming would have awakened the children and filled them with terror.

- The pastor was close by to help kill it.

- It provided food for the pastor's family and friends.

How many times in life do we focus on the negative aspects of a hardship, rather than consider ways to be thankful? I was not happy that a huge python roamed around my little bush house. I hated the thought, but I could be thankful for the way in which the events unfolded. God says, *In everything give thanks,* but many times we refuse to look at the good things in a challenging or fearful situation. Rather, we focus on the difficulty.

If God tells us to be thankful in all things, then I need to look at the situation with a different heart. Can I search for evidence of God's caring hand? I believe there are treasures to be found that show his mercy and love if we choose to look. Thankfulness not only transforms our attitude, but it also changes our heart. Seeing his merciful hand will carry us through difficult times and give us joy in his goodness.

Snakes still frighten me. But to our knowledge, we never had such a large visitor in the house ever again. Our slithering foe went from predator to plate. I was thankful about that too.

Prayer

Father, I ask that you help me to learn joy in my difficulties, to always pray, and to discover what it means to give thanks in all circumstances. Give me eyes to see the many ways that you care for me. You are my God. Thank you for always being with me and working out all your purposes for my life.

Personal Reflection

1. When you experience something frightening, do you look for evidence of God's caring hand?

2. What three directives does God give us in 1 Thessalonians 5:16-18? How can you be thankful for everything, even if it's something difficult?

3. Read James 1:2-3. What does it say we should do during a trial? Why?

First Landing

Wise words bring many benefits, and hard work brings rewards.
(Proverbs 12:14 NLT)

Smoking breaks during airstrip work were a common occurrence. With homegrown tobacco and a foot-long piece of bamboo, a communal smoking pipe was a common tradition among the men. Passing around the pipe, the male workers would have a smoke while sitting under a tree they were digging out on the airstrip. One by one everyone took a smoke while billows of smoke permeated the air.

When they were tired, we would find many of them sound asleep for an afternoon nap under a tree. For hours each day, we might see workers disappear and return later in the day to do more work. It certainly wasn't our Western way of clocking in and out. We decided it wasn't worth fussing about because work in the tropical heat was exhausting. We had also learned that the other workers would do their own fussing at those who weren't doing their portion of the work.

We paid everyone when they finished a section. If they wanted to complete a section in one month or six months, the pay was the same. They worked at their pace, and we learned to live with that. Normally the work moved along at a good pace, but when we went on home leave, they did nothing on the airstrip as they waited for our return.

During the airstrip-building process, when several sections were completed, the pilot decided to do a flyover to see how things were going. The locals were lit up with excitement when they saw the plane. They yelled and whooped with enthusiasm as they watched it do a sweep over the area. The pilot dipped the wings a couple times and created even more enthusiasm. It proved to be a great way to motivate the crowd to work even harder.

When fifteen hundred feet were completed, the airstrip was inspected to see if we were ready for a first landing. Finally, it was ready. We waited at another mission station on landing day. Standing by our high-frequency transceiver, we heard our pilot, Roy Hoey, call us and say, "I'm on the ground at Yehebi."

"How did it go?" we asked.

"No problems at all," he said. Thirty minutes later, he was picking us up to move us, our children, and all our gear. No more arduous seven-hour walks through the jungle to get there. After two years of hard work and waiting, we moved permanently to Yehebi – the new name for the airstrip site. Thankfully, those years allowed us to learn the language and share the Word of God each morning.

The next week, Roy brought a small, brand-new kerosene-run refrigerator for us. Its sparkling whiteness looked out of place in our little jungle house, but I was thrilled. Now we could have a cold drink in the tropics, frozen meat in the freezer, and a way to keep food fresh. Our young daughter was so excited I had a hard time keeping her from opening the door every five minutes. Not long after, a cast-iron wood-stove was also flown in for us. Baking bread would be so much easier. Life had certainly changed for the better for our family.

Even though the airstrip was open, we still had four hundred feet to finish. With weight restrictions on the plane due to a short airstrip, we needed to finish the remaining distance. Nevertheless, the worst was over, and our goal of moving into the Gobasi area was realized. Over the next several months, the rest of its length would be completed as well.

The task of building an airstrip had been daunting. The payoff was landing on it the first time. All that hard work was worth it. Now, the Gobasi tribe would have a permanent location on the map.

Life can have spells of intense labor as we work hard toward goals: a college degree, our first home, a job promotion, getting a teenager through difficult years, or finally getting out of debt. How rewarding it is when we accomplish what we've worked so hard for! Accomplishing a goal is life-giving. Proverbs reminds us that *a longing fulfilled is a tree of life.*[25] The ability to work hard is a gift. When God placed Adam in the garden of Eden, he told him to work and care for the garden.[26] God has made us to work. When we complete a goal that God has set before us, it's a huge accomplishment. I believe he is as happy as we are.

Prayer

Lord, you have ordained work. Thank you that you have said that all hard work brings profit. It is a gift to have the ability to set goals and to reap the rewards of our labor. In times of intense labor, give me the strength to persevere. In times of weariness, help me to not give up. Help me to honor you in the work that I do.

Personal Reflection

1. How does it feel when you have worked hard and reached a personal goal?

2. Work was ordained by God when he placed Adam in the garden. Read 2 Chronicles 15:7. What does that verse say about work? Have you seen your work rewarded?

3. According to Proverbs 16:3, what should we do before setting goals?

---

25   Proverbs 13:12 NIV
26   Genesis 2:15

Thatch Bug Dirt

Work willingly at whatever you do, as though you were working for the Lord rather than for people. Remember that the Lord will give you an inheritance as your reward, and that the Master you are serving is Christ. (Colossians 3:23-24 NLT)

A thatched roof looks cool in tropical-themed designs on travel shows, but when you live under one, it's a different story. Not only does it not last long in a hot and wet environment, but it also presents other problems for those living under it.

When a summer team arrived to help us build a new house, one of the guys walked through the door, looked around, and made a mindless comment.

"Hey, why did we come here to build you a house? What's wrong with this one? It looks cool."

My attitude soured toward this young college kid's opinion, but I decided to keep quiet and let him think about what he wanted. He had no clue what living here was like. It wouldn't be long before he realized some of its difficulties. He just needed to wait until the next tropical rain.

The roof on our temporary house was covered with the long leaf of a palm tree in the area. Dozens of long palm leaves are removed and folded lengthwise. Then they are pinned together along the frond's rib. Hundreds of these are made to cover a large roof. Then the ribs are tied with vine to the rafters. Working along the bottom of the rafters, they work upward until they reach the ridge of the house. Then they add a ridge cap at the top to close the gap. The thatch works great for a time, but then it begins to deteriorate in the tropical environment.

By this time, we had four small tarps covering parts of our thatched jungle roof. Not only was the thatch old, but it also leaked every time we had a rainstorm. We ran around moving things away from the water dripping through the worn-out thatch, or Dale would stuff more leaves in where we had leaks. The tarps were only a temporary fix to hold us over until a more permanent home could be built.

It wasn't long before the guy who said the house was "cool" soon realized it had many drawbacks. Waking up sore because he slept on the round-timber floor, he stumbled out the first morning feeling the aches and pains of a bad night.

"That sure was a rough night of sleep. I could feel every bump on the floor."

For several summers, work parties came to help us and lived in this house with us. One group of eleven young college students came to help work on the airstrip, nine men and two women. Another summer, another team arrived to help us build a more permanent house. These teams were a huge help to us. They were all willing to work hard under rough conditions.

Both teams arrived with great enthusiasm. They came ready to tackle whatever came their way, and we were grateful and blessed for all their help. They slept scattered all over the floor on thin foam mattresses. They washed in the river and helped haul in water for us to drink and cook with. They had meals of oatmeal and rice almost every day with limited variety. And the outhouse with the hollowed-out tree trunk for a seat was less than a comfortable place to take care of business. Every day they went out to work alongside the Gobasi tribe; one group helped with the airstrip work, and another group two years later helped build a more permanent home for us.

When the first team arrived, we sat around in a circle on the round-timber floor to eat our meals. It wasn't long before everyone noticed little dark droplets falling everywhere from the ceiling.

"What's this?" someone said as he pointed to the little black dots.

"Well, it's thatch bug dirt."

"Thatch bug what?"

"It's thatch bug dirt; the poop from bugs eating the leaves covering the roof."

"Seriously? Bug poop?" They all looked at each other with disgust on their faces.

"Yes."

The "dirt" dropped everywhere from the roof. It would end up on bedding, in the kitchen, any place under the roof. I kept the silverware in a closed plastic container to keep it clean. Our drinking water was in a closed yellow cooler with a tap safe from bug droplets. It was just another one of the things we learned to tolerate.

Since paper napkins were a luxury hard to obtain, I sewed everyone a cloth napkin to use at meals. Those became important to them once the presence of thatch bugs was discovered in the house. Taking their napkin, they covered their food or drink to make sure no bug dirt fell from above. No one wanted to see a black dot or two floating around in their water or Kool-Aid or adorning their pile of rice.

Everyone that second summer set to work on building a timber-frame house for us. The hard work they did that summer provided us with a good house for our family for many years, and now serves the church for various events. Even though that young man thought the house looked quaint and cool, he soon realized it was not a house for the long term. In the end, he pushed himself the last several days before leaving to get as much done on the house as he could, even waking up at 5:00 a.m. on the last day to work before the plane arrived to take him home.

Although we had both made quick judgments, the young man learned we indeed needed a new house. I learned he was a fine, hard-working young man who went through rough living and boring food to help build us a house.

These summer workers (and others over the years) gave us a huge boost of help and encouragement. It was an adventure for them, but it was also a sacrifice to live in rough conditions and work from daylight to dusk most days. Instead of a relaxing summer break, they chose to serve. We were thankful they listened to God calling them out to assist us. It was just another way that God helped us in the work. God uses people in numerous ways to accomplish his tasks, and it may not be something grand. It might be eating lousy food, sleeping in a crowded hut, and working hard to help a missionary in the jungle.

Prayer

Father, thank you for those willing to give up their comfort and help in hard places. Thank you that when we serve others, we are really serving you. You see all that we do, and no job is too small. Give me a heart to serve in whatever capacity you have called me. Help me to be willing to deny myself, take up my cross daily, and follow you.

Personal Reflection

1. Sometimes God's plans may not be grandiose; they might be something out of the ordinary. Have you felt God calling you to do something unusual?

2. What do you learn from Colossians 3:23-24 about work?

3. God never promises our service for him will be easy. What does Matthew 16:24 say about following Jesus?

4. When God asks us to do something difficult, we are blessed with the satisfaction of serving him, of new spiritual growth, and of learning from those experiences. In the process, we may bless another person too!

Rustic Outhouse

Rejoice in the Lord always. I will say it again: Rejoice!
(Philippians 4:4 NIV)

I hated outhouses, especially at night. They were dark, with hidden, unknown life forms. Three things were necessary for our outhouse: bug spray, toilet paper, and alertness. Roaches loved to hang around the outhouse, and who knows what other critters I might find?

With no plumbing, we needed to build an outhouse. A ten-foot-deep hole was dug, and a tiny house and floor were built over it. Ingenuity comes into play when you lack materials and nearby stores. One day while working on cutting down trees for the airstrip, my husband noticed that the workers had chopped down a hollow tree. *Hmm,* he thought, *I think we could use this for the toilet seat in the outhouse.* He decided to cut a piece to the right height from the fallen hollow tree. Then he worked manicuring it with his chain saw to make it into the perfect rustic potty seat. When attached over the hole, it became an excellent provision in the middle of nowhere for a somewhat comfortable seat.

During the day, I was fine with an outhouse; during the night, I dragged my husband and his machete out with me in case I needed him to eliminate unwanted critters.

Our small children were afraid of the outhouse and refused to use it, so they used a potty seat in the house. However, one day our two-year-old son walked in and saw our large carton of toilet paper. He decided that it was quite fun to watch the toilet-paper rolls disappear into the darkness below as he dropped them one by one down the hole. I imagined he watched as the mounting faint gleam of white appeared at the bottom. When he was finished, he had thrown our treasured stash of about fifty rolls down the deep, dark hole. Not one was left. Before we even knew what had happened, all our toilet paper had disappeared.

In the middle of the jungle, we knew we were in for a long wait for more, so we found used papers in the house, cut them into pieces, and scrunched them until they were soft. We used that paper in the out-house until another supply arrived.

Unfortunately, the next flight brought more of the same – cut-up phone books from mission headquarters. They couldn't get toilet-paper rolls in time for the next flight, so it was weeks before we had the real thing. Our cutie firstborn son taught us that, yes, we can live without toilet paper! The other thing I learned was to never put your whole stash of rolls in the outhouse. From then on, I only took a few out there from our household supply.

Sometimes life is just a lesson that things can go wrong, but no one is to blame. We didn't get angry at our little boy whose curiosity led him to have a little fun. He had no clue what his actions meant for the rest of us. Surely, God has a sense of humor in these things too. At the time, we had a team of six summer workers with us who also learned how to scrunch up paper for use in the outhouse. It became a funny topic of discussion as they also adjusted. Life will always throw unpleasantness at us. Some things are only a frustration that we can laugh at and remedy as best we can.

Prayer

Father, give us thankful hearts when life takes an unexpected turn. Help me to have patience when unpleasant events happen and give me a sense of humor that shows grace. You have commanded us to rejoice always; give me a heart attitude that sees joy even during life's complications.

Personal Reflection

1. What attitude do you display when an unexpected complication happens? Do you have a sense of humor, or do you display anger and frustration?

2. God gives us a simple solution of how he wants us to respond to what happens in our day. Read Psalm 118:24.

3. Pastor Chuck Swindoll says, "A refreshing sense of humor is never distasteful, ill-timed, or tactless. Instead, it lightens our spirits and energizes our thoughts. It helps us step back and not take this fleeting life quite so seriously."[27]

---

27 Chuck Swindoll, www.insight.org/resources/insights-by-topic/humor.

One Another's Burdens

*Husbands, in the same way, treat your wives with consideration
as the weaker partners and show them honor as fellow heirs of
the grace of life. In this way nothing will hinder your prayers.
Finally, all of you be harmonious, sympathetic, affectionate,
compassionate, and humble.* (1 Peter 3:7-8 NET)

"A village upriver is bringing a man down to see you. He cannot
walk, so they are floating him down the river on a raft." Some of
our village friends had gotten word that a sick man was being brought
down to see if I could help him.

I wasn't sure what to expect, but I suspected a tropical ulcer. Common
in humid tropical environments, these sores are also called "jungle rot"
by some. This bacterial infection can cause large, circular, ulcerated skin
lesions. I had seen a vast number of these in the last few months. They
can become so large and painful that a person cannot walk. A cut, a
scratch, or an insect bite can be the not-too-serious beginnings of such
an ulcer. Without proper hygiene or medicines, they can soon develop
into a large infection. Even poor nutrition can be a factor.

Sure enough, the man had a huge ulcer on his lower leg. It had
become so serious that he could only walk with a stick and with great
pain. Fortunately, the river raft saved hours of carrying him through
the jungle.

In our earliest months here, I bandaged five or more of these infections a day. After washing the oozing sore and leg, I sprinkled antibiotic
powder on the sore. Then I covered it with gauze pads and wrapped a

bandage around the leg to secure it. Oral medication was given to heal the infection. Although it responded well to antibiotics, it could take weeks for such a large ulcer to heal completely.

These ulcers needed to be dressed twice each day, every morning and every evening, to keep the bandages dry. I watched the pain on the sick people's faces leave and the smiles return as they got better. This became a way to build relationships and learn names. Their lives were so hard, and this was one way I could help.

After months of dressing all these sores and helping with other sicknesses, I got up one morning and saw the crowd waiting for me at the door. Instead of having a heart of compassion, I wanted to run and hide.

"I can't go out there; I cannot dress sores today," I said to my husband. In a moment of dread, the stress of this daily care had become too much. I could not face another oozing leg ulcer.

My husband looked at me without hesitation and said, "I'll do it."

Dropping his plans for that morning, he went outside to pass out medicines and bandage legs. I stayed in the house, hidden away. For at least a week, he dressed sores twice a day to give me a break. After a respite from the demands, I felt I could continue. In all our following years, we never saw such an abundance of tropical ulcers as we had during this early time with the Gobasi tribe.

We both had times where we needed to help each other. With no outside sources of help, we had to pick up the slack when the other was stressed, sick, worn-out, or even discouraged. If we ignored each other's needs, the work and ministry could fail.

We had to be vigilant in how the other was doing and take steps to ensure that the other spouse was doing well.

If my husband had told to me, "Pull yourself together and get out there," he would have ignored my plea for help. He knew I was overburdened and he stepped in to relieve my load. Marriage is a partnership; we love and care for each other. To be sensitive to our spouse nurtures the well-being not only of the person, but of the relationship also. Scripture tells us to *carry one another's burdens, and in this way you will fulfill the law of Christ.*[28] Certainly we should obey that command, especially in the marriage relationship.

---

28   Galatians 6:2 NET

Prayer

Lord, thank you for being the author of marriage. In your wisdom, you created a wife for Adam to be his companion through life. Help me to be sensitive to the needs of my spouse, to give sacrificially, and to love unconditionally. May we learn to live in harmony together with you as our leader. Help me to be sympathetic, affectionate, compassionate, and humble in my marriage relationship and in my friendships. May our marriage bring honor and glory to you.

Personal Reflection

1. Are you sensitive to your spouse's needs?

2. Do you recognize when your spouse is under a stressful load? Are you willing to put aside your plans to relieve him or her?

3. Showing love and respect to your spouse nurtures your marriage relationship. What does 1 Peter 3:7-8 tell us about how we are to respond to others?

4. Read Ecclesiastes 4:9-10. How would this passage relate to the marriage relationship?

Panic in the Night

Those who live in the shelter of the Most High will find rest in the shadow of the Almighty. This I declare about the LORD: He alone is my refuge, my place of safety; he is my God, and I trust him. For he will rescue you from every trap and protect you from deadly disease. He will cover you with his feathers. He will shelter you with his wings. His faithful promises are your armor and protection. Do not be afraid of the terrors of the night, nor the arrow that flies in the day. (Psalm 91:1-5 NLT)

It was 3:00 a.m. when I was jarred awake by another one of my husband's violent coughing spells. For over a month, he'd had a relentless cough. During the night, his prone position made his breathing worsen. This time, instead of the usual long, gasping intake of air, he made a horrible sound as he struggled for breath. I knew his airway was blocked completely.

Oh no, he's choking on his own phlegm; he could die!

I jumped up in a panic because I knew he had no air. By this time, he had sat up in the bed desperately trying to get a breath. Without time to think, I hit him on his back hard several times to loosen up the phlegm that blocked his breathing.

A large work party had arrived for the summer, so I yelled out for someone in the house to bring me a flashlight. Without electricity, the darkness of the jungle night prevented me from seeing anything.

Still he didn't breathe.

I banged on his back several more times without success. Finally, in total desperation, I stood up in the bed, got behind him, and leaned down over him to do the Heimlich maneuver. With him sitting and me standing in the bed, it made for an awkward position as I bent to get a good grasp. I grabbed both my hands together in a fist, and I pulled under his ribs with all my strength. After several times of plunging my fists under his chest, he raised his hand up to indicate that I should stop. His airway had cleared enough for him to get air. He sat there several minutes drawing in labored breaths, trying to recover.

By this time, the entire house was awake. We had a house full with six summer workers – four single men and a couple. They had come to help us build a more permanent timber house. All of us slept in this little jungle house with only thin-platted bamboo walls between us. Privacy was non-existent, and everyone heard the commotion of Dale's struggle and of me in a massive panic. We all gathered around in relief when Dale was breathing again. A prayer of thanks was in all our hearts – especially Dale's – that he was breathing again.

After his breathing steadied, I boiled some hot water on our little gas Primus to make a vaporizer. Adding a little mentholated ointment to the water, I made a tent with a towel for him to get under. I hoped the hot, moist steam might help him breathe better and loosen the mucous in his lungs. With our good friend Phil, who had come to help us, the three of us sat up the rest of the night for fear of another choking spell. We got our two children back in bed while the others settled back in for more sleep.

Dale had struggled for over a month with this cough that only continued to worsen. His daily coughing spells grew longer and more intense as he struggled for breath to come. The stress began to wear on me. Each time he started to cough, I would tense up. I listened and waited in anticipation for that whoop sound and intake of air to be sure he was okay. He was not getting better. The violent coughing exhausted him as he struggled to continue with managing station work and a large team of summer workers. It was obvious his body was not fighting well, and the previous night's choking had terrified me.

In the morning, I radioed one of our missionary doctors. Pushing to get him evacuated, I did not want to deal with another horrible choking spell. Within a couple of hours, our MAF pilot, Roy Hoey, rearranged his schedule and arrived to fly him to our mission's hospital. The airstrip had only been open for five months before someone in our own family was the first to be medically evacuated from our small jungle location.

He stayed in the home of two missionary doctors, Mark and Judy Fitzmaurice, and their children. He and another doctor there had differing opinions on his sickness – maybe severe bronchitis, tuberculosis, or possibly whooping cough. They called on the radio transceiver (our only way to communicate with the outside world) to ask us if we had whooping cough in our area, since a village nearby had reported it in their area. Several local children did have severe and violent coughs, so I think we had whooping cough cases as well.

Tests showed that he did not have tuberculosis. The violent coughing and struggle for air made us think it was whooping cough. After several medications, he returned to the station. It was months before that cough was gone and his strength returned to normal.

Terrified that my husband could have died, I tried not to go to that place of fear. Instead of being all alone when it happened, we had the support of others – especially our friend who sat up with us the rest of the night. We had no 911 to call, no nurse on duty, and no quick way out for help. Our sole means of getting to a hospital was by plane – only when it was daylight and only if the weather permitted a flight. I saw God's gracious care that I wasn't all alone when this happened.

Following God doesn't mean we don't have times of fear, worry, difficulty, or even sheer panic. We do. We were here to bring the gospel to a tribe that needed Jesus. We weren't only fighting sickness; we were also fighting the dark spiritual realm around us. Two months before this night, the first Gobasi had become a Christian. I'm sure Satan wasn't happy that we were invading his long-held territory where deep belief in and fear of the spirit world reigned. Attacking the young missionary family could stop the work. I would not have been able to live in this isolation alone with two small children if he had died that night.

We often felt the forces of evil and the darkness all around us, but those forces don't have the last say; God does. And God says, *"Be strong and of good courage; do not be afraid, nor be dismayed, for the LORD your God is with you wherever you go."*[29] Sometimes God will take us into

29   Joshua 1:9 NKJV

the dark places of our soul to build our trust in him and in his ability to care for us. During life's challenges, Satan wants fear to dominate our hearts and minds. Fear is a tool he loves to use to hinder the work of God in our lives. Fear opposes faith. Yet even amid fearful things, we can rest in the knowledge that God is there. The rest is in his hands.

Prayer

Father, thank you for your presence with us during fearful times. Help me to learn what it truly means to place my concerns and anxieties into your hands. I ask that you help me become a person of prayer. Guard my heart from fear and help me to learn complete trust in you. Thank you for the peace that you have made available for us.

Personal Reflection

1. What do you fear?

2. Read Philippians 4:6-7. What does this passage say will conquer fear? What will guard your heart?

3. What does the psalmist declare about God in Psalm 91:1-5? What does God promise in these verses?

Healing Magic

Anyone who believes in God's Son has eternal life. Anyone who doesn't obey the Son will never experience eternal life but remains under God's angry judgment." (John 3:36 NLT)

Dale had walked to the village one day to visit with a sick lady and her family. Bolbai had come to church and expressed interest in becoming a Christian, but now she lay sick with a high fever and severe head and neck pain. The situation did not look good.

"Can I pray for your wife, Bolbai?" my husband asked.

"No, we want to do our healing magic on her," the husband told Dale.

In animism, when someone gets sick, dies, or calamities happen, they believe the cause is either sorcery or an angered spirit. Their lives are lived in fear as they make efforts to appease the spirits. By using traditional methods steeped in their ancestors' past, they hope to satisfy an angry spirit. For sickness, it is healing magic.

So, at his request, we did not publicly pray for his wife. She was extremely sick, probably with cerebral malaria, the most severe neurological complication of an infection of falciparum malaria. This was common in the area where we worked. I was giving her medications according to the doctor's instructions, but she had not improved. We had seen several people with this severe head and neck pain die within a few days.

With their custom of using the spirit medium for their healing magic, we would ask their permission to pray publicly for the sick person. We gave them a choice: did they want prayer, or did they want to do healing magic? If the person was healed, then it would be attributed to their magic and not prayers to God (if both were done). At their choice we did not pray publicly for her, although we prayed in our home for her. For the next two nights, they had séances for Bolbai using their traditional healing practices.

Early in the morning two days later, someone came with the news: "Bolbai is almost to die." I gathered a few things in a string bag and headed for the village.

As I entered the crowded bush hut, I saw Bolbai. She lay on the raised platform of the cookhouse in the far corner. Her mother, husband, and other family sat around her. She was now in a coma. She was emaciated with her face contorted in its dying state. She didn't have long to live.

"Come! Come!" the family yelled. All her family sat around her shouting in her ears to call back her spirit.

"Come! Come!" another yelled in her ears. The air was tense and somber.

Her mother sat beside her and held two small branches with the leaves still attached. She hit Bolbai hard on the stomach several times in succession with the branches. "My child, my child, my child!" she wailed over and over. She paused, only to repeat her wailing and beating.

This last effort was a desperate attempt to try to call her spirit back. The healing magic had not worked, but maybe this would. As I watched this scene unfold before me, many things went through my mind. The hopelessness was obvious, yet this is how they had lived for centuries – living and dying without hope. Bolbai was a young mother, probably not yet thirty, with two little children. They would be left motherless.

I moved forward to give her another dose of medicine without hope that it would make a difference. Burning fever had overcome Bolbai's body. We had done all we could. Her life was in God's hands, no one else's – not mine, not the doctor's, not the spirit medium, not the family yelling to call her spirit back.

I left the village and returned to my house. She died a short while later. We heard the mother's mourning wails all the way to our house. Bolbai had entered eternity.

Life is but a breath. We are here, and we are gone. Job said, *"Only a few years will pass before I take the path of no return.*"[30] Was Bolbai ready? Are we ready? Just like the village thought they could control her destiny by using their healing magic, we may think we control our destiny too. We can refuse God, just as Bolbai's family refused prayer.

I see Jesus as a gentle Savior. He looks toward us with an outstretched hand offering true life to us, but he never forces us to accept it. We must reach out to him. That choice belongs to us alone. He says, *"I am the way and the truth and the life. No one comes to the Father except through me.*"[31] He has a right to that claim because he is the only one who conquered death by his resurrection to life. He holds the keys of our life and our death. He owns the world and everything in it. Will we acknowledge him as our sovereign Lord?

Will we accept the peace, the hope, and the new life that he offers? I hope so. I know he is mine; I hope you know that he is yours.

Prayer

Thank you, Jesus, for being the sacrifice for my sin and that through you, I can be justified before God. Your death was the penalty for my sin that grants me eternal life with you. I only need to ask. Thank you for your great love and forgiveness.

Personal Reflection

1. Considering John 3:36, have you believed, or have you excluded God from your life? What are the consequences of these two choices?

2. We have a desperate need for salvation because our sin has completely separated us from God. What does Romans 3:10-18 tell us about ourselves?

3. God's divine judgment remains on us because our sinful condition is irreparable by ourselves. Only when we embrace faith in Jesus' sacrifice and humbly ask for forgiveness of sins is his wrath removed. Read Romans 3:23-26.

---

30   Job 16:22 NIV
31   John 14:6 NIV

Section Seven

Jungle Family

We lived isolated and alone, but we had a larger community of mission families that supported us and others in their church-planting efforts. Mission headquarters, based in the highlands area of the country, bought any supplies we needed and packed them for the plane. Then our Mission Aviation Fellowship pilot flew those things in to us on a biweekly basis.

Doctors were available at noon by high-frequency radio if anyone had an emergency or needed advice. Office workers printed our literacy materials, and mechanics helped us order parts and keep things running. Others received and sorted our mail, ordered fuel we needed, and helped us with things that we could not do from our isolated location.

This was a visual reminder of the functioning of the body of Christ. Each position had an important part to play, and everyone was needed: the bookkeeper, the shopper, the mechanic, the pilot, the doctors and nurses, the station manager, and the field leaders. Those who hosted and fed traveling visitors, the man who gathered our mail and readied it for a flight, and the work parties that came to help us were all important. Their work enabled us to do what we did.

Our own family was growing too, in size and in number. During our second term, we moved into a more permanent, sawn-timber house with an iron roof, louvered windows with screens, running water, and solar power. And yes, even an inside toilet! My parents visited one summer, and my dad built us a bed, two couches for our living area, and a corner hutch. For our children he built a bunk, a slide, and school desks. We had a much better living situation for our family.

Overdose

Likewise the Spirit helps us in our weakness. For we do not know what to pray for as we ought, but the Spirit himself intercedes for us with groanings too deep for words. And he who searches hearts knows what is the mind of the Spirit, because the Spirit intercedes for the saints according to the will of God. (Romans 8:26-27 ESV)

My husband walked into the bedroom and saw our two small children sitting on the floor with an open medicine bottle and antacid wrappers scattered on the floor. Surprise turned to horror as he realized our three-year-old daughter and almost-two-year-old son had gotten into the medicine bag.

"Carin! Come quick!"

I knew something was wrong when my normally calm husband yelled. Rushing up to the bedroom to see what had happened, I was sickened at what I found – the entire bottle of chewable Camoquin (an anti-malarial) empty and nineteen antacid tablets missing. Mentally I calculated how many amodiaquin should have been in that bottle. I knew the implications of what was happening while my mind and heart screamed, *No!*

While I was outside doing laundry, my husband was sitting in the house, chatting with the men. We both thought the other one had the children. What had been the wonderful gathering of several missionary families at Christmastime now turned into a crisis.

My one overwhelming fear over the last several years was that our young children would get into the medicines we kept. Having various antibiotic and malaria treatments around because of our isolated living helped prevent major emergencies, not only for our family but also for those in the tribe. Dale built several high shelves to store everything out of reach.

However, on this trip the excitement of being with friends for the holiday caused me to forget my usual precautions. Our friend's house had just been built, and there were no shelves or furniture to store things. Our mattress was on the floor, and so was our suitcase with a zipped bag of necessary medicine.

Now my worst fear had come true.

We scrambled into action. Our teammate, John, immediately got on the HF radio and called out to anyone who might be listening. It was the day after our Christmas. The call was heard by the radio network administrators who immediately called a doctor in the highlands by telephone to turn on their HF radio and talk with us. After John explained the situation, the doctor said, "You must make them vomit right away, or this could be fatal." Hearing those words struck terror in my heart. Sobbing, I tried to stay in control.

John's wife, Celia, a nurse, directed us in what to do. Chaos ensued as we tried to force them to drink salted water. Then sticking our fingers down their throats, we tried to make them throw up. We had to get the medicine out of our children's bellies. Celia worked on our son while I helped hold him. My husband worked on our daughter, but she bit his hand several times, refusing to cooperate.

We were desperate as we realized we could lose both of our children if we could not get them to throw up quickly. Time was critical, especially since we did not know how much medicine each child had swallowed.

Our son, Jeffrey, finally threw up medicine until Celia was satisfied the vomit was clear of the yellowish color of the medicine. Our daughter had hardly vomited. She told us she only ate two tablets, but we weren't sure if she was telling the truth or was afraid of getting into trouble if she lied.

Since communication did not happen at the speed it does today, and HF radios were the main means of contacting someone, we were surprised to hear our own mission's doctor come up on the radio. Another nurse within our mission, who happened to be testing out her newly fixed HF radio, tuned in at the same moment we sent out our distress call for help. She knew we had an emergency when the doctor in the highlands area was coaching us on what we needed to do. She then alerted our doctor who ran up to talk with us on his radio. That same nurse then called the station where an MAF pilot was based. Because of the holiday season, there were no plans to fly that day, but his wife heard the distress call and alerted her husband who was enjoying Boxing Day[32] by fishing on the river. He then rushed back to get the plane readied for a flight.

The previous day, Christmas, had been such a fun-filled day for our families, and now we found ourselves in a life-and-death crisis. It soon became evident that our son showed serious signs of toxicity. We still could not get our daughter to cooperate. Our son was becoming lethargic, and fear began to overwhelm us. It seemed like a horrible nightmare, but it wasn't; it was real. I was in anguish to think I might lose one or even both of the children.

It is during these times that our trust in God is at its most vulnerable. Fear can overwhelm us when we are in the middle of a crisis, and it can be hard to even think or pray. When our mind can't absorb what is happening, we still look to God. If our prayers can't form, we have the promise that *the Spirit himself intercedes for us with groanings too deep for words.*

Prayer

Father, I know you are with me, even in a great crisis. When I am struggling to pray, thank you that your Holy Spirit intercedes for me according to your will. In times of weakness and distress, help me to feel your presence and guide me through with your great hand.

---

32 Boxing Day is a holiday celebrated by Great Britain and some of its commonwealth countries on the day after Christmas, December 26. Our pilot was Australian, so it was a holiday for him.

Personal Reflection

1. In a time of crisis, how do you respond? What sustains you?

2. Read what the psalmist says in Psalm 116:1-4. What is the first thing he focuses on and where has he placed his hope?

3. God tells us he is a stronghold for us in trouble.[33] Are you spending time in prayer and fellowship with him? Are you reading and meditating on his Word to gain strength for difficult days?

---

33   Psalm 9:9

A Rainbow with A Cross

But I will sing of your strength; I will sing aloud of your stead-
fast love in the morning. For you have been to me a fortress
and a refuge in the day of my distress. O my Strength, I will
sing praises to you, for you, O God, are my fortress, the God
who shows me steadfast love. (Psalm 59:16-17 ESV)

Our wait for the emergency flight for our son's evacuation seemed like an eternity. His face became flushed, and he progressed to a semi-conscious, unresponsive state as the drugs entered his system. The pilot flew to the hospital base to pick up two missionary doctors who waited at the grassy airstrip with a bag of medical supplies. When they climbed into the Cessna plane, the three took off for our remote location.

After two and a half hours from the time Dale found the children with medicine, we finally heard the plane as it buzzed over the small airstrip where we had spent our Christmas. I fought back sobs as we hurried out to meet the aircraft. The plane landed, and two missionary doctors rushed out.

I knew my son's condition was serious when the doctor stood on the airstrip, took one look at our boy, and immediately started an IV drip. The doctor's grim face spoke more than any words could. His body remained limp as the doctor inserted the needle, and he never even whimpered. The doctor said he hoped the IV drip would dilute the medicine in his blood enough to save his life.

Our suitcases were thrown into the baggage pod, and we climbed inside the Cessna plane. One doctor sat next to my daughter and me, and one doctor sat next to my husband and son. The hospital was an hour away. By this time, we knew our son was hanging on to life by a mere thread. As he lay in my husband's arms, the doctor never took his fingers off his pulse. We learned later that this type of overdose causes cardiac arrest, and Jeffrey was already experiencing heart arrhythmia. The doctor was watching for signs of the heart going into arrest, which would require a shot of adrenaline.

The flight seemed endless as we flew over dense jungle. Even the pilot was somber. By this time, we were sure our daughter would be fine, even though the doctor next to her still checked her pulse occasionally. Our little boy was the one in big trouble.

As we flew, all was silent except for my quiet sobs and the hum of the plane's engine. I'm not even sure I could pray much at that point, but I knew prayers were streaming up to heaven by our co-workers and those who had heard over the high-frequency radio.

Halfway through the flight, the pilot turned around and motioned toward the jungle below. As we looked out the airplane window, we saw the circle of a beautiful rainbow sparkling on the trees below. In the center of the rainbow lay the shadow of the plane resembling a cross. Upon seeing that rainbow and cross-like shadow, I knew God was speaking. It was his supernatural reminder that he was with us, no matter what. What a comfort to us in this time of uncertainty and crisis.

Finally landing, a vehicle waited to take us to Balimo Health Centre in the lowlands of Papua New Guinea. We were met by another friend and missionary nurse who took us to her home. We laid our son on a mattress on the floor of her living area. By this time, his little body began to twitch uncontrollably from the poison in his system. As the doctor waited with us, he gave the nurse instructions to keep administering the drip, have a shot of adrenaline handy, and monitor him all night by checking his pulse every fifteen minutes.

"Call me if there are any changes," he said.

I couldn't bear to ask him how many pills a lethal dose would be. I didn't want to know. I knew our boy was fighting for his life. The doctor was somber and didn't give us any false hope as he walked out the door. All night, we took two-hour shifts checking his pulse and watching him to see if there was any change.

At 6:30 the next morning, the doctor knocked on the door. Relief was written on his face that he hadn't been called during the night. As he walked in the door, the stirring woke our sleeping son. He sat up, weak from the ordeal, but in good spirits. A smile crossed his face as he looked at us. Spotting a can of peanuts on the table, he asked if he could have some. His body had struggled for over eighteen hours, and death nearly overtook him. Yet by a series of miracles, God spared our son.

That afternoon as we were thanking God and talking with the doctor, I finally worked up the nerve to ask him, "How many amodiaquin would have been a lethal dose?"

"Ten," he said.

Jeffrey had eaten at least twenty-three.

That day the Lord orchestrated a string of miracles to save our son. On the day after Christmas, when people's focus was not on HF radios and normal activities but on the holiday and family, God moved in undeniable ways. Had my husband not gone into the bedroom to retrieve ointment, we might not have known the children had gotten into the medicine until it was too late. The first doctor was available for the call from the radio-network administrators at the same moment our hospital's missionary nurse decided to test her HF radio. She heard our distress call and the doctor coaching us, which started a chain reaction of connections that enabled us to get help faster. As a result, she alerted the two doctors and the pilot's wife on another station using a smaller VHF (very high frequency) radio. If the pilot's wife had not turned on her radio that day when there were no plans to fly, she would not have heard the nurse calling for the emergency. All these things caused the plane to arrive at least one hour earlier than it could have, thus enabling the doctor to give our son an IV drip that diluted his blood, and possibly saved his life.

If our nurse friend, Celia Fletcher, had not made him throw up until the liquid was clear and without sign of medicine, he could well have died before the plane even arrived. Amazingly, the doctor even thought it was possible that the antacids might have had a neutralizing effect on the poison. Had none of these things happened as they did, it is likely our son would have died.

When our son recovered, we heard of another little missionary boy who also accidentally overdosed. While our son lived, that little boy died. We struggled with survivor's guilt while being incredibly grateful too. Why did God orchestrate a miracle for us, while those parents lost their son? My simple answer is, I don't know, but it is tied to the divine sovereignty of God. Our finite minds cannot understand an infinite God or his purpose or plans. Had we lost our son, how would we have fared? We do not know. God spared us a tremendous loss that day.

God is still a God of miracles. My son is evidence of that, and I've never since seen a similar rainbow while flying over the jungles of PNG.

Prayer

Lord, you are still a God of miracles. Thank you for your hand of mercy upon us, orchestrating events according to your plan for us. You see and know what is happening in our lives, and you will act according to your sovereign will. Thank you that whatever takes place in my life, I know that you are with me.

Personal Reflection

1. What can we learn from the following verses about the supreme authority of God? Psalm 115:3; Romans 11:33-36; Psalm 33:11; Daniel 4:35.

2. What does God say about death (or the death of those we love) in Psalm 139:15-16?

3. Has there been a time when you needed to trust in the goodness and sovereignty of God? Have you seen God work a miracle in your life or family?

A Day in the Life

*What gain has the worker from his toil? I perceived that there
is nothing better for them than to be joyful and to do good
as long as they live; also that everyone should eat and drink
and take pleasure in all his toil—this is God's gift to man.*
(Ecclesiastes 3:9, 12-13 ESV)

"Where are you going?" we asked as a local family walked past
our house. The husband, with his wife and children in tow,
headed toward the river. The woman carried their baby in a string bag
as a younger child hurried alongside to keep up. Happy to oblige with
an answer, they told us.

"We are going to the garden."

"You go," we replied. It might seem rude to a westerner, but it was
a common greeting here. If we were visiting in the village, they would
ask us, "Where are you going?" or "What are you doing?"

A day of work in the garden meant clearing trees and brush, planting, or harvesting. At the end of the afternoon, the family returned with
their bounty. String bags might be full of taro or sweet potatoes, or a
huge cluster of bananas might be hoisted and carried on their shoulders
for the next meal. String bags bursting with firewood were hauled in by
the wife. Seasonal foods were also gathered during harvest: breadfruit,
pitpit, galip nuts, pandanus, and many other foods.

When a sago tree is ready to harvest, a family will spend days in the
jungle collecting its starch. After chopping down the tree, they beat the
fibers of the trunk into a pulp. Then the beaten fibers are placed in the

bark trough, and water is poured over them while they beat them with a stick. The sediment of starch that runs down is collected at the bottom and becomes the damp, flour-like starch that they eat. Sago was, and still is, a staple of the area; this important food source helps them survive during times of drought.

When they build a house, they cut hardwood trees to the right length and haul them in for house posts; they cut black palm trees for floors and siding. Sago-leaf bundles are gathered for their thatched roof, and vines from the jungle are used to tie on their roof.

Tree fibers are collected to process into string and weave their bags, which are used for carrying food, firewood, and their babies. The men make their bows and arrows for hunting game.

They carve and chip out trees for canoes and paddles for transportation on the rivers. Many early mornings we watched from our porch as men or families paddled canoes down the river to fish, dive for prawns, or gather young, black palm shoots or tree fruit.

For centuries, they passed down survival skills to the next generation. There was little monetary economy. Although they might trade items or sell something at the government post, money was scarce. They knew how to subsist in a steamy jungle, and they lived solely off the land and its resources. Without great effort, they would not eat.

In the Western world, provision for our families requires diligence and hard work also. We do not live off the land as this isolated tribe did, but all of us work hard to pay our bills, to eat, and to keep a roof over our heads. Instead of paddling through a river, we weave through heavy traffic. Rather than searching the jungle for food, we labor at a job and buy food in a grocery store. Whatever sphere of the world we live in, work is a part of life, and God reminds us that *in all hard work there is profit.*[34] When times of weariness come, the help and strength of God is available. In the end, we find joy and a sense of accomplishment as we provide for our loved ones.

---

34   Proverbs 14:23 NET

Prayer

Thank you, Father, for giving us bodies and minds with great capability to work. Keep me mindful that the reward of toil is the provision for my family. Help me to find satisfaction and joy in my labor. Give me hands that are diligent, a mind that is sharp, and a heart that is eager in the responsibilities that you place before me today.

Personal Reflection

1. What gain or satisfaction do you see from your work?

2. Read again Ecclesiastes 3:9, 12-13. King Solomon, often remembered as the wisest man who ever lived, tells us two things that are best for life. What are they? What does he say is a gift from God?

3. Read Psalm 128:1-4. What does God promise to the man who fears the Lord and follows his commands? How is that person's labor blessed?

4. What contrast do you see in Proverbs 10:4?

Amalgam of Cultures

After these things I looked, and here was an enormous crowd that no one could count, made up of persons from every nation, tribe, people, and language, standing before the throne and before the Lamb dressed in long white robes, and with palm branches in their hands. They were shouting out in a loud voice, "Salvation belongs to our God, who is seated on the throne, and to the Lamb!" And all the angels stood there in a circle around the throne and around the elders and the four living creatures, and they threw themselves down with their faces to the ground before the throne and worshiped God. (Revelation 7:9-11 NET)

"How do you live out there by yourself?" People asked me that question many times, even other missionary wives.

"Don't you get lonely? I could never live out there alone."

Loneliness is a struggle when you live isolated for months on end. I have four answers to that question. First, yes, I did get lonely, especially without like-minded fellowship and extended family. It can be easy to feel forgotten. Living away from all you know and those you love is difficult for a missionary. Second, when God calls us to a specific job, he enables and upholds us for that task. We were both rather introverted, so the isolation was maybe less of an issue for us than it might be for someone else. Third, we made friends where we were and became an active part of the village. We had plenty of interaction with others, but they were those of another culture and language. Every day I engaged with my house helpers, the young women who helped me with household tasks. They became my closest friends, and they were an important part of my everyday life.

Lastly, our missionary community became our family. In three terms of living overseas, we went home to the United States only twice in almost thirteen years. When you live for years without going home to family, your fellow missionaries become your family-away-from-family. Highlights for us were visiting other missionaries or having visitors come to us.

We looked forward to the yearly missionary conference where many of us would gather for a week's retreat. These and other get-togethers of our smaller area team would give us encouragement. At times, I would visit another missionary friend who also had young children, or we would chat on the HF radio during the weekend. Our children loved being with other missionary kids who all spoke the same language.

Not only did the country have over seven hundred languages and tribal cultures, but the mission we worked with was an amalgam of different cultures also. We were Australian, New Zealander, American, British, Dutch, German, and Swiss. A group of networking missions created a diverse international team in this one area of Papua New Guinea. Yet we were united by Christ with the goal of reaching and helping these distinct tribal cultures and languages.

English was the common language for us, but we found that terminology and meanings were often different. When we first arrived as young Americans, we felt overwhelmed adjusting to so many nationalities.

Australian biscuits versus American cookies.

American napkins versus Australian serviettes.

British-teapot cozy versus American tea-bag dunking.

Some of their lingo raised our eyebrows, and some of our terminology raised theirs. It was confusing at times, but our common bond united us, and we learned to interact with grace and understanding of our cultural differences. Together we learned to love American cookies, Australian pavlova, British tea, homemade German spaetzle, Swiss chocolate, and New Zealand roasted lamb.

When our third child was born at our mission's hospital, an Australian midwife delivered him, assisted by a Papua New Guinean nurse, who was on a station with a naturalized German-Australian manager, where Dutch and Australian doctors worked!

Did we have cultural mishaps? You bet! On one memorable occasion, I made hot tea for a British man who came to help with practical work on our station. After he drank his tea, he said, "I'll make my own tea from now on. That was the worst cup of tea I ever drank."

That was blunt and to the point. From then on, he made it himself. When he needed his tea break, he ran into the house to make his own "cuppa."

Or, our Australian friend once told us, "You Americans put peanut butter on everything."

"Well, we don't understand how you think Vegemite is edible." Sometimes the banter between us could get rather feisty. Yet usually it was done to understand the other and enjoy sought-after fellowship.

Americans value a strong work ethic and independent thinking. Yet the country's culture we lived in valued strong relationships; they made group decisions with the clan. Our co-workers from other nationalities had similar but different worldviews and values. We learned from each other and formed great friendships during these years.

Unity amid diversity is the challenge of every missionary's career. A richness of life comes from interactions with those from different worldviews and ways of doing life. We gain an awareness that changes our perspective on how we view our own culture, as we learn from each other. Every culture has good things from which we can learn. Our world is diverse, yet Christ and a biblical worldview bring us together in unity. A true bond with Christ makes us one in a world that longs for peace and acceptance. Someday, all believers from diverse cultures, languages, and peoples will unite in heaven as the family of God. What a great reunion that will be!

Prayer

Lord, thank you for showing no favoritism and loving all nations and peoples. Give me a heart that desires to walk in humility with those who are different from me. Help me to accept and show your love to them.

Thank you that someday, all believers from every nation and language will worship at your throne.

Personal Reflection

1. In Revelation 7:9-11, who is described worshipping at the throne? Where were those people from?

2. Considering God's love for every person and nation, why is it important to accept people who are different from us?

3. What does Philippians 2:1-4 teach us about humility in building relationships with others?

Great Catch!

*For this reason the LORD is ready to show you mercy; he sits
on his throne, ready to have compassion on you. Indeed, the
LORD is a just God; all who wait for him in faith will be blessed.*
(Isaiah 30:18 NET)

"Wow! How did you catch all of those? What did you use for bait?"
That typical male question looked for the secret of a great
haul. While we awaited the birth of our third child, we lived for a month
in a house on the mission's hospital station. The doctor came to check
on me since my pulse had been elevated for a few days. Our baby was
due any day. On that early morning, we'd had a sleepless night when
the missionary doctor showed up at our door.

As he walked through the door, he saw the bucket that Dale had
placed near the front door to carry out to the trash. Inside lay last night's
catch – nine dead rats.

"I caught them all using the same piece of meat; I tied it on with
dental floss," Dale said.

"I need to try that."

Most of these old missionary houses had been around for decades.
Rats found hiding places during the day in the ceiling and in the
bamboo-platted walls. During the quiet of the night, they roamed the
house in search of food.

Several weeks earlier, I had flown out with our two children to
await the baby's birth. Dale waited to join us in a couple weeks (as per
mission policy). Staying in this old house with friends, we slept in a

bedroom across from the kitchen. After the children were tucked into small beds in the same room, I crawled under my mosquito netting to get some sleep. Eight months pregnant and stifling tropical heat were not a good combination. The room had no ventilation or breeze, so I was miserable. Dosing off, I was soon awakened by a noise from the kitchen. Rats scuffled in the kitchen over some crumb of food.

Great. No sleep tonight.

Before long, one squeezed through the bedroom door and ran under my bed. At intervals throughout the night, I heard the rat population in the house.

The next morning at the breakfast table, I said to my hosts, "Did you hear the rats last night?"

"No."

"Well, you must have a family of rats living here. I heard them in the kitchen all during the night. One even ran under my bed."

"Oh. We didn't hear anything."

My friends soon left to go back to their home country, so I moved further down the house into their back bedroom, hoping to get better sleep away from the flow of rats. Then I contacted Dale to ask him to bring rat traps when he flew out to join us for the baby's birth. I couldn't wait for him to arrive to take care of the rat problem.

Each evening I cleaned and put away anything the rats might eat. If vegetables or fruit were left on the counter, they would find them. Nothing could be left out. At night, I stuffed things in the little refrigerator, or put things away into lidded containers. Then each morning I washed the counters to make sure they were clean before preparing food.

After Dale arrived, he looked around the kitchen to see where he should place the trap. He saw a hole in the kitchen ceiling and figured that must be their opening to explore at night, so he placed the trap below it on a shelf high on the wall.

After we nodded off to sleep, we soon awoke to the familiar sound of the trap going off.

Wham!

Dale got up to check the trap. Sure enough, we caught one little guy. Dumping that departed rat into a bucket, he reset the trap and returned to bed. All night long with the same piece of bait, the trap went off until nine furry rodents of various sizes were caught. Each time Dale would get up, dump another in the bucket, and reset the trap. In the wee hours of the morning, the house became quiet, and we finally got some sleep.

Who catches nine rats in one night with one piece of bait?

I was certainly thankful when my husband came to take care of us. There are just some things a lady refuses to do, especially a very pregnant one. After that night, we had no more trouble with rats. We got much-needed sleep because the Lord showed us his help and mercy that night.

About a week later, our third child, a boy, was born in the little mission hospital called Rumginae Health Centre. With the rats gone and our baby born safely, I felt a sense of relief. Things had turned out okay.

Sometimes we have short but difficult seasons in life. We have no option but to bear up under the added stress. We know at some point in the future this too will pass. Part of maturing as a Christian is learning to deal with life's frustrations with an attitude that accepts where God has us for a time. The temptation to harbor negative feelings will come, but we need to take things one day at a time. If we get through one day, we can get through another. We can choose to have faith that God will get us through whatever difficulty we face. That will make all the difference in our ability to cope, and our family and those around us will learn from our example.

In the end, we saw God's uncanny ability to answer a prayer.

Prayer

Thank you, Lord, for telling us that your compassion never fails. You see and know our struggles, and you will never abandon us. In a difficult season, give me perseverance and the ability to get through one day at a time, knowing that this season will also pass.

Personal Reflection

1. We all experience temporary seasons in life; some are good and some are difficult. Have you had a time in your life

when you were in a difficult but temporary season? How did you deal with that?

2. What are two things in Isaiah 30:18 that the Lord says he will show us? Who will be blessed?

3. Read Psalm 103:13. If the Lord looks upon us with compassion, then he understands our difficulties with compassion too. Our struggles do not escape him. Has there been a time when you have seen the Lord's uncanny provision for you?

Cockatoo Alarm

My brothers, if anyone among you wanders from the truth and someone brings him back, let him know that whoever brings back a sinner from his wandering will save his soul from death and will cover a multitude of sins. (James 5:19-20 ESV)

Church services rarely went without drama, and this Sunday was no different. A screaming baby, a wandering dog, or an ear-deafening tropical downpour were most of the distractions. However, this time we had a new drama to deal with – a cockatoo.

After the singing finished, this parrot perched on the window opening where all the ladies sat. Only ten feet ahead of me, I could see him clearly. At first, he sat quietly, looking around. Then he bounced by throwing his head forward, extending his yellow crest, and shrieking. Loudly. The message was interrupted by his commotion.

Someone shooed him away, but before long he returned.

He flew back to sit in the same spot, but it wasn't long before his agitation got the best of him, and he started another dance.

"He's angry and crying for food because he wants to eat," my friend told me. "He belongs to a family in the village as a pet." After a while, he dozed off to wait for his human parent. I thought he was adorable. Where else in the world could you enjoy such a display?

We often saw the birds of the area, especially the long-beaked Papuan hornbill and the Sulfur-crested cockatoo. Papua New Guinea is known for its exquisite birds of paradise, but those stayed hidden in the jungle around us. These two birds, however, were sometimes kept as pets in the village if caught at a young age.

One bird was black and the other white, and their personalities were as different as their opposing colors. The black hornbill was a relaxed bird, content to hang around and watch, but the cockatoo's flamboyant personality made his presence known through his loud and obnoxious behavior. These large, snow-white parrots were beautiful with a gray beak and feet. A cluster of yellow feathers on top of their heads extended and fanned out when they felt excitement or agitation. The local word for this parrot, *Ulo,* is the same word they use for the color white.

Cockatoos lived in the trees across the river from our house. Early in the mornings, we heard their shrieks and screeches as they flew around enjoying the morning sunrise after their night of sleep.

One afternoon while many people hung around our house, we heard the shrieks and squeals of a family of cockatoos down at the bend of the river. We looked over to see them flying around the top of the tree where they had been perched. In a panic, they were disturbed about something.

Neither Dale nor I had any clue what was happening, but the men immediately knew the meaning of the parrots' behavior.

"They see a snake and are afraid," one of the men said.

A snake in search of a meal wanted a cockatoo for dinner. The cockatoos flew around in a panic squawking to warn each other.

"Let's go find it."

The men left in the direction of the birds. A big snake meant dinner. About an hour later, they returned to show us their prize. With the snake wrapped around his neck, a young man carried the dead reptile in for us to see – a thirteen-foot-long python. That evening the village cooking fires had roasted meat on the menu. They never wasted an opportunity to hunt for food.

Families are important, even a family of cockatoos. When one bird sensed a killer snake, its cry of panic alerted every bird that danger was near. No cockatoo died that day because their warning served a useful purpose for those that weren't aware that peril was close. If one cockatoo would have ignored the panic and kept dozing on his limb, he would have been in the python's belly for dinner.

Just as the cockatoos alert and protect each other, our families and friends do the same for us. If they think something harmful is in our lives, they will raise their concerns. Do we listen to their warnings? We often choose to ignore the warnings that come from our loved ones.

Many times, when we've made a mess of things, we will look back and see that someone close to us had raised their concerns. We can ignore them, or we can consider if their warning is legitimate. Perhaps they expressed worry about one of life's most important decisions: a marriage partner, hurtful patterns or habits, financial choices, or any other critical life choice. God can and does speak through our family and friends, and we should weigh their concerns against his Word. A warning is something we should consider when it comes from those who know us best and love us most. Ignoring and moving forward without examination may lend itself to future heartache.

Pray and seek God's guidance to gain a sense of conviction that the choice we are making is right for us. Don't doze on a limb and ignore the voice of a loved one who has sounded an alarm.

Prayer

Thank you, Lord, for my family and friends who are part of life's gift that you have given me. Give me a wise and humble heart that knows when to listen to the warnings and advice of those who love and care for me. Guide me through all of life's decisions, so that I will live my life completely for you and accomplish the purpose that you have for me.

Personal Reflection

1. If your family or a friend is worried about something going on in your life, are you willing to listen and pray about their concern?

2. The Lord also warns us if we have a sin in our life. Read Genesis 4:1-8. What sin did Cain have in his life? How did the Lord warn him? Did Cain heed the Lord's warning?

3. Has there been a time when you were thankful that you listened to the warnings of a loved one?

The Unseen Realm

A final word: Be strong in the Lord and in his mighty power. Put on all of God's armor so that you will be able to stand firm against all strategies of the devil. For we are not fighting against flesh-and-blood enemies, but against evil rulers and authorities of the unseen world, against mighty powers in this dark world, and against evil spirits in the heavenly places. Therefore, put on every piece of God's armor so you will be able to resist the enemy in the time of evil. Then after the battle you will still be standing firm. (Ephesians 6:10-13 NLT)

"Wake up! You're having a nightmare."

It was another bad night. Awakened in the middle of a dark night, I heard stressful sounds coming from my husband. Trembling in the bed, he moaned out several times in distress while still asleep. Rolling over toward Dale, I laid my hand on him to wake him. Whatever the nightmare was, we needed to pray.

"I dreamed a demon was batting me around, and I couldn't move or call out to Jesus," he said.

We both suffered at times from nightmares. Dale had one recurring dream where he dived into the river to save one of our children from drowning. We had both dreamed of death while we watched, helpless to save someone, or that a demon kept us from breathing. At times we experienced other weird and strange dreams that kept us from peaceful sleep. Or, our children would awake, yelling for us in the night, until we would go and console them. They had bad dreams too. In one week, I had emotional nightmares three nights in a row.

Restful sleep often seemed elusive, and we sensed we were under a spiritual attack at these times. The lingering, oppressive heat was a constant challenge, but these nightmares were very unsettling.

Some nights we would awaken to the sound of flying foxes flapping outside our house. Although this was normal nocturnal activity for them, the creepy part was that one of them liked to land on the window of our bedroom. We would lie in the bed and listen to the eerie sounds of this bat as it licked our screen. Other times more than one would land on the roof of our house, and their claws would scrape on the metal roofing, preventing the peaceful sleep we longed for.

Over the span of several months, I also experienced numerous internal struggles: an overall sense of depression, anger, self-condemnation, and an impatient spirit with my children. I prayed, read Scripture, and confessed my sin, but nothing seemed to fix my struggles. I read books that might help, but these overwhelming feelings hung over me like a dark cloud. I tried with diligent prayer and self-effort to control these feelings because these struggles were affecting our family life.

One morning I prayed, "Lord, if this is a satanic thing in my life, please show me somehow." I had done everything I knew to move past this. Exhausted from the day, that same evening I went to bed early. As I lay in bed to sleep, I felt that something had entered the room. I sensed its presence standing there, watching – a dark, heavy presence. I perceived its evil.

I did the first thing I could think of: I jumped out of the other side of the bed and ran out in fear. No brave quoting of Scripture or claiming the power of God. I ran out to find Dale.

When Dale and I sensed the power of satanic forces, we would pray together to claim the power and authority of our heavenly Father. He alone had the power to make the Enemy flee and the power to break through the spiritual darkness in this isolated place that had been held captive for thousands of years. We were in a battle with the unseen powers of darkness, and Satan wasn't giving up his long-held territory in a remote jungle tribe without a fight. There were times when we felt worn-out and battle-weary; the work itself was difficult, but so was the spiritual battle.

I believe that I had been oppressed and under an attack by Satan as he filled my mind with lies, anger, and self-condemnation. Once realized, we began to pray against it. Months later God sent an older and wiser couple to help me pray through many things. For the rest of that year, I embraced the truths in God's Word. Every day I claimed his promises for me. Things improved as my mind and heart were renewed by God's promises and the power of his Word.

We are all in a spiritual battle. It may not be as intense or as blatant as in this jungle stronghold, but Satan has numerous ways that he will attack, distract, and cause havoc. His subtle ways can be ignored or brushed off, but we know the Bible acknowledges Satan's evil: *Your enemy the devil prowls around like a roaring lion looking for someone to devour.*[35] He is the believer's most vehement enemy. He will find ways to attack our lives. That is why it is so important to understand why all believers can *put on the full armor of God, so that you can take your stand against the devil's schemes.*[36] He has crafty and secret ways to attack us. We may not always recognize his influence in our lives, but when we experience uncanny struggles, discouragement, self-condemnation, or intense internal difficulties, we need to consider that this could be a spiritual attack in our life. We don't have to fight alone. God has provided a path in his Word to fight these attacks. Let's embrace the weapons he has made available to us and gain the victory.

Prayer

Lord, I submit myself to you as the one power and authority in my life. I resist any attacks and schemes of the Enemy to influence and hinder your will in my life. Today and every day may I seek to put on the armor of God. Help me to stand on your truth alone. Give me your peace and righteousness as I humbly submit to you. Father, I ask that you protect my mind from Satan's lies and give me a love for studying your Word. Put a spirit of prayer in my heart today as I seek you.

---

35 1 Peter 5:8 NIV
36 Ephesians 6:11 NIV

Personal Reflection

1. Can you recognize any areas in your life that could be under Satan's attack? What lies from Satan have you believed?

2. From Ephesians 6:11-12, what is *not* our struggle? And what four things are we struggling with?

3. Read Ephesians 6:14-17. What are the six pieces of armor and how does each one protect us from the Enemy?

Family Life

A house is built by wisdom and becomes strong through good sense. Through knowledge its rooms are filled with all sorts of precious riches and valuables. (Proverbs 24:3-4 NLT)

One day, when our daughter was about four, I heard a repetitive and faint "squeak, squeak" sound in the house.

What is that?

I went to our bedroom and found our daughter sitting on our bed with something in her hands.

"Janelle, what is that?"

She opened her hands and showed me a little, gray, baby rat. She held it like a treasured pet, stroking its fur. I, on the other hand, was disgusted. All the years we spent eliminating bush rats that invaded the house at night, and now our daughter was cuddling one on our bed!

Nope. Not happening.

"Where'd you get that?"

"My friend gave it to me."

"You are not playing with a nasty rat; go give it back."

After a bit of discussion on the issue, she stomped out at being told to return her little furry friend. The local children loved to play with baby animals – rats, birds, cassowaries – and they would often bring things around for our kids to see.

During this same year, our children brought in a container of live grubs given to them by the friend who often helped me cook over a fire. They were eating them alive. These fat little grubs were considered a delicacy, even uncooked. I never had the stomach to eat one grub, but my own children ate them like our local friends did. They did as they learned in the culture.

Our children grew up learning the culture as their own. As our little family grew, so did some of the traditions of our life in this isolated location. Since we did not leave our location for months at a time, life was simple. They had no visits to Grandma, no invites to birthday parties, and no school programs to participate in. Holidays were simple too.

It became important to create a few special moments for our children. Friday night became our family's VHS movie night, with all equipment run by our generator. Sunday afternoon became our day to relax or take a long swim in the river. It also became the day for a special treat.

I always kept a stash of treats for Sunday – whether it was candy sent to us in a parcel or a Coke or chips stored in the back of the pantry. Sunday was the day to pull out something nice for everyone to make the day special. If the treat stash was bare, I spent the afternoon making chocolate-covered donuts, candied popcorn, or some other dessert for us to enjoy.

Living in the jungle meant that our children grew up with all sorts of unusual adventures.

- They grew up traveling on jumbo jets and flying in six-seat Cessna planes.

- They had "aunties and uncles" from countries all around the world, so there was a blur between blood family and mission family.

- They had a grassy airstrip next to their house where they watched Cessna planes land and take off on a regular basis. A plane's arrival bringing supplies was the village's big-event day.

- They lived and functioned well in two cultures and became what has been termed "third-culture kids" (having a blended culture of their own).

- They were the richest kids around, even though they lived simply and without most things American children enjoy.

- They knew and understood how the poorest of the poor live in a third-world country.

Our three oldest children spent all or most of their formative years in another culture. Before leaving the country, our son stood in a canoe to paddle and tried to climb a coconut tree like the local boys.

Were they deprived? By our Western worldview and standards, yes. Yet our children were given what most adults will never experience – the gift of living as friends in a culture vastly different from their own and incorporating some of that culture into their lives. They learned compassion for those less privileged, and they watched a people steeped in animism embrace Jesus as their Savior. Those simple years contained a richness and an adventure I will always miss.

Life in our Western civilization can overwhelm us. I see exhausted parents carting their children to multiple events each week, managing two jobs, and trying to keep the bills paid. With the demands of raising a family in our culture, we fall into bed exhausted.

Raising children is the hardest and the best job on earth. How will we train them to become responsible, loving adults? What important things do we want to teach our children? I hope my children learn that their best life is not found in what this world offers; it is found in a relationship with Christ. I want them to learn that life is not about serving self but serving others. I hope they find the purpose that God has planned for their lives and that they fulfill that purpose. Life is about loving God and loving others. That's what matters, and that's what I hope my next generation learns.

Busyness of this world can lead us away from what is important – teaching the next generation. Children learn from our example.

Prayer

Lord, thank you for children and for establishing the family. Help me to be a wise parent and build a strong home on the foundation of your Word and truth. Give me a gentle and kind spirit with my children, even when I am busy and exhausted. Help our home to be a joyful and peaceful place where our children can thrive.

Personal Reflection

1. Chuck Swindoll said, "Children are not to be 'jerked up' (as my mother put it), but to be cared for with gentleness and detail . . . and lots of it."[37] Are you gentle and patient with your children? Or does busyness leave little time for them?

2. According to Proverbs 24:3-4 (NLT), a home with wisdom has *precious riches and valuables*. What *good sense* things will help build a strong home? What changes can you make in the home that will benefit your family life and your children?

3. How are you teaching your children to become responsible, loving adults?

---

37   Charles Swindoll, *Wisdom for the Way: Wise Words for Busy People* (Nashville, TN: J. Countryman, a division of Thomas Nelson, Inc., 2001), 13.

Malaria Attack

So we do not lose heart. Though our outer self is wasting away, our inner self is being renewed day by day. For this light momentary affliction is preparing for us an eternal weight of glory beyond all comparison, as we look not to the things that are seen but to the things that are unseen. For the things that are seen are transient, but the things that are unseen are eternal.
(2 Corinthians 4:16-18 ESV)

"Mommy, I have a headache. Can you give me medicine?"

For months our daughter, Janelle, had had a vague sickness. She had constant low fevers, ear infections, a cough, cold symptoms, and she complained almost daily of headaches. Our normally active girl was not herself. I had flown with her to Rumginae Health Centre to see the mission's interim doctor. Over the months she was treated with several rounds of antibiotics, but nothing helped. I was beside myself with worry. What was going on with her?

Six months later, I flew out with her again, this time to see our permanent doctor who had returned from his home leave. He gave her a checkup, and everything seemed okay. Then he took a malaria blood slide and went with the lab technician to look at it under the microscope. He felt she had a recurrent strain of vivax malaria, which displayed itself with milder symptoms. Rather than the high fever, chills, and severe symptoms normally suffered with a malaria attack, she experienced vague symptoms with a low-grade fever. He discussed changing our family's weekly anti-malaria treatment. Instead of one drug per week, we started taking two drugs a week to prevent malaria.

That did the trick. Once her medicine changed, she improved within a couple of weeks.

We lived in an area with this lethal disease. Everyone in the tribe suffered from its symptoms at times – high fever, chills, headaches, sweats, body aches, and lethargy. Severe symptoms could lead to unconsciousness and death. In our area, there was also chloroquine-resistant malaria, a form of malaria that did not respond to chloroquine treatment.

We often struggled with fever and sickness from malaria. Fevers usually meant malaria, especially if nothing else was obvious. If one of us got a high fever, the first thing we learned to do was to consult with the doctor and start a course of malaria treatment. Usually we got better within three to four days, but sometimes our bodies weren't able to fight it as well.

When our oldest son was almost three, he became sick. I treated him with the oral medicine, but he did not improve. His fever remained high, and he was lethargic. The medicine was not killing the infection. After talking with the doctor on the HF radio, he said, "You're going to have to give him quinine injections."

"But I've never given an injection."

"You're going to have to do it," the missionary doctor said.

Before going to live in isolation, I had been taught by a nurse to give injections for emergencies. It could mean life or death for whoever needed it. I had practiced with her on a lemon, but I had never given a shot to a person.

Who would have thought I'd have to give my first injection to my own son? Without his responding to the oral drugs, it was important to give him the stronger drug. I had all the medicines on hand that the doctor ordered. With great dread, I pulled out the items from the cupboard. After preparing the syringe, I drew up the medicine. With my son crying at the sight of a needle, I took a deep breath and gave the injection while Dale held him.

Over the course of several days, he began to improve.

When our third child was born, he struggled with malaria as a baby and as a toddler. Several times I had to treat him for fevers. When he was about seven months old, he got so sick with malaria that he stopped drinking milk and didn't wet his diaper for an entire day. I knew that meant he was dehydrated. Alone in the jungle, I sat with him in my arms rocking him. I dripped water into his mouth with a spoon to force it into him; I had to keep him hydrated. I worked to keep his fever under control and made sure he kept his medicine down. I'd seen the local babies die quickly from fever and dehydration. I was afraid. For hours that day, I held him, wept, and prayed for him to get better.

In the Lord's timing and mercy, he started to improve.

We all suffered from malaria; it was something we learned to deal with. No matter what measures we took, we would get bitten by a disease-carrying mosquito.

The Christian life involves a concept that does not come natural to us. In Jesus' words to his disciples he said, *"Let him deny himself and take up his cross daily and follow me."*[38] We naturally prefer that life goes well. Yet Jesus said that his followers need to take up their cross daily. The cross is a symbol of death, and with Jesus, it is also a symbol of his sacrifice. As we take up our cross, we are telling Jesus that he is worth the suffering and difficulties we face. In the process, *"If you give up your life for my sake, you will save it."*[39] We build a bond with Jesus that deepens our relationship with him. As we lean on his strength, those roots of faith start to grow deep and anchor us to a loving Savior. God's purposes are at work for his glory, not ours.

Prayer

Lord, you have told us to deny ourselves, to take up our cross, and to follow you. I want to follow you. Help me focus on eternal things and the purpose that you have for me. Even amid suffering, give me strength to remain steadfast by praying and trusting you. Thank you that my troubles here are temporary, but my joy when I reach heaven will be forever.

---

38   Luke 9:23 ESV
39   Matthew 16:25 NLT

Personal Reflection

1. What positive things has God taught you during the hard times in your life?

2. According to 2 Corinthians 4:16-18, what is happening to us inwardly as we go through difficulties? What should we fix our eyes on?

3. Read Psalm 119:71. What does the psalmist say he learned from his suffering?

4. Is someone in your life struggling? How can you pray for them today?

From A Pilot's Vantage

For we walk by faith, not by sight. (2 Corinthians 5:7 ESV)

I just knew that my husband and three children were going to crash. Tears blurred my eyes and sobs caught in my throat as I grabbed an umbrella to hurry outside. Rain pelted my legs as I rushed to the grass-covered airstrip. The sky had only thick, ominous clouds. It was the last light of day. If the small Cessna didn't land soon, darkness would prevent them from landing, and my family would die. I heard the buzz of the plane as the pilot tried to find our short runway.

My family had left for a day to fly out to see a dentist, and I had stayed behind alone. When the pilot called earlier to check the weather, I said, "The weather is bad. There is rain and full cloud cover overhead." As I stood at the edge of the airstrip, I heard the plane circling overhead. The pilot would not be able to find me, and the village friends with me, or land in this bad weather.

But wait, didn't I know Bruce? Wasn't he a well-trained pilot, familiar with the treacherous terrain? Hadn't he flown every day for years without an accident? Yes, Bruce was an excellent pilot, and I should trust his judgment. Yet somehow, that wasn't much comfort as I scanned the dark sky and felt the rain splash at my feet.

Several village friends stood with me when they knew Dale and the children were in the plane and the pilot was trying to land. We listened together as the plane circled over us. A few made the traditional click sound that meant they were a little worried too.

After several anxious minutes of standing outside, we saw the plane pop down through a cloud, circle the area to position for landing, and then touch down on the grassy airstrip. I breathed a huge sigh of relief as I watched the Cessna taxi over. I told Bruce how worried I had been (obvious with my puffy eyes).

He raised his eyebrows and said with confidence, "It was clear up there. Your area was covered in rain, but there was blue sky everywhere else. I knew I would have no trouble landing."

All my worry was unfounded, and my fear had spread to those around me. Bruce could see what I couldn't from a pilot's vantage – the clear sky all around with only patches of bad weather over our area. Isn't trusting in God similar? God sees the full picture of what is happening in our lives – our past, present, and future. To him, all is crystal clear. His plan for our lives is unfolding with purpose and direction, even if we are in the middle of a storm and see only clouds. God sees what is beyond with clarity. We may not always know why he allows certain things, but he sees from eternity's perspective.

I was thankful for the pilot's expertise to get my family home safely. I should have trusted in his knowledge and experience. God taught me a great lesson that day: he knows our vision is limited, but what a joy to know that his power and knowledge is endless. We need to walk by faith and trust him. Our ability to place things in God's hands is one of the most important lessons we can ever learn as Christians.

Prayer

Thank you, Father, for seeing the beginning and the end. Your knowledge is endless, and your power is beyond my understanding. You see with clarity what I cannot see. Give me eyes of faith to trust you through life's storms. In times of trouble, let prayer be my strength.

Personal Reflection

1. Have you experienced a difficulty and then later saw with clarity how God led you through it?

2. One of the Hebrew names of God in the Old Testament is

El Roi. It means "the God who sees me." You are cherished by God. Read Psalm 139:1-6 to see how much he sees and knows you.

3. Not only does God see you, he also sees everything that happens on earth. Read Job 28:24 and Psalm 33:13-15. What do you learn from these verses?

4. Worry can incapacitate us. It can also affect others around us. Try to memorize Philippians 4:6-7 as a reminder for those days when you are prone to worry.

Jungle Church

Building a church among the Gobasi tribe seemed a daunting task. We were Bible-college graduates, but we weren't trained to plant a church. Yet that was our goal. In sharing the gospel, we wanted to build a nucleus of believers within the community. How do you go from knowing no one and not speaking the foreign language to having a living community of believers? How do you engage in a culture so different from your own that the result is an active church?

In the earliest years, we built relationships. We learned their distinct tribal names, we bandaged their sores, and we learned to eat their food. We learned phrases to communicate. We worked with them. We visited their homes, and we sent food when they were sick. We laughed with them, and we cried with them. We gave them access to us, and we became their friends.

The most basic church-planting strategy rises or falls on building relationships. The tribe began to trust us as we lived among them, and love and truth began to break down the barriers of their worldview as the power of the gospel reached into their hearts.

Taboos

And in this way I desire to preach where Christ has not been named, so as not to build on another person's foundation, but as it is written: "Those who were not told about him will see, and those who have not heard will understand." (Romans 15:20-21 NET)

"I was afraid of the spirits when I was a young boy. When I was four, my mother died. Then, when I was ten, my father got a bad sickness, and he died too. With both my parents dead, my father's youngest brother looked after me."

Such is the story of many young children in the village. Too frequently, death and sickness are a harsh reality even to the young. In an animistic culture, death doesn't happen because of disease; death occurs because someone in the village inflicted them by using sorcery, or an angry spirit caused them to die. Fear of the spirit world is ingrained into their worldview from the time they are young.

Sefasui, the young boy who lost his parents, was a teen when we first met him. He, along with his uncle and aunt, came to work on building the airstrip. Once everyone arrived for that work, the older men of the village told everyone, "Don't eat the bamboo shoots or the black palm shoots over on the spirit hill, and you cannot drink the water from the two streams here either. If you do, the spirits will become angry. Then you will get sick and die." These things were considered taboo along with many other things.

Everyone in the tribe listened to the old people.

Animistic tribal groups believe that all things in the natural world have a spirit and soul. Trees, plants, animals, and other natural objects have spirits that connect them to the world they live in. They believe these unseen beings need to be appeased. If a spirit becomes angry, bad things will happen. Because of this belief system, they have rules and taboos on how to live. They might leave an offering of food under a particular tree where they think the spirits dwell; they do magic for a bountiful crop when planting a garden; they don't drink from certain streams. They perform rituals for conception or for hunting, so that they have successful outcomes. Sickness doesn't come from a germ or an infection; it comes from a sorcerer in the village or from the spirit world. These beliefs affect every part of their lives. They see these evil forces as the source of power for their well-being (by placating them) or for their destruction (by breaking a taboo or by causing anger). They live in constant fear and never experience true peace.

During the morning service before each airstrip workday, Sefasui sat near the front to listen. A pastor from a nearby tribe worked with Dale to translate the message into a dialect of language that the Gobasi could understand.

One morning, a couple of years after our first contact with the tribe, when the message was finished, Sefasui spoke up. He said, "I want to leave the old ways and become a Christian." Usually decisions were made as a clan, but he went against cultural norms to become a Christian without discussing this decision with others.

Years later, Sefasui related this story to us:

When I heard God's Word, I began to think I should become a Christian. I thought about what you said. Everyone discussed it at night in the village. While we worked on the airstrip, the pastor told some of us younger boys that "nothing will happen if you drink from those streams." Several of us decided not to listen to the old men, and some of us went to drink the taboo water in secret. We didn't want to walk the long path where everyone fetched their water, so we drank from the taboo stream when no one was looking.

Nothing happened. We didn't get sick. We didn't die, so we knew the old men were wrong.

Then one day you said, "If you believe in Jesus, then when you die, you will gain eternal life." I thought about these things.

When I became a Christian, I no longer felt the evil spirits. I wasn't afraid anymore.

The power of the gospel changed this young man's life. A little boy who lost both parents to what he thought was caused by sorcery or angry spirits learned that there was a good Spirit called Jesus who had greater power than any unseen being. He was drawn to the light of the gospel with a simple faith. No longer bound by the fear of angry spirits, he believed in a God who cared for him and could give him peace.

"After I became a Christian," he said, "I saw it wasn't good to steal. I was scared to do those things and stopped. I wanted to do good things."

To this day, over thirty years later, he has been a faithful Christian. With only a little training, he still works as a pastor to his people. When the fear of the spirit world left Sefasui, it was because of the knowledge and truth of Christ and the peace that comes from the indwelling of the Holy Spirit. God's power is stronger than anything in this world, and the saving faith of Jesus Christ overcame the darkness and chains of this world. All men and women everywhere need an opportunity to hear that God loves them and has come to this earth to save them.

Only a few months later, more of Sefasui's clan decided to follow the Lord.

Prayer

Lord, thank you for those who go into foreign cultures to share the gospel with others. Give them strength to do the task you have asked of them. We ask that through their ministries many will come to know you as their Savior and Lord. We ask that you give us a heart for those around us who are lost, and give us boldness to share the gospel.

Personal Reflection

1. How does 1 John 3:7-9 exemplify Sefasui's life and the change that came over him when he became a child of God? Who do we belong to if we keep on sinning? What

does it say about those who are born of God? What did the Son of God come to destroy?

2. What fear left Sefasui once he believed in Christ?

3. Many believe we should leave these primitive cultures alone in their traditions. Read Matthew 28:18-20. Why is it important to share the gospel with those who have no opportunity to hear it?

The Spirit Medium

And I will give them singleness of heart and put a new spirit within them. I will take away their stony, stubborn heart and give them a tender, responsive heart, so they will obey my decrees and regulations. Then they will truly be my people, and I will be their God. (Ezekiel 11:19-20 NLT)

Three spirit mediums lived in the village. The oldest, a man named Abulai, was obvious in the crowd of people working on the airstrip. Each morning before work began, we held a simple service to teach them a short message about the Bible. That is also when we kept a record of who came to work that day.

Most people came when they heard the call for work – two pieces of metal clanged together. Abulai, however, always showed up late and sat on his haunches in the back. A smile never crossed his face, and he scowled as he waited for work to start. Years of his belief system and hard life had taken a toll on him. A small, skinny man with a weary-worn face, his best years were behind him. His drooping earlobes, stretched from years of wearing a large ear decoration, were no longer adorned with the traditional bamboo disc. He must have felt like he looked – angry and worn-out.

Months of airstrip work went by. Clearing the jungle of trees and brush to make a landing strip for a plane was hard, gut-wrenching work for everyone, including my husband, who spent the bulk of his days chainsawing trees.

Abulai showed up every day for work, but I don't remember talking much with him; I spent most of my time with ladies and children. However, his young son, Soiyal, used to hang around us all the time. He watched me bandage sores, pass out aspirin, or hand-wash my clothes in the wheelbarrow. Or, he and other children would play with our two young children. Yet his father only watched from a distance and did his work. He didn't engage much with us.

A spirit medium such as Abulai held a powerful position in the village. If someone was sick or had died, the family went to the spirit medium so he could reveal the sorcerer. In an animistic belief system, no one dies because of sickness; they become ill or die because someone did sorcery against them, or because they angered a spirit. The spirit medium enters a trance and asks the spirit world which person committed sorcery. Violent retaliation by the village against anyone accused of sorcery usually ended in that person's death. Everyone depended on the village spirit medium to reveal the sorcerer among them.

After the airstrip was completed, we moved as a family to live there permanently. A year later after one of the morning church services, six people made a unanimous decision and said, "We all want to follow Jesus. We want to leave the old ways behind." Two of those were Abulai and his wife, Suya. They understood that Jesus offered them freedom and peace. To leave the old ways behind meant leaving their ways of violence, fear, and treachery. For Abulai, it meant leaving behind his power and influence over the village as one of its spirit mediums. It meant leaving the séances, the rituals, the magic, and the violent ways of his ancestors. In a life that offered no hope and no peace, this new life offered them so much more.

"We want to follow this talk of Jesus," they said.

It had taken years to realize this dream and see God sweep through the hearts of some to turn them to faith in Christ. It was a great moment for them and for us.

The change was dramatic. From his former self, Abulai's entire countenance changed. His scowl was replaced with a smile, and he had a joy and peace on his face I'd never seen. Rather than sitting in the back, he fully engaged with us and attended church. Baptized in the Siu River with his wife and others, they became some of the first Christians in the Gobasi tribe.

While on earth, Jesus said, *I am come that they might have life, and that they might have it more abundantly.*[40] What a wonderful thing when the Lord transforms a person's life. He promised to put a new spirit within us. With the indwelling of the Holy Spirit, he empowers us to leave behind our old ways and embrace all the newness of a life in Christ. He transforms our hearts and minds in a way that only God can do. No more do we follow the ways of this world; no more do we need to follow the demands of false religions; no more do we need to live in bondage to Satan and in fear of death. True faith in Christ offers us so much more than the world ever will. Praise be to God for his transforming salvation!

Prayer

Thank you, Lord, that the transformative power of the gospel changes our lives forever. You take the burdens of our sin, and you grant us forgiveness. You remove our fear of death and give us the hope of an everlasting life with you. You are our peace, our truth, and the foundation upon which we stand. We praise you today for your great salvation.

Personal Reflection

1. In what ways has the transformative power of the gospel changed your life?

2. In the verses in Ezekiel above, what is the contrast between the two hearts mentioned?

3. What simple truth can we learn from Romans 10:9?

---

40   John 10:10 KJV

My Friend Suya

Jesus said to her, "I am the resurrection and the life. Whoever believes in me, though he die, yet shall he live, and everyone who lives and believes in me shall never die. Do you believe this?" (John 11:25-26 ESV)

Suya was married to the village spirit medium Abulai when we first moved out to live with the tribe. I noticed her among the women because of her outgoing personality. Her husband, on the other hand, had walked around with a scowl etched on his face. He was scary looking. They had one son and two daughters. After several years, they had become some of the first Christians in their tribe.

When we moved out of our dilapidated, thatched-roof hut, we built our new house on stilts, seven feet off the ground. Underneath I did laundry in a twin-tub washer that was powered by a generator. The clothes agitated with soap on one side, and I rinsed them out by hand in a large basin of water. Then the other side of the twin tub spun out the water. Washing clothes underneath the house protected me from the intense tropical sun.

Throughout the day people walked past our house. If they spotted activity, they came to see what was happening. One day as I was washing, Suya and a few of the ladies hung around to chat while they watched me work. After a while, I tried to listen to their conversation to see if I understood it. Then I interjected a comment into their discussion.

"You understood our talking!" Suya clapped her hands in glee.

She was as happy as I was that I could understand simple conversation.

Each week I held a Bible study for the ladies, and Suya attended. I worked hard to get my lesson together, since I was still not fluent in the language. I kept it simple so we could all understand. We started the study with simple songs in their language, and then I taught a short lesson. All these spiritual concepts were new to them, and the lessons challenged their way of thinking. Most who came were ladies who wanted to learn about "God's talk." Either they were already Christians, or they weren't yet but were interested in hearing more.

Sometimes during our time together, I would take a crafty thing to teach them, such as stringing a necklace or sewing. One week I passed out spools of thread and needles, and we sat together and sewed. Because these simple items were difficult for them to obtain, they were small ways I could help them.

Of all the ladies, Suya paid careful attention during our meetings. At the end of each lesson, I often asked questions to see if they understood. Most were too shy to respond, but Suya loved to answer.

We often heard about fights erupting in the village between husbands and wives, so I later decided to teach on marriage. I worked to put together a lesson for the ladies on how to be good to their husbands. I shared a couple Scriptures on marriage. Then I gave several examples in the culture of how they could do something nice for their husbands.

"One good thing you could do for your husband is to sew up the holes in his clothes. Or, if his string bag is old and no good, you could weave a new one for him. You could gather plenty of firewood and have it ready for cooking." I gave several other ideas of how they could show goodness to their husbands.

The next time I saw Suya, she sat weaving a traditional string bag. She had twisted bush materials into twine and had scattered in little scraps of black and red yarn to add a pop of color.

"Oh, you are making a string bag. It looks nice," I said.

Her eyes twinkled as she smiled and said, "I'm weaving this for my husband."

I smiled back and said, "That's good!" I was thrilled that she was absorbing the simple lessons I taught. One of the great joys for us was in watching the transformation that the gospel had brought to those who accepted the truth of a Savior. We saw lives change for the better in this isolated little tribe.

Early one morning after we'd eaten breakfast, one of the ladies from the village came to our door and told me, "Suya died in the night."

"Suya died?" I couldn't believe what I had just heard.

"Yes, she had a big sick and died fast. Her husband had gone to another village, and she died in the house while he was away."

About 7:00 the night before, a couple of women had come to tell me that Soiyal (her son) had a fever, so I gave them a couple aspirin to give to her son. If it was evening and nothing seemed serious, I usually told them to come see me in the morning if they needed more medicine. Yet somehow, I had confused Suya and Soiyal's names, and only heard the word for *fever,* not "big sick" (their terminology for something more serious).

"I thought you said Soiyal had fever last night."

"No, Suya was sick. Suya died."

The names were so close that I misunderstood everything, it seemed. If I had realized she had been so sick, I would have walked to the village to see her. I was so sad that my friend had died. Did she lay dying thinking I didn't even care about her? Did they tell me she was dying, and I didn't understand? I wished I could have done something. For days, sadness and guilt held my heart.

My mom had a phrase that she told me many times when I commiserated over something that had happened.

"Carin," she would say, "the Lord allowed that."

God knew I misunderstood, and he allowed the mix-up. He says, *Every day of my life was recorded in your book. Every moment was laid out before a single day had passed.*[41] God has written out the total number of our days before our birth. It was the right time for him to take Suya, and nothing I could have done would have changed that. God in his sovereignty and infinite wisdom chose to bring Suya to her heavenly home.

Through my sadness I did rejoice in one thing: Suya was one of the first Christians in the Gobasi tribe and one of the first to enter God's

---

41   Psalm 139:16 NLT

eternal realm. What joy she must have experienced when she saw her Savior! For that I was so very thankful.

Prayer

Lord, thank you for being a sovereign God. You control all things, even life and death. Nothing happens on this earth that is not first measured through your hands of love. Thank you that you are *the resurrection and the life,* and that those who believe in your Son, Jesus, will live eternally with you. What a great hope we have that someday we will dwell in your eternal realm.

Personal Reflection

1. Our physical body will die, but our spiritual body is raised to new life in Christ. What promise has God given in John 11:25-26 to those who believe in him?

2. When we speak of the sovereignty of God, it means he "orders everything, controls everything, and rules over everything." God is sovereign over life and death. Read Psalm 139:1-16. What do you learn from that passage?

3. Have you experienced the unexpected death of a friend or loved one? What gave you hope during that time?

The Little Ones

Jesus traveled through all the towns and villages of that area, teaching in the synagogues and announcing the Good News about the Kingdom. And he healed every kind of disease and illness. When he saw the crowds, he had compassion on them because they were confused and helpless, like sheep without a shepherd. (Matthew 9:35-36 NLT)

Life and death hung in fragile balance in PNG, and infant mortality was high. Malaria, meningitis, and pneumonia were common diseases. A baby could be lost within a week if they didn't get needed medicine; dehydration was deadly as well. Most mothers had lost at least one child. Many had lost more.

One afternoon, a husband and wife walked in from another area to ask if we could help their adopted son. When she removed the string bag suspended from her head, she pulled away the sides of the bag for me to see her child. I peered in to see a thin baby boy nestled inside in obvious distress. From our conversation, I guessed he was about four months old.

"Has he had any medicines?" I asked. I knew they had walked from the government post where there was a small medical clinic.

"Yes, they gave him medicine, but he is not getting better. We walked here to see if you could help him."

"Did they give him injections?"

"No, they did not give any injections. They put only medicine in his mouth," she said.

I took his temperature and respiration. His temperature was 105 degrees with elevated respiration and pulse. His breathing was labored. He looked malnourished and underweight. His little legs and arms had no baby fat. This little guy experienced a rough start to life. When his birth mother had died, this woman from the family had adopted him. They said the mother died of an infection after his birth.

With his fever so high, I gave him liquid acetaminophen right away. We needed to bring his fever down, and the mother let me sponge-bathe him to try to bring down his temperature. I radioed for the doctor, and he ordered antibiotic syrup and quinine injections, which I gave him.

The next morning when the mother brought him back, he had improved somewhat. I weighed him in at only six pounds. I gave him more medicine, but by the evening, his respiration had shot up again. I could do no more; I had given him all the medicine I could.

The next morning the adoptive mother and father came with him to the house. With tears she said, "My baby died." The father stood off to the side and tried to hide his tears. They had no children of their own, and this little boy was their hope for a child.

The previous day the mother had showed me the baby's medical record booklet. Mothers usually carry these booklets when they go to a clinic so medical workers can see the record of the child's health and document treatment. I checked the medical treatment the baby had before coming to us. The record showed that all this little boy had been given at the government clinic were vitamin drops and cough syrup. Nothing else. No antibiotics. No malaria treatment. For weeks, this baby had been sick, and she had tried to get him help. With her lack of medical knowledge and reading skills, she trusted that they were giving her baby proper medicine. When she realized he was not getting better, they walked for a day to see if we could help. He was too sick for me to help him, and he needed help that I couldn't give. I didn't know if the clinic was out of medicine or if they were afraid to treat him because of his size. He probably died of severe pneumonia and dehydration.

As she walked away with her dead baby boy, I heard her chanting wails. "Come . . . Come," she cried. "Come to your house . . . Come drink milk . . . Come . . . ."

They left to go back to their village and bury their child. I felt grief for them, disappointment, and anger. I grieved because they had lost their only baby. I felt disappointment because I had not been able to help; he needed expertise that I couldn't give. I experienced anger because the baby had received only vitamin drops and cough syrup at the government clinic when he needed and deserved so much more. Life isn't fair. In my mind, with proper medical help that child should not have died. Yet he had. This was a place of suffering.

Onez was another little boy whose mother brought him to me for help. At five months old, he had a high fever and respiration, probably pneumonia. He was weak and seemed to be dying when I saw him. We treated him for malaria and pneumonia. Sometimes when these sick babies came in, it was difficult to predict the outcome. If the parents waited too long before coming, they might die. If they came early enough and then faithfully came for the medicines, their children had a better chance of getting well.

For two weeks this little guy was on medicines and slowly began to improve. I asked the mom if she would like supplemental feedings for him to help him get stronger. Each morning, I would make up a milk formula and add vitamin drops and a little cod-liver oil. Even after his medicine treatment was completed, his mother brought him faithfully every day for weeks to get his extra feedings. He needed whatever nourishment he could get to build his strength, and his mother was diligent.

Then we left for a three-week trip. When we returned, the change in him was dramatic. He had filled out, gained fat, and looked stronger. Instead of a pitiful expression, he now gave us big smiles. I continued to give him feedings once a day for a few more weeks. When the ladies of the village saw the change in little Onez, they came with their babies too.

"Can you help my baby?"

One of the things I loved the most was helping these little ones. The babies who couldn't help themselves and these mothers who didn't have any options deserved my best effort. Although these times were stressful and hard while caring for my own family, I could not turn away from a dying baby. It didn't matter that I felt inadequate; I had to help.

I believe God used these times, as difficult as they were, to build a bridge of love with the Gobasi people. It's not only our words but also our actions that will help people respond to God's love. Each day we needed to show love to our village community. We failed at times because we were stressed, tired, and still learning, but God honored our efforts with a growing number of people coming to Christ in faith.

Jesus showed the perfect example of love and compassion. People were drawn to him, and large crowds followed him. *When he saw the crowds, he had compassion on them, because they were harassed and helpless.*[42] Jesus understood their burdens and their pain. In this world, we become the hands and feet of Jesus, and it's important that we do our best to show love and compassion to a lost and dying world. Jesus' presence changed the world forever, and we can too, one person at a time.

Prayer

Thank you, Jesus, that you were the perfect example for us. You showed compassion and love to those who came to you. You healed the sick, and you cared for those who hurt. Give me a compassionate heart. Help me to think of others and give time to those who are lost and hurting.

Personal Reflection

1. We are all wired differently. Does compassion come naturally for you? Or do you need to work at it? How do you display compassion to your spouse, your children, or your friends?

2. What three things did Jesus say in Matthew 9:36 about the crowds he felt compassion for?

3. Read Micah 7:18-19. List the ways the Lord has ultimate compassion on his children.

---

42   Matthew 9:36 NIV

God Plants His Church

Now all glory to God, who is able, through his mighty power at work within us, to accomplish infinitely more than we might ask or think. Glory to him in the church and in Christ Jesus through all generations forever and ever! Amen. (Ephesians 3:20-21 NLT)

"Abulai wants you to come pray for him. He is sick in the village." One of the men came one morning to tell Dale. Of course he would go to pray, so Dale left for the village.

Abulai, one of the former spirit mediums, had been baptized a few years earlier. When my husband arrived at his house, Abulai lay outside in the sun. The village people would often lay outside under the tropical heat if they were sick or had chills from malaria. Abulai looked terrible. Dale visited, and they chatted briefly. Then he prayed with him for God to heal him.

"I feel better already," he said as soon as Dale finished praying.

Dale thought that he didn't look any better, as he lay on his mat. But by the next day, he had improved significantly and had turned a critical corner toward recovery.

It took five years after Dale's first trek in 1982 into the Gobasi tribe for God to begin building his church there. Now we had a nucleus of Christians. When Sefasui chose to follow God, only a few months later others from his clan soon followed. They approached Dale and said, "We want to become Christians and be baptized." Abulai had been in this first group.

This is what we had hoped for, and the Lord blessed our efforts. In the following year, eight believers were baptized. Later, more followed. Then one Christmas three years later, more decided to follow Christ, and a large group of fourteen were baptized in the river. We started to see a change and happiness in the community. The Christians had their struggles and failures, but we saw God working to change the hearts and minds of many in the village.

The most amazing thing we saw was that three of the spirit mediums in the village were among the first to become Christians. If some in the village still wanted to do their séances and sing-sings (a gathering of different villages where drinking, traditional dancing, and unsavory things happen), they had to arrange for someone from one of the other villages to come.

Then one day some of the Christians came to Dale and said, "We want to have a Bible school like the Samo tribe has."

This was not something that Dale had planned for this soon in our ministry. We had hoped to work harder on language acquisition for a few more years, and other projects as well, but the people were adamant that this is what they wanted. They wanted to learn more, but how could that be added to our other responsibilities? Yet their strong interest in having their own Bible school swayed our plans.

On the first day of Bible school, every Christian in the village showed up – twenty-nine people! We were thrilled, but many children came in tow as well. The challenge was to teach over the chaos of the little ones.

Dale taught a chronological study, which was designed to lay a foundation for faith in Christ in both the Old and New Testaments. The chronological teaching taught on the beginnings of creation, man's fall into sin, Cain and Abel, Noah, and other main events in the Old Testament. Then the New Testament study taught on the life and death of Jesus. Dale also taught on topics: marriage and family, good and evil spirits, life and death, and others as the need arose. Bible school was taught all morning for two weeks each month, and then there were two weeks off for them to have time to work their gardens and maintain other life tasks.

By this time, I was keeping busy homeschooling our three children and working on literacy primers. I held weekly meetings with the women, taught sewing classes two afternoons a week, and did medical work as needed when we did not have a health worker. The needs of our growing family and church kept us busy.

When we felt God calling us to an unreached tribe, we had no practical experience in church planting. We read stories and talked with others, but how do you share the gospel and build a church among former cannibals?[43] The task seemed impossible. Who were we to think we could accomplish such a thing? But by the grace of God, one day at a time, a community of believers grew. God uses people to help accomplish his purposes, and we were humbled to see all that he did.

If we are God's people, we want to follow where he leads. At the moment of our salvation, the Holy Spirit indwells us, and we are given power that *works in [us], both to will and to work for his good pleasure.*[44] What seemed impossible in our own efforts became possible as we learned to lean on God's guidance and power. Our weaknesses allow for his enabling power, and he brings peace to our fears. When we obey God, he shows his power in extraordinary ways. We have all heard the phrase that "God won't give us more than we can handle." I would rather say this: God may give us more than we can handle, but with his power and enabling, we can accomplish the task he has purposed for us. No religion on this earth offers the relationship that our God gives. And that is a powerful thing.

Prayer

Lord, help me bring you glory so that others will see your beauty, your perfection, and your worth. Thank you that whatever task you ask of me, your mighty power is at work within me to accomplish your purposes. Please give me a willing and obedient heart.

Personal Reflection

1. Describe a time when God asked you to do something that you felt was impossible or beyond your ability.

43　Cannibalism had already stopped when we got there only because of the government's police presence close to their tribal border.

44　Philippians 2:13 ESV

2. According to Ephesians 3:20-21, what helps us accomplish more than we can ask or think?

3. Read Philippians 2:12-13. There are two parts to these verses: our part and God's part. What are we to do and what does God do?

Yanked Out, Dug Out, and Replaced

Therefore, since we are surrounded by such a huge crowd of witnesses to the life of faith, let us strip off every weight that slows us down, especially the sin that so easily trips us up. And let us run with endurance the race God has set before us. (Hebrews 12:1 NLT)

While working in the house one afternoon, my friend Bufui came running up to the door. Frantic and bleeding, she called out, "Jeffrey's mother, my husband stabbed me. We argued, and he cut me in the leg!"

The village called me not by my name, but by "mother" and the name of our firstborn son. I was known as "Jeffrey's mother." Though our daughter was our first child, the firstborn male had higher status. Every mother was called by the name of the eldest son. Superstition was also connected to calling someone by their given name; they believed it brought that person to the attention of evil spirits.

We lived in a culture where the women had low status. They were good for bearing children and for working in the garden. Marriages had difficulties, and the husbands often lashed out in abuse.

Bufui's upper leg was bleeding from the knife wound. Young and newly married, she and Mode were hardly out of their teenage years. Both had strong personalities, and Mode was known for having a temper. A fight between them escalated until he lashed out and stabbed her. I knew Bufui well, since she worked for me prepping vegetables, starting the woodstove, and doing other chores in the home to free me up for other tasks. I cleaned and bandaged her wound and wrapped gauze around her leg to keep it clean. Thankfully, it was not a deep cut. While she calmed down, Dale went up to talk with Mode.

Another afternoon a lady came to us bleeding from a gash on her head. In a fight with her husband, he had hit her with something hard. Sadness and dejection covered her face. She sat down on a log near the house while I examined her scalp. With her hair matted with blood, I couldn't see the cut on her skull. Grabbing some water and a cloth, I washed off the blood and then shaved some of her hair to get a better look at the gash. Drying the shaved spot, I then bandaged her wound.

"Come again tomorrow," I said to her. I needed to check it for a few days to make sure it was not infected. When she returned the next day, her face brightened with a smile.

Often we would hear other unsettling things from village life. One morning a Christian who had been appointed a deacon came to talk with Dale.

"Togobi and Selemini are having marriage troubles," he said.

"What kind of troubles?"

"The husband says his wife is angry all the time, swears, and he doesn't think she is a Christian. He wants to divorce her," he said. "But the wife tells me he is mean to her and asked two men to kill her."

This came as a surprise to us. We worked closely with this couple and knew them well. But being a foreigner in the culture meant things could be happening under the surface that we did not realize.

The church leaders arranged a meeting to discuss the problem. One way the tribe settled disputes was to let everyone share their concerns. Then a unanimous decision would be made. During these discussions, it was revealed that a single woman was trying to move into the wife's territory. The husband, susceptible to her influence, wanted to divorce the wife. (If I had been the wife, I might have been angry and mean too!) Over time, things worked out, and they did not divorce.

Other things arose that caused us grief as this young church grew in maturity. Yet some new believers knew intuitively that certain behavior was wrong.

One day a friend came to the house and said, "Yowami let her baby die." Often, they never revealed the whole story, so I prodded for more information.

"How did the child die?"

"She hung it over the fire. The baby cried for a while, and then he stopped."

The mom had made a fire, hung the baby in its string bag from a rafter above, and it died from smoke inhalation. This mom had just given birth to twins, one boy and one girl. She let the boy baby die. Superstition was connected to the birth of twins. They believed that when twins were born, one baby was a bad spirit, so they would kill one of them.

During this same year, we heard that another baby had been left to die over a fire. A mom with three sons left the fourth son to die. If they did not want a baby, they would suspend it over the fire to die from smoke inhalation.

Then we learned there was an incident of adultery between two confessing believers. During the church service on Sunday, the offended wife came running into church with an axe to attack the other woman. Dale and a few of the men had to hold her back from causing harm. Both offended spouses were furious with their partners.

The church needed further teaching on family life. The men could treat their wives brutally, but the women could be just as heartless with their babies. Immorality, homosexuality, and adultery were a common part of tribal culture. A tribe that lived for centuries bound by old traditions and behaviors was heinous in their dealings with other humans. Their initiation of young boys, previous cannibalistic behaviors, warring between tribes, sorcery killings, and brutality with their wives and babies were behaviors from the mind of Satan.

The gospel had made a dramatic change in the lives of many, but teaching still needed to be done. More understanding on leaving their sinful ways behind needed to be imbedded in their hearts and minds as they let the Holy Spirit transform their lives. The roots of their former belief system needed to be yanked out, dug out, and replaced with the truth of the gospel of peace.

Conviction of sin happens as we gain a better understanding of God. Sin is not just something that offends others, but sin is against a holy God. Psalm 51:4 reminds us that *against you, and you alone, have I sinned; I have done what is evil in your sight* (NLT). The truth of the Word of God makes a dramatic change in our lives when we come to know Christ, but continual growth is needed as he reveals our weaknesses and lack of understanding. Our Savior came to give us freedom, joy, and fullness of life. A deepening relationship with Christ happens as we deal with sinful behaviors and gain the freedom of a new life.

Prayer

Thank you, Lord, for giving me the indwelling of the Holy Spirit to convict me of wrong habits and behaviors. Help me overcome the sins that easily trip me up and yank out the roots of my belief system that do not honor you. Give me courage as you reveal my weaknesses and lack of understanding. Transform me to become more like you.

Personal Reflection

1. How did your life and behaviors change when you became a believer in Christ?

2. The weight of sin slows down the life of the believer. What were the physical and emotional effects of David's sin in Psalm 38:3-8?

3. Hebrews 12:1 speaks of *sin that easily trips us up* (NLT), but we hear excuses for wrong behavior: "I can't change; it's who I am." What do Romans 12:1-2 and 2 Timothy 2:21 tell us about changing?

Bush Spirits

Late one afternoon, Sagay walked down the steep path alone to put a fishing line into the river. As he neared the water, he heard a strange noise behind him that filled him with terror. That noise could only mean one thing – a warrior bush spirit. He was sure it had come to attack and kill him. He wished he had not gone to the river alone. Frantic, he jumped around and screamed in panic for someone to come help him.

My husband and a few others were outside our house when they heard him screaming down near the river. Several men stood on the high ledge 150 feet above the river to call out to him while others went down to find him. He did not calm down or stop yelling until someone got to him.

Sagay was already an old man when we arrived to live among the Gobasi. His life as a tribal man was ingrained in him from the time he was a small boy. He had participated in cannibalistic raids, and he grew up with the horror stories of being ambushed by spirits. Encountering one meant certain death. The spirit world was as real to him as his own life. When the others finally coaxed him back up from the river, they learned that another man was further down the river fishing with his son. Sagay mistook that father calling for his son for the sound of a warrior spirit trying to kill him.

Another time the village men brought down a young teen for us to help. When we saw him, he was in a catatonic-type state. He couldn't talk and he hardly moved, and his face held a look of terror. We were told that the night before he had a dream about the spirit world, and it had terrified him so much that he had gone into this unresponsive state. From what we could see, he did not appear sick, nor did he have a fever, but something was obviously wrong. It took hours before he was normal again. Later, this young teen, Wobow, came to Christ and became a part of the church.

Because there was a deep fear of evil spirits, no one walked the jungle alone. They believed they were most vulnerable to an attack from a bush spirit when alone. For them, there was comfort and protection in numbers. Even if we were walking home from the village alone, several people would follow us home because they did not want us walking alone either. Neither did they use first names to address each other for fear of drawing the attention of evil spirits to someone by using his or her name.

The spiritual realm is real. These and other incidents showed us the power and control that the evil spirits had over people's lives. Satan controls with fear, and we saw that fear over and over. Some say that we should leave these cultures alone or that we shouldn't spoil their traditions and way of life. Those who say such things have not seen what we have seen – the abject fear, the hopelessness, and the stark brutality. Where is the hope in such a culture? Would those who say these things want to live this lifestyle? It's a coldhearted person who wants to leave them to their ways without sharing the power of the gospel. God came to set the captives free, and it is our job to be a witness even in difficult places.

Yet in the middle of all this fear, now there was hope. When Abulai's wife, Suya, died, he mourned her death. Without her, he was left to care for his teenage son and two daughters. One day when returning from his garden with his children, I saw him walk past our house. Then I heard his grieving wail. It was traditional to wail when mourning the passing of a family member. I knew he missed her.

I walked outside and said to him, "Suya died, and you are grieving."

"Yes, I'm crying. My wife died."

"I'm sorry," I said. "I'm sad too. Suya died, but now she is looking at Jesus. Suya is not dead. She lives now in God's place (heaven). She was a Christian, and she is happy now, looking at Jesus." In my simple way, I tried to encourage him.

He looked at me, and then repeated what I said. "She is living in God's place now. She is not dead. She is happy."

"One day when you die, you will see Suya again."

He looked at me and smiled. "Later, I will see her again in God's place," he said. Then he walked away happy at that thought. Now there was hope in a little tribe, not just fear and death.

We all need hope, and with Christ hope abounds. As believers, we have the full assurance of eternal life when we die. It's a gift to all who believe that Jesus has paid the sacrifice for our sin. It's a simple faith that even a forgotten tribe can understand from a missionary that struggled to string cohesive sentences together. The most glorious truth we can realize is that we are loved by a God who sacrificed his own Son to die for a world that needed life. Because of Christ, we have new life in this world and eternal life when we depart this earthly life. Jesus took all the punishment. We only need to believe, reach out, and accept it from his hand.

Prayer

Thank you, Jesus, for offering eternal life to those who believe in you. I praise you that through the power of the cross, we now can have hope and peace. Thank you that because of your death, Satan and the powers of darkness have been defeated. Because of you, I have new life on earth and the glorious hope of eternity with you.

Personal Reflection

1. Satan is the author of fear and death, but Jesus is the Savior who gives life and peace. Read Ephesians 6:12. What does that verse say about the struggle we have in this world?

2. Has there been a time when you felt the forces of spiritual darkness around you? Describe how that felt.

3. Romans 15:13 says, *Now may the God of hope fill you with all joy and peace as you believe in him, so that you may abound in hope by the power of the Holy Spirit* (NET). Describe how the God of hope filled your life with peace and joy.

Faithful Provision

Enter his gates with thanksgiving; go into his courts with praise.
Give thanks to him and praise his name. For the LORD *is good.*
His unfailing love continues forever, and his faithfulness con-
tinues to each generation. (Psalm 100:4-5 NLT)

"Gogali has a very big sick. Can you come and help her?" someone from the village asked. Quickly gathering a few things, I put them in a woven string bag and headed up the hill to the village with several of the women.

As I entered the dark hut, Gogali lay on the floor semi-conscious. She was pregnant and looked near death. After taking her vital signs and asking the family questions, I returned home to call the missionary doctor on the HF radio for advice. Suspecting malaria or meningitis, he advised immediate injections for malaria treatment and antibiotics. Returning to the village, I gave her the needed shots.

The next day, as I climbed up the rough-hewn log steps into the house to give her another round of injections, my nostrils were assailed with the stench of sweaty bodies and the smell of sickness. The hut was small, made of round timber with a thatched roof, and had one small window that could be pushed out and held open with a stick. Probably not yet thirty years old, Gogali lay still in the middle of the room.

Around the edges of the room several of the village women were sitting and waiting for the inevitable – death. She breathed what some call the "death rattle." Oblivious to her surroundings, her breaths came in short gasps high in her throat as she struggled for air. I knew death might be soon. I gave Gogali her next dose of injections as everyone watched in silence. Out of the quietness someone said, "She gave birth."

"Where is the baby?" I asked.

"Here," Basai responded.

I stepped over to see Basai holding a premature baby girl. Wrapped up in rags and sleeping peacefully, she was unaware that her mother was dying. She weighed less than four pounds. The lady cuddling her was childless. I saw a gleam of hope in her eyes. She desperately wanted a child, and she knew that no one would want a baby whose mother was dying. In an animistic culture, too much superstition and fear were connected to such a baby: Did this baby cause the mother's death? Was this baby actually a bad spirit? Sickness didn't kill, only sorcery or angry spirits did.

No one would want her. In the past, babies like this were hung over the fire to die from smoke inhalation.

A few hours later, someone came with the news: "Gogali died."

A few years earlier, Gogali had decided to follow Christ. We took comfort knowing her suffering was over, and she was in heaven. As the village prepared for the burial, I felt the gloom of everyone and forgot about her tiny baby.

Almost two days later, the Lord reminded me. With people always gathering around our house, it was easy to get information.

I went outside and asked, "Where is Gogali's baby?"

"Basai has her," someone in the crowd responded.

Happy to hear that the baby was still alive, I said, "Can you ask Basai to come with the baby?"

Before long, she came with the baby inside a traditional string bag. With its long strap secured on her forehead, the baby lay against Basai's back as she walked up to the house. Taking the bag off her head, I peered in at this tiny girl.

Alive with no mother to feed her, she slept.

"Has anyone nursed her?" I asked.

"No. I tried to feed her with my breasts, but I have no milk."

We needed to act quickly to help this baby. I went inside the house to boil water and pulled out my medical books to find a recipe for milk formula. After mixing it, we used a dropper to dribble formula into her mouth. After we fed her, I sent Basai home with a jar of boiled water, milk powder, and some spoons all in a clean container. I explained what she needed to do to feed her – especially the need for cleanliness. Then I instructed her to return early the next morning for more milk.

When Basai arrived the next morning, she had followed all my instructions. Many frustrations and complications arose in helping the women with their children because instructions for cleanliness, consistent medicine, and proper food were not followed. I was very pleased with how Basai had done and checked the baby. Then I went to make a bottle for her.

We asked village ladies to wet-nurse the baby, but no one wanted to help. Too much superstition was still connected to a baby whose mother had died. No one was brave enough to feed this tiny baby.

Twice a day Basai came to get milk for her adopted baby. I prepared the bottle, and Basai fed her. (I could not send a bottle home with her because the government would not allow bottles in a village setting without proper sterilization.) Between these visits, I gave her a little stash of milk powder, boiled water in a clean jar, and spoons stored carefully for cleanliness.

This became our daily routine, and soon the baby began to gain weight. Her parents were delighted with her, and they named her Yuwasop. She was the baby they had longed for. As well as feeding her the milk, Basai also offered her breasts to the baby for comfort. The women of the village laughed because they knew she had no milk, but I encouraged her to keep trying. I had read that some adoptive mothers had been able to obtain milk by nursing. I wasn't sure it would work, but we had nothing to lose. This baby could still die.

Weeks later, one day when Basai came to the house for formula, she ran up in excitement and said, "My milk came in! My milk came in!" She sent a stream of milk into the air to show me. God knew Yuwasop needed a mother's nourishment and had provided in a miraculous way.

By helping Basai and little Yuwasop, I saw a God that is so faithful. He gives us the tools we need (like medical books or a doctor's wise advice) when we worry about what to do next. He cared for the tiniest little one that no one wanted by giving a barren woman the bravery to go against culture and love this infant. He proved faithful when Basai was laughed at by the village, and provided milk for her to nurse her baby when it seemed impossible. He brought happiness to a barren woman and love to a tiny baby because he cares about what we need.

What a deep joy he brings us when we walk hand in hand with him in faith!

Prayer

Almighty God, thank you for surprising me and providing for me in supernatural ways. You alone are worthy of praise. Give me a thankful heart to praise you for all that you have done in my life. I praise you for your goodness, your love, and your faithfulness to me.

Personal Reflection

1. Can you remember a time when the Lord helped you or a family member with what seemed like a supernatural provision from him?

2. What three attributes of God are mentioned in Psalm 100:5? Why do you think it is good to dwell on the character of God in our daily life?

3. Read 1 Chronicles 16:23-27. What do these verses tell you about praising the Lord for what he does?

Battleground

Rejoice in our confident hope. Be patient in trouble, and keep on praying. (Romans 12:12 NLT)

Three deaths in eleven days had shattered the three villages in our community. Now, only a few days after the last death, a Christian man was overtaken by a sudden sickness. He lay sick in his house.

A spirit medium had a vision and said, "The spirits are angry. The second lady died because her husband walked through the spirit ground and did not leave any meat for the spirits. Now, a fourth person will die."

According to their animistic worldview, if several deaths happened in a village, then the spirits were angry. To appease them, they needed to move away and start another village. Even the Christians became afraid and talked of moving.

Everyone trusts that the spirit mediums are speaking truth when they identify someone who commits sorcery in a village. By entering a trance, they communicate with the spirit world and gain access to "information." When someone gets sick or dies, it is because of sorcery by another person in the village, or it is caused by an angry spirit. When a sorcerer in the village is identified, their tribal custom is to kill that person. Rather than seeing it for what it is, a brutal murder, they see it as protecting others in the village.

When this spirit medium said a fourth person would die, fear spread like a fire through the three small villages that lived around the airstrip. We were dismayed when we heard talk that everyone might move away. After my friend Suya died, a young girl died from a sickness while we were away at a missionary retreat. Then another woman got sick and died the day after our return.

Now the man who lay sick was a friend who had become a huge help to us. He had learned to handle all the station work so that Dale could focus on ministry and teaching the Bible school. Now it looked like he might die. Our hearts were heavy as we tried to help him, but he didn't improve with medicine. After a few days, we arranged to have him flown out on a medical evacuation to be treated at the mission's hospital.

If everyone moved away, our ministry would change.

All we could do was pray. We knew this was a serious situation, and we pleaded with the Lord to heal our friend. It did seem uncanny that we had so much death and sickness in such a short time. That had never occurred since we had lived with the tribe, but we knew from Scripture that Satan had power to bring on sickness, if the Lord allowed it (Job 1-2). We were in a crisis and a spiritual battle. Every adult affected by death or by sickness had become a Christian, and all these deaths were attributed to the spirit mountain that was close to where we all lived.

Dale preached the next Sunday on God's power over life and death. He said, "The spirits don't hold the power over life and death. Only God has that power. He has marked out all the days that we will live."[45] He encouraged them to trust God and to stand strong. God had freed them from the power of the spirits, and he is the one who held life in his hands. With our friend close to death, we knew God allowed this, even as another death seemed imminent.

But we did wonder, *Where are you, God? Where is all the power we keep telling the Gobasi you have?*

During this time, we were also dealing with an unknown sickness with our daughter – low fevers, ear infections, cough, cold, and constant mild headaches. Her body didn't seem to be fighting off anything. Even after several rounds of antibiotics, she still had a low fever and constant headaches.

Six months later when nothing had helped her, I considered jumping on the next plane out to do whatever it took to get her proper medical attention. One morning I felt the Lord saying to my heart, "Satan is trying to gain ground in your life through your worry and fear over

45　See Psalm 139:16.

Janelle." God was saying, "Do not fear." I felt like the man who went to Jesus and said, *"I do believe, but help me overcome my unbelief!"*[46]

Dale and I read Scripture together and prayed against Satan gaining ground in our lives and in the lives of our village friends. Fear is such a strong emotion, and it can control many aspects of our life. The tool that had kept the Gobasi tribe in bondage for centuries was now knocking at our own door.

We sensed we were all under severe spiritual attack. Not just us, but the tribe as well. Satan wanted to discredit everything we had done by getting the people to move away. We prayed and looked to God to answer our prayers for help. We felt our child and our ministry were at stake, and it was a struggle to fight discouragement and fear.

We also believed that the Gobasi Christians needed to deal with their fears and leave their old traditions and behaviors behind. They needed to learn what it meant to trust in God and to confront the Enemy. Our village friends needed to fight their fear of the spirit world to walk in the freedom Christ wanted to give them.

Several months later, two things happened. Our daughter was diagnosed with a low-grade malaria, and her anti-malarial medicine was changed to two different drugs. That brought her back to her happy self. Then months after he had been flown out to the hospital, our sick friend returned and stepped off the plane. It had taken months for him to heal from a serious brain infection, but now he was on the road to recovery. God had answered all our prayers.

At some point in our lives, we will all face trials and affliction, even severe spiritual warfare. We should not be surprised when God says, *"You will have many trials and sorrows. But take heart, because I have overcome the world."*[47] Sometimes God puts us in a time of waiting when we do not see clear solutions or answers. Yet we can be sure that he hears our prayers, and we know he often works in ways that we cannot see. These are building-times in our lives as we learn patience during a time of suffering.

During those times, don't give up. Fight the discouragement through reading and meditating on God's Word. Don't allow the Enemy to

---

46   Mark 9:24 NLT
47   John 16:33 NLT

control you with fear. Rather, use that time to learn patient endurance as you continue to trust and hope in God. Continue daily in prayer. His work of sanctification in our lives is not always an easy process, but we can trust that he is working out his purposes in our lives and in the lives of those we love.

Prayer

Lord, thank you for hearing my prayers. Thank you that when I don't see a clear solution, you are still working out your purposes for me. During difficulties, help me to rejoice in you as my hope, give me patient endurance, and help me to be diligent in prayer.

Personal Reflection

1. Describe a time when you experienced a difficulty that sparked fear in your life.

2. According to Romans 12:12, what three things are we to do?

3. David fled for years from King Saul who wanted to kill him. Read Psalm 18:1-6 where he thanked God for delivering him from many difficulties. How did David describe God? How does this passage speak to you regarding difficulties you might experience?

The Spirit Tree

*Since you have heard about Jesus and have learned the truth
that comes from him, throw off your old sinful nature and your
former way of life, which is corrupted by lust and deception.
Instead, let the Spirit renew your thoughts and attitudes. Put
on your new nature, created to be like God—truly righteous
and holy.* (Ephesians 4:21-24 NLT)

"We want to go cut down the spirit tree and give it back to God."
The Christians discussed confronting their fear of the spirits.
If their fear of the spirits was greater than their trust in God, they had
not truly left their belief system behind to embrace their new relationship with God.

"If you cut down the tree, you will cut your own spirit. Then you will
die," some in the village said to the landowner. The spirit tree grew on
land that belonged to one of the Christian men in the church. That tree
was believed to be the same spirit that was with the man who owned the
land. If the tree was cut down, then he would die too. The landowner
had become one of the earliest baptized Christians.

"No, we are going to cut it down," he said.

As the Christians disclosed more of their secrets to us, the men
revealed the names of the two spirits who lived in that area. They were
associated with a large bamboo patch and a sago tree. The focus of their
animistic worship in this area was that sago tree, which was the place

where they left offerings to appease those spirits. This hill, which they called Asabi, was especially feared for causing death and sickness.[48]

These three recent deaths and sickness brought this fear to the forefront, causing everyone to want to move and start new villages elsewhere. However, the Christians decided that they wanted to cut down the sago tree. Because we felt that outside pastors could lead the Christians through the process better than we could, we flew in two senior pastors from other tribes to help the church with the process of confronting the spirit ground. Both pastors said they had to deal with spirit grounds like this in their own tribal areas.

Before walking to the hill, the Christians met with these pastors in the church to pray. Then the Christian men set out to walk the thirty minutes up the hill to the tree. Praying again at the location, the first man started chopping down the sago tree. After the tree was cut down, one of the women processed the pulp for making sago, their staple flour. The Christians then cut the taboo bamboo shoots and ate them. Before that day, even the Christians would not eat those bamboo shoots. This day seemed like any other day in the bush, processing sago and eating bamboo shoots.

But it wasn't.

The Christians in the tribe had confronted their greatest fear: they had chopped down the spirit tree and eaten food from that spirit ground. Their faith to "give God back the spirit mountain" and rebuke Satan would begin to work in their lives as they internalized the freedom that the Lord had given them. They didn't need the spirits to help their garden grow; they didn't need to fear making the spirits angry; they didn't have to obey the taboos. All they needed was to trust God. He loved them, and he would help them.

Years later, on a return visit to the area, we met with Sefasui, the first Gobasi who had become a Christian as a young teen. After we had returned home to our country, he had become the pastor for the tribe. His years of faithfulness blessed us as we saw him carry on the work of the church.

"Why did you want to become a pastor?" we asked.

---

48   We were never told about this hill when we chose a place for the mission station. We almost unknowingly named the airstrip location Asabi!

"When we cut down the spirit tree, I saw that nothing happened. No one got sick, no one died, and nothing happened to the landowner. I saw God's power. I knew his power was great. That's when I decided I wanted to become a pastor."

He had first broken a taboo by drinking water from a local stream as a teen, which helped him see that the traditions were wrong, and he decided to become a Christian. Then when he joined in cutting down the spirit tree, he saw God's power over the spirit world. He grew in conquering his fear and trusting in a powerful God. To this day, he is still a pastor to his people.

Knowing the truth of the gospel brings freedom and new life. As the Gobasi church moved toward embracing their freedom in Christ, it was necessary that they confront the spirit ground. Their old belief system held them in fear, and unless they took a stand, they would stay in bondage. This step would change their way of thinking about the spirit world and show them that the true God had great power. They no longer needed to fear.

Satan wants to keep us in bondage to fear and lies. We saw that played out in a very literal way among the Gobasi tribe. But God wants us to live in freedom and truth. God wants to dismantle our wrong belief system and replace it with his truth. He says *that anyone who belongs to Christ has become a new person. The old life is gone; a new life has begun!*[49] He renews our mind, our thoughts, our beliefs, and our actions. He changes who we are. The miracle of new life in Christ is a metamorphosis. Instead of an ugly, fat caterpillar lugging along on a branch, we become a colorful, beautifully designed butterfly that flies off into freedom.

The Gobasi tribe experienced their freedom in Christ the day they chopped down the spirit tree. What a wonderful life God gives to those who trust in him!

Prayer

Thank you, Father, for bringing us truth. You break our bondage to sin and the lies of Satan, and you carry us into freedom and new life. Thank

---

49   2 Corinthians 5:17 NLT

you for your love, forgiveness, and mercy toward me. Renew my mind, my thoughts, and my actions. Help me to live a holy and righteous life that honors you.

Personal Reflection

1. Is there a sin or belief system that is keeping you in bondage? What might you need to do to change your life?

2. What does Ephesians 4:21-24 tell us we are to throw off? Who renews our thoughts and attitudes? Who are we created to be like?

3. Read Ephesians 2:1-10. In these verses, there is a great contrast between those who are dead in their sins and those who are alive in Christ. List all the wonderful things that God has done for you according to this passage.

Epilogue

And now, just as you accepted Christ Jesus as your Lord, you must continue to follow him. Let your roots grow down into him, and let your lives be built on him. Then your faith will grow strong in the truth you were taught, and you will overflow with thankfulness. (Colossians 2:6-7 NLT)

We lived in PNG for three terms, almost thirteen years, and then returned home before our fourth child was born. In many ways, it seemed too soon to leave. Yet the larger church we worked with was entering a new era, and established ministries were being placed in the hands of trained Papua New Guinean pastors. This was a good thing; the baton had passed. We also had educational needs for our older children. Our decision to leave was a difficult one. We could have done more work, but in the final years we sensed that God was transitioning both us and the church to new responsibilities and ministries.

Months ahead, we told everyone we would not be returning as we had from our previous home assignments; we felt they needed time to digest this news and think through what it meant for them. Then we arranged for a trained Papua New Guinean pastor to settle in and take over the church work for a few years after our departure. On the morning we left, everyone came at dawn to gather at our home.

"I'm sad that you're going back to your village."

"Yes, I am very sad too."

As we walked around telling our friends goodbye, we heard that familiar click sound they make when they feel sad or distressed.

The plane arrived mid-morning. As we piled our luggage in and buckled up, everyone gathered at the airstrip to watch us leave. When we taxied down the airstrip and prepared for takeoff, the tears began to flow. Our years of ministry here had come to an end. The engine roared to life as the pilot pushed for full rpm. Once the plane rose in the sky, we passed over to see everyone waving. The pilot took another pass around them before we flew out of sight. We were leaving behind our PNG family and the only home our children had ever known. We didn't know if God would allow us to ever see them again.

When we returned to the United States, Dale helped at our mission's base office. We did the usual American things – purchased a house, put the kids in school, drove in a car pool, and worked at raising our four children. We lived in a big city with a postage-stamp-sized yard, but I loved it that God gave us a home that bordered a conservation area with no neighbor behind us. It reminded me of the jungle.

Less than a year after our return, I walked out into our new back-yard and sat on the grass. No one came to watch me, or sit with me, or chat with me. I was alone.

I missed our little tribe and all those staring eyes that had become so familiar. I thought I would be a missionary for decades, yet God had a different plan. We had planted a church, and he had called us home.

What would I do now? I sensed something new and intimidating that I believed God wanted me to do. In fact, it filled me with fear.

Several times I sensed God clearly saying, "I want you to write."

But I didn't want to write, and through many tears I resisted. It became another fear I had to overcome and trust into God's hands. In his gentle way, God nudged me forward to write about our years in Papua New Guinea.

"You are the only one who can tell these stories."

One day after much resistance my husband said, "If you don't start writing, God will stop talking." That thought scared me more than writing did. If I continued to fight, my disobedient spirit would harm my relationship with God. So, I felt myself being called on another hard journey. By faith, I needed to write.

These are those stories.

It's been over twenty-five years since the Christians confronted the spirit ground. Yehebi station is still a place where no roads go, but cell-phone technology has crept in. Now there is a cell tower a few miles away. Although expensive, we can talk briefly on the phone to the people there. Who would have thought that would ever be possible?

The Gobasi church is alive and growing. In a recent call, the younger pastor said, "The church is too small; we need to build a new building. Many people are attending church, and now we have no room." Outreaches to other Gobasi villages are happening and bearing fruit, but now it is driven by the pastors and the people.

Much to our joy, the Lord has blessed us with trips back. On a visit back in 2013, one of our Gobasi friends that we'd known since he was a teen said, "When your family left, I was very, very sad. I cried and cried." He dragged his fingers down the front of his face to emphasize the crying.

"But today, I am happy. You are here with us."

Now there are two Gobasi pastors and a third young man in training. God has done the work of building and sustaining his church there. Just as with any church, there have been ups and downs. Yehebi is still in an underdeveloped area of PNG with only basic schooling and sporadic medical care. It is still buried in remoteness and forgotten by many.

As of this writing, we are involved in a large program back in PNG with a couple visits a year as we supervise an oral storytelling program for multiple tribes – including our Gobasi friends. God brought us back again to help. We always sensed that God had another part for us in PNG, although we didn't know what that would look like. Dale is supervising workshops, and I am writing. God has given us new challenges once again.

God is in the business of making us more like Christ and strengthening us to live out his purpose for us. His goal is to shape and mold us to be more like Jesus every day. God can take anyone and turn them into what he wants them to become if they are a willing vessel in his hands.

I love the fascinating story in Exodus 3 when God appeared to Moses in that burning bush. Raised in the glory of Pharaoh's courts with all its privileges, Moses lived in a lonely desert. He had become a fugitive – a murderer hiding in the wilderness and tending sheep. The passion he once had for his Jewish people died along with the man he murdered who had oppressed them. Now he wandered with his father-in-law's animals. His memories must have haunted him.

Then, God appeared to him in that forlorn desert and shattered who he thought he had become. *"I am sending you to Pharaoh. You must lead my people Israel out of Egypt."*[50]

Moses must have thought, *What? Who, me? But I've made a mess of things. I'm only good for wandering around with sheep now. I'm hiding in the wilderness because I'm a murderer. Don't you remember that? I know you must have the wrong person. Find someone else.*

Moses stood in fear and doubt. It had been too long since he had walked the courts of Egypt and too long since he had observed the oppression of his people. He was an old man, but I sense that the passion for his oppressed people rose within him at this possibility. He listened, but replied, *"Who am I to appear before Pharaoh? Who am I to lead the people of Israel out of Egypt? . . . Then what should I tell them?"*[51]

God knew Moses had zeal for the Jewish people of his birth. God knew he was a leader, and it was time to reignite that passion. God had an astounding purpose still for Moses.

God told Moses to tell the Israelites, *"I AM WHO I AM. Say this to the people of Israel: I AM has sent me to you." . . . "This is my eternal name, my name to remember for all generations."*[52]

Just as God wanted to use Moses, he wants to use us too. We know from the book of Exodus what a great man Moses became to the people of Israel as he obeyed God's voice. He became a messenger from God. He freed his people and became a great leader to them.

God is not past or future; he is ever-present and never-changing. He is all-encompassing and all-sufficient. He is infinite and sovereign. He is majestic and holy. His is the name that is above *all* names. He sees. He knows. He controls. He never changes. He is who he is. Always. Without fail. Forever and forever, he is.

"I AM WHO I AM."

What a glorious truth that we can see and know the God who is.

50   Exodus 3:10 NLT
51   Exodus 3:11, 13 NLT
52   Exodus 3:14-15 NLT

Meet the Author

Carin LeRoy and her husband have been in ministry with Pioneers since 1981. They worked in a church planting ministry in Papua New Guinea for almost thirteen years, during which Carin developed literacy primers for that language, ministered to the women and children, and added three children to their family. They have since worked in Orlando, FL, serving in several roles within the Pioneers staff. They continue to visit Papua New Guinea to encourage the church, as the Lord has enabled them. At home, Carin also teaches piano. They have four grown children and six grandchildren.

Photos

The LeRoy family in 1994

Dale with our son, Matthew, on a visit in 2016

Two young teens we met during the first
trek into Gobasi territory, 1982

A Papuan Hornbill

Gobasi men in ceremonial dress, 1987

A small cooking house

Missionary Aviation Fellowship

An aerial of Dadalibi village, 1983

Gobasi children, 2009

Language learning, 1985

Temporary bunk beds for our two children, 1985

A Gobasi man in ceremonial
dancing dress holding a kundu
drum, 1987

Village, 2016

Pastor Sefasui (left)
and Pastor Kilas,
2013

A young boy
with greens,
2013

Printed in Great Britain
by Amazon

18082672R00172